D0934360

Retiring Wealthy in the 21ST Century

How to Beat the Coming Retirement Crisis

Also by Gordon Pape

INVESTMENT ADVICE

Building Wealth in the '90s
Low-Risk Investing in the '90s
Making Money in Mutual Funds
Gordon Pape's 2000 Buyer's Guide to Mutual Funds
    (with Richard Croft and Eric Kirzner)
Gordon Pape's Investing Strategies 2000
    (with Richard Croft and Eric Kirzner)
Gordon Pape's 2000 Buyer's Guide to RRSPs (with David Tafler)
Gordon Pape's 2000 Buyers Guide to RRIFs and LIFs (with David Tafler)
The Best of Pape's Notes
The Canadian Mortgage Book (with Bruce McDougall)

CONSUMER ADVICE

Head Start (with Frank Jones)
Gordon Pape's International Shopping Guide (with Deborah Pape)

HUMOUR

The $50,000 Stove Handle

FICTION

(With Tony Aspler)
Chain Reaction
The Scorpion Sanction
The Music Wars

NON-FICTION

(With Donna Gabeline and Dane Lanken)
Montreal at the Crossroads

Visit the Gordon Pape Web site at
http://www.gordonpape.com
for free CBC radio transcripts,
your financial questions answered,
weekly mutual fund audio commentaries,
book and newsletter excerpts, and much more.

GORDON PAPE

Retiring Wealthy in the 21ST Century

How to Beat the Coming Retirement Crisis

Prentice Hall Canada

Canadian Cataloguing in Publication Data

Pape, Gordon, 1936–
  Retiring wealthy in the 21st century: how to beat the coming retirement crisis

Rev. ed.
Previously published under title: Retiring wealthy.
Includes index.
ISBN 0-13-020638-5

1. Retirement income – Canada – Planning. I. Title. II. Title: Retiring wealthy.

HG179.P37 1999   332.024'01   C99-931825-X

Prentice-Hall Canada Inc.
Scarborough, Ontario

Prentice-Hall, Inc., Upper Saddle River, New Jersey
Prentice-Hall International (UK) Limited, London
Prentice-Hall of Australia, Pty. Limited, Sydney
Prentice-Hall Hispanoamericana, S.A., Mexico City
Prentice-Hall of India Private Limited, New Delhi
Prentice-Hall of Japan, Inc., Tokyo
Simon & Schuster Southeast Asia Private Limited, Singapore
Editora Prentice-Hall do Brasil, Ltda., Rio de Janeiro

ISBN 0-13-020638-5

Editorial Director, Trade Group: Andrea Crozier
Copy Editor: Nick Gamble
Production Editor: Jodi Lewchuk
Art Direction: Mary Opper
Production Coordinator: Barbara Ollerenshaw
Page Layout: Arlene Edgar

  2 3 4 5   F   03 02 01 00 99

Printed and bound in Canada.

Visit the Prentice Hall Canada Web site!
Send us your comments, browse our catalogues, and more.
www.phcanada.com.

To my wife, Shirley
with the promise that the slowdown
years are coming!

Contents

Acknowledgements

No book is written in isolation. Every author must call upon others to help bring a work to fruition.

In some cases, the assistance comes from experts in particular fields. In this regard I would like to say thank you to Charlie Black at the Canadian Life and Health Insurance Association, to Revenue Canada for answering several specific questions and for the useful advice found in several of their publications, and to the accounting firm of Ernst & Young for providing tax rate information.

Also thank you to John Thibodeau of Media Profile and the people at the Canadian Home Income Plan for their help on the subject of reverse mortgages.

And a special word of thanks to Lea M. Koiv of the Mississauga, Ontario office of the accounting firm of PricewaterhouseCoopers for her valuable assistance and guidance on the subject of individual pension plans, and the potential problems involved in transferring money out of defined contribution pension plans.

Also my thanks to the editors and production people at Prentice Hall Canada for their usual professionalism in bringing this book to reality.

Preface

When the first edition of *Retiring Wealthy* was published in 1991, the climate for retirement planning was very different. After more than a decade of study, the federal government had just introduced a massive overhaul of our entire retirement savings system which, we were assured, would finally put pension and RRSP contributors on an equal footing. "Fairness" and "flexibility" were the watchwords of the new system. A dollar saved was to be worth a dollar, no matter what type of plan it went into. Inflation was to be removed from the system through the annual indexing of contribution and pension limits starting in 1995–96. It was indeed going to be a brave new world.

Well, something happened along the way. Actually, a few things, including soaring government deficits through the early- to mid-nineties and a growing awareness in Ottawa of the demographic time bomb represented by the baby boomers. Almost as soon as the new program was launched, the retrenchment began, first under the Conservative government of Brian Mulroney and later at the direction of Liberal Finance Minister Paul Martin. Many of the planned reforms were postponed, watered down, or eviscerated. Moreover, the cash-strapped federal government decided to open the RRSP cupboard to allow people to dip into their savings to fulfill desirable socio-political goals, such as housing and education—without making any effort what-soever to inform them of the serious financial consequences of using their money in this way.

Now, as we enter a new century, the promise of 1991 has given way to the harsh reality of 2000. Governments can no longer afford to be as generous in their tax support for retirement savings. Nor is the private sector picking up the slack. The era of lean and mean in the corporate world has meant reduced frills for employees, and pension plans have not escaped.

So the twenty-first century in Canada is shaping up as a "do-it-yourself" time as far as retirement planning is concerned. We're going to have to increasingly depend on our own resources if we are to live our years after work in the comfort and dignity we all desire. Increasingly, governments will direct their support only to the poorest segments of our aging society. Private pension benefits will become more stingy, with less employer involvement. As life expectancy increases, the dream of early retirement will become more of a will-o'-the-wisp.

Against this backdrop, I felt it was time to revisit *Retiring Wealthy* and to prepare a totally new edition that would provide solutions to the complex new problems we face, and help Canadians prepare for the new retirement world of 2000+. This book is the result. I believe you will find here everything you need to know to put together a workable retirement plan that is perfectly suited to your personal needs, and that meets the daunting challenges we face in the coming years.

I hope the result will be many years of happy retirement for you.

Gordon Pape
Toronto

1

You May Not Like
the Future

*Cessation of work is not accompanied
by cessation of expense.*

— Marcus Cato

IT IS JUST AFTER 5 P.M. ON JANUARY 6 IN THE YEAR 2050. EMMA HARRIS checks the thermostat in her apartment. Fifteen degrees Celsius. She shivers, goes into the bedroom, and puts on another sweater. She'd like to turn up the heat–the early darkness makes the winter chill worse. But she can't afford it. Electricity costs too much. An extra sweater costs nothing.

Emma Harris is 85 years old. She lives alone in a one-bedroom apartment in midtown Ottawa. She is in excellent health, and why not? The advances made by medical science over the past 50 years have been nothing short of miraculous.

Alzheimer's, the scourge of the elderly in the twentieth century, has been completely eradicated thanks to a remarkable gene therapy developed 40 years earlier. Diabetes has been conquered. Cancer, while not completely vanquished, has been greatly diminished as a killer–more people now die in car accidents each year. Heart disease and stroke remain serious problems, but their mortality rate is also way down.

Emma heads toward the kitchen. Her step is lively and her pace brisk. The once-crippling afflictions of old age are only a distant memory now. Arthritis, osteoporosis–both have succumbed to effective new treatments developed soon after the turn of the century.

The impact of the huge strides in health care is reflected in the life expectancy of the average Canadian. A baby born this year, 2050, can expect to live to age 93. A woman reaching age 50 is likely to survive beyond her one hundredth birthday.

At her annual check-up last month, Emma's doctor told her she could live at least another 20 years in just about the same state of health as at present. "Maybe even longer, if we use this new cell regeneration process they're developing," he added.

Emma's heart sank at that news.

She opens the cupboard and takes out a tin of macaroni and cheese. She hates macaroni and cheese; has done so ever since her mother served it three times a week when she was a child. But it is one of the few food items she can afford.

When she retired from her office job 20 years before, she received what at the time seemed to be a modest but adequate pension. But there was one serious flaw in it, she discovered over time. It wasn't indexed to inflation—in fact, hardly any pensions in the private sector were. That hadn't seemed like a big deal originally, and since she'd stopped work inflation had averaged just 2 percent a year. But, like water dripping on a stone, over time it had done its damage. Her pension income would now buy just about half of what it did at the time she retired.

She pours half the contents of the tin into a pot and puts the rest in the fridge for tomorrow night's dinner. As she does, her eyes automatically go to the spot beside the door where Oscar's food and water dishes used to sit.

She misses Oscar. She'd had that old cat for sixteen years before he finally curled up in the sun on his favourite chair last summer and quietly passed on. She'd thought about getting another cat—she'd always enjoyed the companionship of a pet. But it was just too expensive. She could hardly afford to feed herself, after all.

The macaroni and cheese is hot now. She sits at the counter and picks away at it. Life is lonely. She wishes she could see her daughter in Toronto more often, or at least speak to her. But she had the phone disconnected last year. Too costly, and rarely used.

After eating, she washes the plate and goes into the sitting room to turn on the television. It's the one luxury she still allows herself.

The news is on and a politician is being interviewed. An election is coming up, and the ruling party is trying to win a third term. Their message to the people of Canada is: "You've never had it so good."

Emma watches for a while as the politician goes on about the quality of life in the mid–twenty-first century. "Canadians are living longer, healthier lives than ever before," he intones, somehow implying that his government is responsible for these blessings.

Emma sighs and changes the channel.

Longer, healthier lives indeed. Longer, more miserable lives would be a better description. And the government certainly isn't doing anything to make it easier.

Her mother died at age 73. Emma envies her.

2

The Barriers to Success

Prosperity is a great teacher;
adversity is a greater.
— William Hazlitt

THE WORLD OF THE MID-TWENTY-FIRST CENTURY MAY BE JUST AS bleak for many Canadians as it will be for Emma Harris. The idea that they may spend their final years in semi-penury may seem unthinkable to most people now in the prime of their working lives, but it is a very real possibility. In fact, unless things change dramatically, we are looking at a major social crisis that will be upon us in less than a generation.

As we embark upon the new millennium, Canadians face huge barriers to the dream of a happy and comfortable retirement. Only those of us who recognize them and take appropriate evasive action are going to be in a position to truly enjoy what many will sarcastically refer to as "the fool's gold years."

Some of these barriers are products of government policy. Some are due to fundamental changes in the economy. Some are a natural consequence of advances in health care and the treatment of disease. Some flow from the demand by shareholders for greater corporate profits. And some are the result of our own unwillingness to accept reality.

The purpose of this book is not to frighten you, but to show you the techniques for achieving a retirement lifestyle that lives up to your expectations. However, for that to happen you must be aware of the problems you will have to overcome along the way. Here are the most important barriers you face.

Retirement Obstacles

Reduced Government Support

During the second half of the twentieth century, Canadians were conditioned to look to governments to provide the basic framework of their retirement income. First came the introduction of Old Age Security in 1952. This program provided a monthly payment to all Canadians, regardless of income, when they reached age 65 and was our first truly universal plan.

But the Liberal government of Lester B. Pearson decided that OAS wasn't enough. So in the mid-sixties, at a time when the economy was booming and budget surpluses were routine, they added a second retirement support program, the Canada Pension Plan. It came into being in 1966, after extensive negotiations with the Quebec government had resulted in that province opting out and setting up a separate Quebec Pension Plan, similar to, but not exactly the same as, the CPP.

The third leg of the federal government's retirement income stool is the Guaranteed Income Supplement (GIS), established in 1967. Just hope that you never have to resort to it, because it is intended only for people in serious economic straits. Unfortunately, as the century unfolds, more people may have to apply for it.

All these programs, plus some supplementary provincial support plans, were designed to ensure that Canadians would be able to maintain at least a minimal standard of living in retirement. But, over time, governments began to realize they had bitten off more than they could chew. The aging baby boom population began to send chills down the spines of policy-makers who looked into the future and calculated what all this was going to cost their treasuries.

The response was to cut back. Not all at once—that would have created too much of a political fuss. The Progressive Conservative government of Brian Mulroney discovered just how potent a force Canada's elderly had become when the grey power movement forced them to back away from their plan to partially de-index OAS payments. The subsequent Liberal government of Jean Chrétien apparently didn't get the message however, and paid the price a few years later when they had to drop plans for a Seniors' Benefit which would have reduced Ottawa's total cost of retirement income support programs by several billion dollars.

But these two well-publicized victories for the over-50 crowd only served to mask the many defeats they suffered over the years, as governments at all levels began chipping away at their retirement programs.

Item: OAS payments are subjected to a special tax, known as the claw-back. The effect is to end the universality of the program, although the politicians refuse to admit it.

Item: The tax credit given to Canadians aged 65-plus is subjected to an income test. As a result, thousands of middle-income retirees find themselves paying hundreds of dollars a year more in taxes.

Item: The age for the mandatory winding-up of RRSPs is reduced to 69. The result is to deprive older people of two years of badly-needed tax-sheltered growth in their plans.

Item: Some provincial governments drastically reduce their health care support programs for older people.

Item: RRSP contribution levels are frozen.

Item: Canada Pension Plan premiums are increased and benefits reduced.

All that is just the tip of the iceberg. Any Canadian who believes governments are finished with their slashing of income support programs is still mentally living back in the 1960s. As the population continues to age, the pressure on finance ministers to cut still more will increase in the early years of the twenty-first century. Rising CPP premiums will add fuel to the political fire, as younger people become more vocal in their objections as they see an ever-growing chunk of their pay cheque going to support an expanding population of retirees. Don't be surprised when a future government responds by putting a freeze on CPP premium increases, paid for by raising the minimum age for claiming benefits and, possibly, by de-indexing payments or imposing a claw-back similar to that applied to OAS.

However it plays out, you can be sure of one thing: government support payments will not be more generous when you retire than they are today. If anything, they are likely to be lower, perhaps much lower, than they are now.

Diversion of Retirement Savings

As the money stashed away in RRSPs grew into multi-billions of dollars in the late years of the twentieth century, cash-strapped governments started to look at these personal retirement plans as an alternative way of funding what the politicians perceived as desirable social and economic policies.

"We can't afford to do it," the rationale seemed to be. "But we can still be heroes by introducing programs that allow people to do it themselves."

And so it was that the first retirement income diversion scheme came into being in the early nineties. It was a time of deep recession and the housing industry was hurting badly. A delegation from the Canadian Real Estate Association went to the federal cabinet with a plan. Let's allow people to borrow from their RRSPs to purchase a home, they suggested. It will cost the federal government nothing. But it will be a huge stimulus to the economy. By unlocking some of that unproductive RRSP money, we'll not only help revive the housing industry, but we'll also give a boost to furniture and appliance manufacturers, retailers, tradespeople, and just about anyone else you might name.

The Tory government of the day bought in. The Home Buyers' Plan was introduced by then–finance minister Don Mazankowski in 1992. It was supposed to be a temporary program, for one year only. But it proved so popular and so successful that it was extended. Then it was extended again. Finally, in 1994, the newly-appointed Liberal finance minister, Paul Martin, made it a permanent part of the RRSP scene.

Canadians loved it. The HBP made it possible for hundreds of thousands of people (including two of my children) to become home owners years sooner than they had expected. No one except a few curmudgeons dwelled on the impact the plan was having on the retirement savings of younger people. The program was a political success and most people were well-satisfied with it. Any potential problems were way off in the future.

The idea was so good that Mr. Martin decided to use it again a few years later. Post-secondary education was in crisis. Governments were cutting back on university funding. Tuition fees were shooting up. Graduates found themselves financially crippled by huge student loans that had to be repaid. The federal government had no more money to throw at education. What to do?

Well, there's always the RRSP well to go back to. So in his 1998 budget, Mr. Martin announced a new plan for diverting retirement savings. Starting in 1999, Canadians would be allowed to borrow up to $20 000 interest-free from their RRSPs for purposes of furthering their post-secondary education, or that of their spouse. A noble use of the money, everyone agreed. More Brownie points for the Liberals, without expending a cent of public money.

There is just one problem with these diversion programs, and the others that are almost sure to follow as the twenty-first century unfolds. They can take an immense toll on the future retirement income of anyone who uses them. Let's take the case of a 30-year-old woman who withdraws $20 000 from her RRSP under the Home Buyers' Plan and repays the loan over the 15-year period allowed by the government. If she had left the money in the plan, it would have grown to $295 700 at age 65, assuming an average annual compound rate of return of 8 percent. But the effect of the loan and the 15-year repayment is to reduce the end value of that $20 000 to just under $170 000.

If she converts her RRSP to a RRIF at age 65 and starts drawing income from it immediately, the impact will be to reduce her annual income by more than $5000. And that deficiency will increase with every passing year. That's the part the politicians never talk about.

There are ways to avoid this financial disaster, which we'll explore later in the book. But the first step is to realize that these RRSP diversion schemes are indeed a serious impediment to retiring wealthy. Only when you acknowledge the existence of the problem can you start taking steps to rectify it.

A Low-Interest-Rate Climate

Low interest rates are a good thing, everyone agrees. They make it easier for people to buy homes, they help to sell cars, they encourage entrepreneurs to expand their businesses, they reduce the carrying cost of government debt—in short, they're good for the economy.

Well, for most parts of the economy. The low interest rate environment that we've experienced since the mid-eighties has not been good news for Canada's older people, nor for those who want to save for retirement with minimal risk.

Low interest rates have translated into reduced retirement income for many people. Economists make the argument that the loss has been offset by a lower inflation rate, but it hasn't happened that way in the real world. Let me give you one illustration to make the point. In the early nineties, retirees could invest their money in ultra-safe five-year guaranteed investment certificates issued by major banks that paid about 8 percent interest. So for every $10 000 that was invested, a person received $800 in annual income.

At the start of 1999, banks were paying 4.7 percent on their five-year GICs. That works out to $470 in income for every 10 000 invested, a drop of more than 40 percent. The last time anyone looked, food stores had not adjusted their prices downward to compensate!

Lower rates mean that those who wish to save for retirement using interest-bearing securities such as GICs and bonds will build their RRSPs much more slowly. And those who rely on interest-bearing investments for income once they retire will have their cash flow greatly reduced.

There are alternative investments, of course. But these inevitably involve a greater degree of risk, something many people have not yet learned to manage effectively.

Less Generous Employer Pension Plans

Unless you work in the public service, the chances that you will retire with a defined-benefits pension plan complete with built-in inflation protection are growing slimmer each year. Not only are such plans very expensive, but they have become so ensnared with government red tape that only the largest corporations can manage them. As a result, most new private sector retirement plans today are in the form of group RRSPs or money-purchase pension plans.

Both these forms of retirement saving have one big drawback—it is impossible to predict the amount of your pension with any certainty until you are within a few years of stopping work. That's because the value of your pension will depend upon how well the invested money performs. There are no guarantees. If the securities that are purchased for the plan do well, you should draw a decent income from it. If they do badly, or if there's a big market crash just before you're about to cash in, you could end up in serious financial trouble.

This means that, for most people who retire in the twenty-first century, pension plans will not be the reliable source of retirement income they were in the past. There are simply too many variables involved.

Longer Life Expectancy

Many people think it would be terrific to be able to live to 90 or older, if they could enjoy good health all the way. But, as we saw with Emma Harris in Chapter 1, long life could end up being more a curse than a blessing if the income isn't available to enjoy it properly. Medical science is doing everything it can to prolong our time on this planet. However, social programs are not keeping pace with the needs of the millions of 60-plus people who will inhabit this country in the century ahead.

To see how serious the problem of an aging population may be, just take a look at the payment tables for registered retirement income funds (RRIFs) that appear on pages 208–209. The way these funds are currently structured, cash flow from a RRIF will inevitably decrease once a person reaches their mid-nineties, and in many cases well before that. It will be tough enough making ends meet with a constant income at that age. What are people supposed to do when the cash flow starts to run out? Our political leaders have not even begun to address that problem.

The growing dream of early retirement further complicates this whole picture. People who will be living longer want to stop work sooner. That means they will have fewer income years in which to put aside the money they will need to support themselves for a much longer period after they stop work. If this sounds like the irresistible force meeting the immovable object, it's because that's exactly what it is. As the century goes on, it will become increasingly apparent to many Canadians not only that early retirement is impractical, but also that they will probably have to work much longer than they anticipated to build an adequate retirement nest egg. A generation ago, 70 was considered to be the normal retirement age. It may become so again.

A Natural Reluctance to Plan Ahead

Of all the retirement obstacles we face, this may be the biggest hurdle. As a general rule, Canadians under the age of 40 put retirement planning way down on their list of financial priorities. There are so many other things that seem to take precedence, from buying a car, to owning a home, to raising children. Retirement is a long way off. We'll get around to it, they say, once the mortgage is paid off and the kids are out of college.

This kind of thinking is a recipe for future trouble. Consider this. If you put $5000 a year for 10 years into an RRSP, between age 25 and age 35, that money will be worth about $72 000 at the end of that period, assuming 8 percent annual compounding (quite possible with mutual fund investments). Suppose you then stop contributing to the plan and just allow the money to continue to grow at the same rate. By the time you turn 65, you'll have more than $725 000 in your plan. That will be enough to generate retirement income of more than $29 000 in the first year of a RRIF, using the minimum withdrawal formula.

Now suppose you contribute nothing to the RRSP until age 35. You then contribute $5000 for each of the next 30 years, to age 65. Again, we will assume an average annual compound rate of return of 8 percent. At retirement, your RRSP will be worth about $565 000. That's right. You will have contributed an additional 20 years, which means you will have paid $100 000 more into the RRSP than the person who started at 25 and stopped at 35. Yet your plan ends up being worth about $135 000 less, and your first year income from the RRIF is about $22 600 instead of $29 000 and change.

You can see immediately how important it is to overcome that natural reluctance to start early. Those who don't will either have to save much more when they are older, or resign themselves to a lower retirement income.

Key Points in Review

1. Don't expect government programs to provide for any more than a small portion of your retirement income. If anything, governments will cut back on their support in the years ahead, not increase it.
2. Diverting retirement savings to some other purpose, such as buying a home, may seem like a good idea at the time. But it will seriously reduce your income once you stop work unless you take appropriate counter-measures.

3. Low interest rates may be good for the economy, but they can be bad for conservative investors and for retirees who depend upon interest-bearing securities for cash flow. New strategies are required to overcome the problem.

4. Unless you work in the public service, employer pension plans will be an uncertain source of retirement income in the twenty-first century.

5. We'll live longer and healthier in the years to come. But unless there's income to support that longer life, it may turn out to be a curse instead of a blessing.

6. Canadians under 40 have a natural aversion to putting aside large amounts of money for a retirement that is many years away. Failure to overcome this tendency will be extremely costly.

3
Getting Started

Castles in the air cost a
vast deal to keep up.

— Anonymous

IT'S HARD TO BELIEVE, BUT SOME CANADIANS' APPROACH TO retirement planning seems to be to buy a lottery ticket, if we can trust the polls. A recent survey done by the CIBC turned up the astonishing information that 11 percent of respondents saw winning a lottery as a key part of their retirement strategy. No information was provided on what they planned to do if that strategy failed.

Other surveys have turned up responses that, while not as dramatic, were almost equally worrisome. For example, a Scotiabank poll conducted by the Goldfarb organization and released in early 1999 found that only about one-third of RRSP investors make the maximum contribution to their plan, and more than four out of ten don't even know what their allowable limit is.

Of course the banks have a vested interest in encouraging people to contribute more money to their retirement plans, because they earn a variety of fees from the assets under management. But in this case, their self-interest coincides with yours.

Let me state it simply: *Every Canadian needs a comprehensive retirement plan.* And the sooner you get started with it, the greater your chances of being able to live your post-working years in the lifestyle you wish.

A comprehensive retirement plan does not begin and end with opening an RRSP. That's just one piece in the puzzle. Here's what you need to do to get it right.

Define Your Goals

Just saying you want to live comfortably when you retire isn't enough. You need to have an understanding of just what that will mean, in terms of your lifestyle and what it will cost to maintain it. The younger you are, the more difficult that is to define. But let your imagination roam for a bit. You know what you like and don't like. Your tastes and your dreams are probably not going to change a lot as you grow older.

From the time we were married, my wife and I knew we would one day like to live by the sea. That wasn't possible through most of my working career, but we never lost sight of that goal. We finally achieved it a couple of years ago with the purchase of a winter home in Florida that looks out on to a bay teeming with dolphins, aquatic birds, fish and even manatees. To us, it is paradise, the place where we want to spend a large portion of our remaining years together.

What do you want when you retire? Something similar? A ski chalet in Whistler? A cottage in Muskoka or the Laurentians? None of the above?

This is not an exercise in idle dreaming. This is an exercise in long-range planning—in deciding how you would ideally like to spend your later years and then building toward those goals.

To get you started, take a minute to complete the following Personal Lifestyle Planner.

Your Personal Lifestyle Planner			
Retirement Age	**Self**	**Spouse**	
Target retirement age			
Number of working years remaining			
Housing	**Yes**	**No**	**Not Sure**
Continue to live in present house			

Housing (continued)	Yes	No	Not Sure
Move to less expensive house			
Move to more expensive house			
Own more than one residence and will continue to do so			
Will acquire a second residence			
Will acquire more than one additional residence			

Lifestyle	Yes	No	Not Sure
More time with family			
Frequent travel			
Winters in the sun belt			
More sports activities			
Gardening			
Reading, watching TV			
Computers, Internet			
Hobbies			
Part-time work			
More active social life			
Boating			
Volunteer/charitable work			
Other (fill in your own priorities)			

Of course, your objectives may change over time. That's normal. If it happens, revise your master plan accordingly. A retirement plan should never be cast in stone; it must be flexible to respond to new conditions and changing needs.

Estimate Your Expense Needs

Once you have decided on your initial goals, you need to put a price tag on them. That will require some detail work, and a time commitment of an hour or two. But you need some numbers in front of you to provide a revenue objective.

There are two ways to estimate your post-retirement income needs.

Less patient readers may use the quick and dirty method. This simply involves using your current family income as a base and multiplying by a target percentage.

The question is, what percentage? Estimates of the amount of retirement income needed to maintain pre-retirement living standards range from 60 to 85 percent of your income in the final year before you stop work.

Higher-income people—$70 000 a year and up—may be able to get by with a lower figure, in the 60 percent range, if they are not planning to live elaborately. But lower-income earners—those with pre-retirement incomes of less than $40 000 a year—may need 80 percent of their salary to maintain their standard of living.

At the outset, I recommend a target range of 75 to 100 percent of pre-retirement income. For purposes of this calculation, I suggest you use 80 percent unless you have especially extravagant retirement lifestyle dreams.

On that basis, the quick and dirty formula would be:

This Year's Family Gross Income x 80%
= Post Retirement Needs

So if your family income this year is $50 000, you'd need $40 000 in today's purchasing power after retirement to maintain your standard of living. Of course, if you want to live even better, it will cost more.

If you want a more precise figure, you'll have to do some additional work.

The Expense Estimator that follows on pages 20–22 will help you make a more accurate projection of your likely expenditures when you stop work. There are some calculations involved, but I think you'll find it worth the effort.

I suggest you make photocopies before filling it out, so you'll have some extra sheets for future updates.

Before you begin, you'll need to know approximately how much your family is spending annually now in each category. If you don't have a current budget, this is a good time to create one.

Use today's dollars when completing the Expense Estimator. I'll explain how to take inflation into account later. Also, leave taxes aside for the present, except for Canada Pension Plan and Employment Insurance premiums.

Here are some other considerations to keep in mind.

Housing. You may still be paying off a mortgage, but look into the future. Based on the current amortization schedule, or on any mortgage paydown plans you may have, will it be fully discharged by the time you stop work? If so, the mortgage component can be eliminated from your post-retirement spending estimates. Under utilities, include the cost of heating, electricity, water, cable TV, telephone (including long distance), Internet service, and any special costs you may have, such as a water softener, water filter, or security system monitoring. The improvements and replacements line is to cover the cost of renovations or new furniture and appliances. Don't underestimate these expenses: many people like to spend time after retirement fixing up their home or buying new furniture, drapes, and carpets. If your lifestyle plans call for you to move to a less (or more) expensive home after retirement, adjust your spending estimates accordingly. Do not include any allowance for profit you may make on the sale of your present home, however—that will be dealt with later.

Recreational Property. You may not own a cottage, sun-belt condo, or vacation property now, but if you want one after you retire you'll have to build in the costs. Many retirees buy a place in the sun to spend the winter months. If this is part of your desired retirement lifestyle, start planning for it now. If you want a rough rule of thumb on the annual costs of carrying such a property, assuming it's mortgaged, use 15 to 20 percent of your estimated purchase price. A condo in the sun-belt will usually cost at least as much to carry as a comparable residence in Canada—what you save in heating bills you'll pay out in higher costs for electricity, property taxes, and maintenance charges.

Food. Your current food costs may not be indicative of what you can expect to pay after retirement. Your children will probably have left home by the time you stop work. Many people also find they eat smaller portions as they age. Meals out may cost less, especially if you and your spouse both work and have lunches away from home five days a week. On the other hand, if your desired lifestyle calls for more socializing and entertaining, budget accordingly.

Clothing. If you and your spouse have to dress for work, whether it's in an office or on a construction site, those costs will be eliminated. You may have to build up your leisure wardrobe, but casual clothes usually cost less than business wear.

Transportation. For most people, the family car is the largest single expense in this category. You'll almost certainly want to retain at least one car when you stop work, so you'd better plan for it. Remember to include all relevant costs: gas, oil, insurance, licence, and maintenance. I've also included a line for public transportation (remember, many communities offer seniors' discounts) and one marked "reserve." This is for money put aside to purchase a new car every five years or so.

Health Care. This is a tough one to estimate. Your personal health costs will likely be higher after you retire and you may not have ongoing group plan protection. Dental care and glasses may cost more and you may have to purchase a hearing aid. However, if you're currently paying large sums for health care—perhaps your daughter just got braces on her teeth—the increase may not be overly dramatic. Make inquiries about the cost of individual health insurance for older people and include this in your post-retirement projection.

Personal Care. Cosmetics, hair care, perfumes, and the like all cost money. Allow for it here. Also include any spending on tobacco and alcohol on this line.

Life/Disability Insurance. If you have a young family, your annual premiums may be quite high at present. However, you shouldn't need as much insurance after the kids have grown up, especially if you've built a solid retirement plan that will comfortably support both you and your spouse through the rest of your lives. Unless you want to use life insurance to leave a big estate to your children, plan to reduce your costs once you stop work. Disability insurance is valuable as long as you're working, but once you retire there is no point continuing it. Any money you're now spending on disability premiums can be directed elsewhere.

Family. Take a close look at what your dependents are costing you now. If you have children in university, for example, you're probably laying out thousands of dollars annually that won't be required in a few years. On the other side of the coin, consider your parents or other close family relatives. Are they in good financial shape, or are they likely to need help from you in later years? Also, don't lose sight of the grandchildren that may come along. They can cost a lot of money in gifts and visits.

Travel. If you want to see the world, or at least the sunny south, after you retire, this is the time to start planning for it. If you don't spend a lot on holidays now, this may be the component of your budget that shows the largest percentage increase.

Recreation. You're probably going to want to be active in your spare time, so don't skimp here. If you're a golfer, you may want to join a club (if you don't belong already) or purchase new clubs. Hobbies can be costly—I happen to enjoy collecting fine wines and I don't intend to give it up when I stop work. Many retirees like gardening, which can be expensive. You may want to buy some compact discs or rent movies. How about some nights on the town? Will you be doing more reading? Do you plan to buy a boat? This is your chance to do all those things you've complained you never had time for, so make sure the money is available in your budget.

Pet Care. Many retired people like the companionship of a dog, cat, or other pet. If that sounds like you, put some money in your budget at this line. Don't underestimate the cost. Vet fees can be expensive, and if your pet requires regular grooming the way our shaggy sheltie does, that will set you back $50 to $75 every month or two.

Debt Repayment. You may be servicing a lot of debt right now: credit card balances, a car loan, investment loans, etc. Include the annual interest cost of everything except your mortgage in the Present Cost column. Your target should be to pay off all your debts before retirement to reduce that outlay to zero, thereby freeing up cash for other post-retirement needs.

Professional Services. You may need the services of a lawyer, accountant, financial planner, and/or investment counsellor when you retire. Budget for those costs at this line.

Donations. If you give regularly to charitable organizations, you'll want to continue doing so when you retire. Include an appropriate amount here.

Canada Pension Plan/Employment Insurance. You're probably paying several hundred dollars each year in premiums. This expense will disappear when you retire.

Retirement Savings. You should be contributing several thousand dollars each year to retirement programs, such as pension plans and RRSPs. This is another outlay that will stop once you retire.

Other Expenses. Most people find they spend at least 10 percent of their income on items for which they can't readily account. Make an appropriate allowance on this line. If you have any unusual expenses, such as alimony payments, also add them at this point.

Expense Estimator

	This Year's Cost	Retirement Percentage	Retirement Cost
Principal Residence			
Mortgage/Rent	_____	_____	_____
Property taxes	_____	_____	_____

Principal Residence (continued)

Maintenance/Repairs _____ _____ _____

Utilities _____ _____ _____

Improvements/
Replacements _____ _____ _____

Recreational Property

Mortgage/Rent _____ _____ _____

Property taxes _____ _____ _____

Maintenance/Repairs _____ _____ _____

Utilities _____ _____ _____

Improvements/
Replacements _____ _____ _____

Food

At home _____ _____ _____

Meals out _____ _____ _____

Clothing

You _____ _____ _____

Spouse _____ _____ _____

Laundry/Cleaning _____ _____ _____

Transportation

Car(s) _____ _____ _____

Public _____ _____ _____

Reserve _____ _____ _____

Health Care

Insurance Premiums _____ _____ _____

Medical Costs _____ _____ _____

Health Care (continued)

   Prescriptions   _____   _____   _____

   Dental Care   _____   _____   _____

   Eye Care   _____   _____   _____

Personal Care   _____   _____   _____

Life Insurance   _____   _____   _____

Family

   Children   _____   _____   _____

   Other Relatives   _____   _____   _____

Travel/Holidays   _____   _____   _____

Recreation

   Memberships/Fees   _____   _____   _____

   Equipment   _____   _____   _____

   Hobbies   _____   _____   _____

   Other   _____   _____   _____

Debt Repayment

   Credit Cards   _____   _____   _____

   Loans   _____   _____   _____

Professional Services

   Donations/Gifts   _____   _____   _____

   CPP/EI Premiums   _____   _____   _____

   Retirement Savings   _____   _____   _____

   Other Expenses   _____   _____   _____

TOTAL   _____   _____   _____

Now that you have some idea of what your costs will be, let's move to the next step.

Review Your Sources of Revenue

Once you have an idea of approximately how much money you will need to retire in reasonable comfort, the next step is to look closely at your likely sources of revenue once you stop work, and see how the cash inflow is likely to match up to the outflow.

Most people can expect to receive retirement income from several of the following sources.

Canada Pension Plan. Virtually all employed and self-employed people are required to make contributions to the CPP. You can begin drawing a pension as early as age 60 under certain conditions, and it is currently fully indexed to inflation.

Old Age Security. OAS payments are made to all Canadians aged 65 and up. However, once your income exceeds a certain level, a special claw-back tax reduces the amount you'll actually get to keep. If you expect to be relatively well off when you stop work, you should reduce your estimated income from this source.

Guaranteed Income Supplement. This federal government program is intended to provide income support to the poorest elderly people. If you follow the guidelines in this book, you will never need it.

Employer Pension Plan. This will be a major component in the retirement income picture for some people, especially public service employees, teachers, and employees of large corporations. Others, such as the self-employed, will have no pension plan at all. Your overall retirement strategy will be greatly influenced by your pension plan or lack of it. If you do have a plan, make sure you understand it well. See Chapter 11 for more details.

RRSP. The importance of an RRSP will be in inverse proportion to the strength of your pension plan. Those with a generous pension program with lots of fringe benefits, such as indexing, will place relatively small emphasis on the RRSP component of their overall program—in fact, their ability to contribute to an RRSP will be severely constrained or even non-existent. But if you don't have a pension plan (or something similar like a deferred profit sharing plan), your RRSP will probably be your primary income source in retirement.

Other Investments. Many people overlook the potential value of having a non-registered investment portfolio in addition to assets in registered plans like pensions and RRSPs. Although a non-registered portfolio should only be built after tax-deductible contributions to registered plans have been maximized, such funds can provide a useful additional stream of retirement income.

Working Income. It may seem strange to talk in terms of income from work after you're retired, but a lot of people earn some income of this type. It may come from consulting work or from starting a second career, perhaps based on a hobby. If you do anticipate this kind of income, don't expect it to continue indefinitely, however. The time will come when you want to completely relax, or don't have the desire or energy to keep going.

Develop a Strategy

When you've completed all these steps, you'll have a reasonably good idea of what you want to achieve, how much it will cost, and where the money will come from to pay for it. Now it's a case of pulling it all together and working out a strategy to make it happen.

Your strategy should be designed to achieve four specific goals by the time you're ready to retire. I call these the four Pillars of Independence. They are:

Freedom from Debt

You want to begin your retirement years completely debt-free. This means discharging any remaining mortgages on property you own, paying off all credit cards, retiring any investment loans, and getting rid of any consumer loans you may still be carrying.

Not owing any money when you begin your retirement will give you a huge financial advantage, for three reasons.

First, interest payments are a drain on what will likely be a reduced income flow once you retire. If you have to put aside a large chunk of money every month to service old debts, you may find yourself having to compensate by reducing your living standard.

Second, loans are more difficult to pay off after you retire. If your income drops, you'll find it harder to put money aside to reduce your outstanding principal. Nor will there be any windfalls, such as an annual bonus, that can be put toward reducing debt.

Finally, carrying debt into retirement puts you at risk. Interest rates have been low in recent years, but any sharp upward move would increase your monthly costs. That would put an additional strain on your retirement budget.

So part of your retiring wealthy program should be directed toward debt elimination. Set up a repayment program that will ensure all your loans are paid off by the time you plan to stop work (even sooner, if at all possible).

Your first priority should be non–tax deductible debt carrying the highest interest rate. For most Canadians, that means credit card balances. Unpaid credit card bills are one of the most expensive forms of consumer loans available, and the interest rates charged by the card companies tend to be very slow in coming down, even when rates generally are low.

So pay off those credit card balances as soon as possible, and make it a point not to allow them to run up in future.

Use the money that has been freed up by paying off your cards to attack other high-interest outstanding loans. A car loan, if you have one, should probably be next on your list.

RRSP loans come next. More people are using RRSP catch-up loans to pick up carry-forward credits, and these can take as long as 10 years to repay. Unlike other investment loans, interest on RRSP loans is not tax-deductible, so paying down the balance should rank high on your priority list.

You should also consider repaying as soon as possible any loans from your RRSP under the Home Buyers' Plan or to go back to school. Although you don't pay any interest on these loans, they can cost your RRSP dearly in terms of lost earnings. See Chapter 9 for more information.

Governments won't like to read this, but student loan repayment beyond the required annual amounts should rank fairly low on your priority list. That's because there is now some tax relief for the interest costs of these loans.

Once all your non-deductible consumer loans have been retired, go after your mortgage. Take advantage of any prepayment clauses in your contract to make the maximum penalty-free payments you can afford. Remember, you can pay off any amount you want with no penalty at each renewal date.

Your final target, once all other debt has been eliminated, should be any tax-deductible loans you've incurred for business or investment purposes. The reason for leaving these until last is simple: once the tax advantages are taken into account, they're the cheapest form of borrowing available to most people.

Home Ownership

I continue to be a strong believer in the financial benefits of home ownership, especially in retirement. There are three main advantages to having your own place—fully paid for, of course.

First, you'll eliminate a major cash drain on your retirement income. If you're a renter or paying down a mortgage now, take a moment to calculate how much of your income goes to meeting those costs every month. If you're like most Canadians, the percentage is significant. One of your primary goals should be to ensure you won't carry that particular cost burden into retirement with you.

Of course, you'll still have to deal with all the other expenses associated with home ownership: property taxes, utilities, repairs and maintenance, and the like. But by knocking rent or mortgage costs off your retirement expense projections, you'll be reducing your financial burden considerably.

The second benefit of home ownership is that it reduces the impact of inflation on your retirement budget. Housing is an important component of the Consumer Price Index. If you don't have to concern yourself with rising house prices or rents, even if the increases are modest, you're a step ahead.

The third advantage of home ownership is that it provides a source of available capital you can tap into if required. Home equity lines of credit and reverse mortgages allow you to use the capital value of your home after retirement, while still living in it. I'll explain how these new financing methods work in Chapter 22.

A Tax-Sheltered Savings Program

We live in a highly-taxed country. However, we have a major advantage over most other nations: one of the most generous tax-sheltered retirement programs in the world. The federal government allows us to put aside large amounts of money for our retirement every year in the form of pension contributions, deferred profit sharing plans, and RRSPs. To encourage us to make use of this program, we're offered two valuable tax benefits: immediate tax deductibility and future income growth in a tax-sheltered environment.

These programs are classified as "registered" investments. That simply means the plan is registered with Revenue Canada and is subject to certain terms and conditions. All other investments you make are said to be "non-registered."

The tax benefits associated with registered plans are so attractive that you'd think every adult Canadian would want to take advantage of them. But that's not the case. According to the 1999 Scotiabank poll cited earlier, only 58 percent of working Canadians have an RRSP. While that's better than a decade ago, it's still way too low.

In a heavily-taxed country, it's absolutely essential to use every break you can get if you hope to retire wealthy. Registered investments are accessible to everyone with earned income. You cannot set up a good retirement plan without them.

A Non-Registered Investment Portfolio

While making maximum use of registered plans is important, you must go further. The government has limited its tax assistance: maximum contributions to registered plans will generate about 70 percent of pre-retirement income when combined with other income support programs such as the Canada Pension Plan and Old Age Security.

However, Ottawa's 70 percent target can be an illusion for many people. It requires 35 years of maximum contributions to achieve that level. And higher-income earners may find their payouts from registered plans, plus their CPP and OAS payments, fall well below the 70 percent mark because of a cap on the amount you can receive from employer pension plans.

All of this suggests you'll need income from other sources to achieve your retirement objectives. Unless you're planning to continue working part-time after you retire, that income will have to come from your non-registered investments: stocks, bonds, GICs, rental properties, Canada Savings Bonds, and the like.

Building a non-registered investment portfolio should therefore form part of your retirement plan. However, it's important to keep your priorities straight. This should be the final item on your retirement list, to be undertaken only when the first three pillars of your structure are firmly in place.

That doesn't mean building a non-registered portfolio isn't important. But you'll find it will be much easier once you've accomplished the first three goals.

To help you assess where you stand now in putting your four pillars into place, take a few minutes to calculate your net worth in the context of a retirement plan.

Your net worth is the total value of all your assets less any outstanding liabilities. Knowing your net worth is critical to formulating your retirement plan. It gives you a financial snapshot of your present situation and helps you set priorities for debt reduction and investment. You should review your net worth position at least once every two years; annually if you're within 10 years of retirement.

Using the information your net worth statement provides will help you establish a program that will eventually enable you to put all the pieces of your retirement plan into place. Once that process is under way, you'll be truly on the road to a wealthy retirement.

Here again, I suggest you make some photocopies of the worksheet that follows before you start so you can update your position in the future. The numbers to include on the asset side should represent the value of each item if it were sold today—you're not projecting future income at this stage.

Here are some additional pointers to help you.

Registered Assets. Include here the current value of any holdings you have in registered plans. RRSPs should be recorded at their market value today. In the case of pension and deferred profit sharing plans, show the lump-sum amount that would accrue to you if you stopped working for your employer tomorrow. This figure should be available from your most recent benefits statement or through the administrator of your pension plan or DPSP. If you have any vested benefits from pension plans with previous employers, include their current value as well. If you've converted any RRSPs into registered retirement income funds (RRIFs) or life income funds (LIFs), they should also be listed here.

Non-Registered Liquid Assets. This category consists of investments that can normally be converted to cash reasonably easily, although not always at their face value. Use current market values in all cases. Use updated bank statements, brokerage reports, and mutual fund statements as your information sources.

Non-Registered Illiquid Assets. In this group, list the current value of any assets that are not easily convertible to cash. Real estate is included here because the sale of property can sometimes take several months. Show the full current market value of any property you own; outstanding mortgages will be deducted in the Liabilities section. Limited partnerships are also listed here, since there is usually no ready market for such units if you need to sell. Business interests should include the value of your ownership position in any company not publicly traded. Vehicles, collectibles, furnishings, and the like should be listed on the basis of how much they could be sold for today if you needed to raise cash.

Liabilities. List the current amounts outstanding on all loans. This will help establish priorities for the debt reduction part of your retirement plan.

If you're married, show the total value of the assets and liabilities of both you and your spouse in all cases.

Net Worth Calculator

Date:

ASSETS

Type	Current Value

Registered

RRSPs _____

Employer pension plans _____

Deferred profit sharing plans _____

RRIFs _____

Subtotal #1 _____

Non-registered—liquid

Cash and equivalent

Savings/chequing accounts _____

Short term deposits _____

Savings certificates _____

Canada Savings Bonds _____

Treasury bills _____

Money Market Funds _____

Foreign currencies _____

Other _____

Subtotal #2 _____

Type	Current Value
Non-registered—liquid (continued)	
Income	
Bonds	_____
Mortgages	_____
Income mutual funds	_____
Mortgage-backed securities	_____
Guaranteed investment certificates	_____
Preferred shares	_____
Royalty trusts and REITs	_____
Other	_____
Subtotal #3	_____
Growth	
Stocks	_____
Equity mutual funds (Canadian)	_____
Equity mutual funds (International)	_____
Gold and precious metals funds	_____
Other	_____
Subtotal #4	_____
Subtotal # 5 (Add subtotals #2, 3, 4)	_____
Non-registered—illiquid	
Principal residence	_____
Recreational property	_____

Type	Current Value
Non-registered—illiquid (continued)	
Income property	_____
Limited partnerships	_____
Business interests	_____
Vehicles	_____
Boats	_____
Collectibles	_____
Furnishings/appliances	_____
Jewellery	_____
Silver	_____
Clothing	_____
Other	_____
Subtotal #6	_____
TOTAL ASSETS (add subtotals #1, 5, 6)	_____

LIABILITIES

Type	Current Value
Short-term loans (non-deductible)	
Credit card balances	_____
Personal lines of credit	_____
Demand loans	_____
Instalment loans	_____
RRSP loans	_____
Other	_____
Subtotal #7	_____

Type	Current Value
Short-term loans (deductible)	
Student loans	_____
Margin accounts	_____
Investment loans	_____
Business loans	_____
Deductible PLC loans	_____
Other	_____
Subtotal #8	_____
Long-term loans (non-deductible)	
Mortgage (principal residence)	_____
Mortgage (recreational property)	_____
Other	_____
Subtotal #9	_____
Long-term loans (deductible)	
Mortgage (income property)	_____
Limited partnership loans	_____
Other	_____
Subtotal #10	_____
TOTAL LIABILITIES (add subtotals #7 through 10)	_____

NET WORTH

(subtract total liabilities from total assets) _____

There it is: the framework you need to put together your comprehensive plan to retire wealthy. Now let's go about making it happen.

Key Points in Review

1. Retirement planning means a lot more than just opening an RRSP. You must have a comprehensive plan if you hope to achieve the lifestyle you want.

2. Don't be afraid to dream. Dreams can come true, if you put a price tag on them and set up a plan to make them happen.

3. You'll probably receive retirement income from more sources than you expect. Do some advance calculations to find out how important each is likely to be.

4. Pay off all your debts before you retire. Otherwise, the financial burden may be crushing.

5. Owning your own home will reduce your retirement costs and could provide an unexpected source of income.

6. Take advantage of the government's tax-sheltering mechanisms by contributing the maximum possible to registered plans. It's one of the most effective ways for Canadians to build personal wealth.

7. Take the time to calculate your current net worth. The knowledge will help you to establish a realistic retirement plan.

4

How Much Money Will You Have?

Lack of money is the root of all evil.

— George Bernard Shaw

THERE'S NO WAY YOU CAN PLAN FOR A COMFORTABLE RETIREMENT unless you have some idea, even a rough one, of how much income you can expect to receive. The younger you are, the more difficult that estimate becomes. After all, who can predict what will happen over the next 30 or 40 years? You might win the Lotto 649, in which case all of this would become irrelevant. But unfortunately, that's not likely. So at this stage, you should at least identify the various sources of income that are likely to be available when you stop work. Then you'll be able to put more precise dollar signs on their value as the years pass.

In Chapter 3, we quickly looked at the various sources of retirement income available to most people. Now we'll start to affix values to each. For now, we'll use today's dollars to keep things simple. In the next chapter, we'll discuss the effects of inflation on your future income needs.

Your goal should be to arrive at a retirement income potential that is at least 80 percent of your current family income. That's on the high side according to federal government actuaries, but I always maintain it is better to have too much money than too little when retirement comes.

Government Programs

Canada Pension Plan/Quebec Pension Plan. The maximum monthly benefit in 1999 was $751.67, or just over $9000 a year, for both the CPP and the QPP. CPP/QPP payments are fully indexed for inflation. If that policy is maintained (which I am not convinced it will be), you'll receive a pension from this source that is equivalent to $9000 a year in today's purchasing power when you retire. If your spouse is also eligible for full benefits, the CPP/QPP will be worth $18 000 a year to your family.

However, don't take for granted that this is the actual amount you will receive. There are several ways in which the CPP/QPP benefit can be reduced, some of which may come as a surprise to the newly-retired. They include early retirement, which reduces your contributory years, and early application for benefits (if you start to draw before age 65, your payments are reduced). You'll find more details on the CPP/QPP in later chapters.

Old Age Security (OAS). OAS payments are made to all Canadians aged 65 and older. During the first quarter of 1999, the amount was $410.82 a month, or a little more than $4900 a year. So a couple would receive almost $10 000 a year from this source. Again, these benefits are fully indexed so if there is no change in policy, the current purchasing power will still be there when you retire.

Whether you get to keep the full amount of your OAS cheque is another matter. Retired people in high income brackets are hit with what the federal government euphemistically calls a "social benefits repayment tax," more popularly (or unpopularly) known simply as "the claw-back." This kicks in if your net income in any year is higher than $53 215. You'll find more details in Chapter 16.

Guaranteed Income Supplement (GIS). You don't want to get this one and it should not be included on your "Sources of Income" list. GIS is support payments provided by the federal government to low-income individuals. Hopefully, you will never need to apply.

Employer Pension Plans

If you are fortunate enough to have an employer pension plan, it will likely be one of your main sources of retirement income. But don't let the fact that you have a plan lull you into a false sense of security. Many people have found to their dismay that what they thought would be a generous pension benefit turned out to be a mere pittance in relation to their total retirement income needs.

The fact is that many Canadians overestimate the amount of income their pension plan will produce. By the time they realize their mistake, it's often too late to do much about it.

That's why it is essential to obtain an estimate of the income you can expect from your pension plan as soon as possible. Obviously, the closer you are to retirement, the more accurate the estimate will be. Your employer should provide you with an annual benefits report that shows your current status. However, any pension projections will be based on your current level of compensation. Few benefits reports attempt to project your income at retirement because of the many variables involved. If you want to get a better fix on what you can expect at retirement, ask the plan administrator to do a projection based on your current income and on the assumption that you will remain in the plan until you retire. This will provide a good estimate of the percentage of your current income you can expect to receive as a pension.

However, such an estimate is only possible if you belong to a defined benefit pension plan—one in which the payment is determined by a fixed formula, normally based on a combination of income and years of service. If your plan is of the money purchase type (also known as defined contribution) or is a group RRSP, the estimate becomes more difficult. In this case, your pension benefit won't relate to your salary or years of service at all; rather it will be a function of how much you and your employer contribute to the plan over the years and how well the invested money performs. Still, you can't build your retirement income estimate without *some* idea of what benefit you might draw from a program of this type, so ask your plan administrator to give it a shot using current contribution levels and a conservative average annual rate of return (say, 6 percent).

Of course, if you have no pension plan, which is the case with the majority of working Canadians, your retirement income from this source will be zero.

RRSPs

If you don't have an employer pension plan, an RRSP (or a combination of them) is likely to be the single most important source of your retirement income. Even if you do expect to receive a pension, RRSP income can form a significant part of your cash flow after retirement.

The first step in assessing the income potential of your RRSPs (I use the plural because many people have more than one) is to calculate how much your current RRSP assets will be worth at retirement. The value of these assets will depend on how well you manage them and what kind of return you can generate. The following table shows how much each dollar now in your RRSP will be worth when you retire, assuming various average annual rates of growth. To be conservative, I suggest you use the 6 percent column for your estimates. If your investments do better, it will be a bonus.

How Your Present RRSP Will Grow

	Future Value of $1 at		
Years Before Retirement	6%	8%	10%
1	1.06	1.08	1.10
2	1.12	1.17	1.21
3	1.19	1.26	1.33
4	1.26	1.36	1.46
5	1.34	1.47	1.61
6	1.42	1.59	1.77
7	1.50	1.71	1.95
8	1.59	1.85	2.14

Years Before Retirement	Future Value of $1 at		
	6%	8%	10%
9	1.69	2.00	2.36
10	1.79	2.16	2.59
11	1.90	2.33	2.85
12	2.01	2.52	3.14
13	2.13	2.72	3.45
14	2.26	2.94	3.80
15	2.40	3.17	4.18
16	2.54	3.43	4.59
17	2.69	3.70	5.05
18	2.85	4.00	5.56
19	3.03	4.32	6.12
20	3.21	4.66	6.73
21	3.40	5.03	7.40
22	3.60	5.44	8.14
23	3.82	5.87	8.95
24	4.05	6.34	9.85
25	4.29	6.85	10.83
26	4.55	7.40	11.92
27	4.82	7.99	13.11
28	5.11	8.63	14.42
29	5.42	9.32	15.86
30	5.74	10.06	17.45

| | Future Value of $1 at | | |
Years Before Retirement	6%	8%	10%
31	6.09	10.87	19.19
32	6.45	11.74	21.11
33	6.84	12.68	23.23
34	7.25	13.69	25.55
35	7.69	14.79	28.10
36	8.15	15.97	30.91
37	8.64	17.25	34.00
38	9.15	18.63	37.40
39	9.70	20.12	41.14
40	10.29	21.72	45.26

To find the value of your current RRSP assets at retirement, use the following formula:

Present Value of RRSP x Growth Factor
= Future Value of RRSP

For example, suppose you have $25 000 in an RRSP today and 30 years remain until you plan to retire. As you can see from the table, if your average annual growth rate is 6 percent, every dollar will grow to $5.74 at the end of 30 years. The value of your existing RRSP assets at that time will therefore be:

$25 000 x 5.74 = $143 500

The table also provides a good illustration of how good money management can greatly enhance the final value of your RRSP. If you achieve an average annual compound rate of return of 8 percent in your plan, every dollar will be worth $10.06 at the end of 30 years. The value of your RRSP in that case would be:

$25 000 x 10.06 = $251 500

At an average annual growth rate of 10 percent, one dollar today becomes worth $17.45 in 30 years and the value of your plan is:

$$\$25\ 000 \times 17.45 = \$436\ 250$$

As you can see, the numbers can become quite impressive.

But what about future contributions? Surely you don't plan to stop contributing to your RRSP now. The next table will enable you to work out the value of future RRSP contributions at retirement, assuming you keep adding to your RRSP every year at the same rate and that you make your new contribution at the start of each year.

Value of Future RRSP Contributions

Years Before Retirement	Future Value of $1 per Year at		
	6%	8%	10%
1	1.06	1.08	1.10
2	2.18	2.25	2.31
3	3.37	3.51	3.64
4	4.64	4.87	5.11
5	5.98	6.34	6.72
6	7.39	7.92	8.49
7	8.90	9.64	10.44
8	10.49	11.49	12.58
9	12.18	13.49	14.94
10	13.97	15.65	17.53
11	15.87	17.98	20.38
12	17.88	20.50	23.52
13	20.02	23.21	26.97
14	22.28	26.15	30.77

Years Before Retirement	Future Value of $1 per Year at		
	6%	8%	10%
15	24.67	29.32	34.95
16	27.21	32.75	39.54
17	29.91	36.45	44.60
18	32.76	40.45	50.16
19	35.79	44.76	56.27
20	38.99	49.42	63.00
21	42.39	54.46	70.40
22	46.00	59.89	78.54
23	49.82	65.76	87.50
24	53.86	72.11	97.35
25	58.16	78.95	108.18
26	62.71	86.35	120.10
27	67.53	94.34	133.21
28	72.64	102.97	147.63
29	78.06	112.28	163.49
30	83.80	122.35	180.94
31	89.89	133.21	200.14
32	96.34	144.95	221.25
33	103.18	157.63	244.48
34	110.43	171.32	270.02
35	118.12	186.10	298.13
36	126.27	202.07	329.04

| | Future Value of $1 per Year at | | |
Years Before Retirement	6%	8%	10%
37	134.90	219.30	363.04
38	144.06	237.94	400.45
39	153.76	258.06	441.59
40	164.05	279.78	486.85

The formula for calculating the value of future RRSP contributions is:

Annual Future Contributions x Growth Factor
= Value at Retirement

To illustrate, let's say you plan to contribute $3000 a year to your RRSPs until your planned retirement in 30 years. To calculate the retirement value of these new contributions at an annual average growth rate of 6 percent, you would multiply that amount by the appropriate growth factor, which in this case is 83.80. Your new contributions would therefore be worth at retirement:

$3000 x 83.80 = $251 400

If you were to achieve an annual growth rate of 8 percent, your new contributions would be worth:

$3000 x 122.35 = $367 050

At 10 percent annual growth—which is not impossible by any means if you manage your money well—the new contributions will grow to:

$3000 x 180.94 = $542 820

At this stage, you know how to calculate the future value of your current RRSP assets, as well as how to project how much the contributions you make for the rest of your working life will be worth at retirement. Now let's put the two together to find the total projected value of your RRSPs.

To do this, add the final value of your planned future RRSP contributions to the estimated final value of the assets already in your plan.

For the 6 percent illustrations I have used, assuming retirement in 30 years, the total final value will be:

$$\$143\ 500 + \$251\ 400 = \$394\ 900$$

With an average annual return of 8 percent, the end value of your RRSPs increases to:

$$\$251\ 500 + \$367\ 050 = \$618\ 550$$

At an annual average return of 10 percent, you'll end up with:

$$\$436\ 250 + \$542\ 820 = \$979\ 070$$

The amount of annual income your plan will generate will depend on how you withdraw the money. Let's assume that when you retire at age 65, you move the assets into a registered retirement income fund (RRIF) and decide to withdraw the minimum amount required by the government each year. You'll find more details about RRIFs in later chapters, but for now we'll assume you start receiving your payments in the year in which you turn 66. The formula for calculating the minimum amount you must withdraw that year is:

$$\frac{\text{Value of RRIF on Jan. 1}}{90 - \text{Your Age on Jan. 1}}$$

(Note: this formula only applies until age 71, after which a specific withdrawal percentage is used.)

Unless your 66th birthday is on January 1, your age at the start of the year will be 65. So your first year minimum withdrawal, using the total RRSP value based on a 6 percent annual average growth rate, would be:

$$\frac{\$394\ 900}{90 - 65} = \frac{\$394\ 900}{25} = \$15\ 796.00$$

Unless your investments take a big fall in value, this amount should increase each year, because the government requires you to withdraw a higher percentage of the plan as you age.

Using an 8 percent annual growth rate, the first year's income from the RRIF will be:

$$\frac{\$618\ 550}{90-65} = \frac{\$618\ 550}{25} = \$24\ 742.00$$

If your investments grew at the rate of 10 percent a year, your first year RRIF income would be:

$$\frac{\$979\ 070}{90-65} = \frac{\$979\ 070}{25} = \$39\ 162.80$$

Non-Registered Investments

If possible, you should try to supplement your retirement income with additional revenue from a non-registered investment portfolio. However, you should only start building such a portfolio after you have maximized your RRSP and pension plan contributions.

A non-registered portfolio can include any type of security or asset— stocks, bonds, mutual funds, real estate, you name it. However, if you want the portfolio to provide some income, you should choose your assets with care. An original Picasso may appreciate in value and look great on your wall, but it won't spin off any monthly cash flow.

The first step in estimating how large a non-registered portfolio you may have at retirement is to work through the net worth calculation, which you'll find in Chapter 3. Subtotal #5 is the key figure to look at, as it is the total of your non-registered liquid assets. The future growth in the value of these assets will depend on a variety of factors, one of which will be taxes. Unlike your RRSPs, you will be taxed on the growth of your non-registered portfolio. But the rate of tax will vary, depending on whether the growth is achieved through compound interest, dividends, capital gains, or rents. Also, you will pay no tax on capital gains until you actually sell the asset. So a stock or equity mutual fund could increase in value over many years with no capital gains taxes being assessed.

Since we are only preparing estimates at this point, let's assume that, with all factors taken into account, your non-registered portfolio is invested mainly in growth securities like equity funds, and that you achieve an average annual after-tax rate of return of 6 percent. You can refer back to the 6 percent column in the table "How Your Present RRSP

Will Grow" to estimate what the value of your present non-registered portfolio will be when you retire.

So if, for example, your current non-registered liquid assets are $10 000 and there are 30 years to retirement, you multiply that amount by a factor of 5.74:

$$\$10\ 000 \times 5.74 = \$57\ 400$$

That represents the value of your non-registered portfolio at that time. However, remember that there may be taxes still to be paid on any portion of that amount that consists of unrealized capital gains.

Suppose you decide to put aside another $1000 a year for your non-registered portfolio—money that you are investing after making your full RRSP contribution. You can use the 6 percent column from the table "Value of Future RRSP Contributions" to see approximately how much that will be worth when you stop work. In this case, the factor is 83.80:

$$\$1000 \times 83.80 = \$83\ 800$$

So, to carry this illustration to conclusion, the value of your non-registered portfolio at retirement would be:

$$\$57\ 400 + \$83\ 800 = \$141\ 200$$

How much will that add to your retirement income? Let's say you decide to invest the proceeds in government bonds with a yield of 5 percent (there are better choices, but we'll keep things simple for now). You liquidate the portfolio for this purpose. Taxes incurred as a result total 15 percent of the assets, or $21 180, leaving you with $120 020 to invest in the bonds. Your annual income from this source would be:

$$\$120\ 020 \times 5\% = \$6001$$

Note: if you plan to sell your home at retirement and move to a less expensive place, add your anticipated profit to your non-registered portfolio total. This money will be received tax-free.

Other Income

If you expect to receive retirement income from other sources (e.g., a share in a business, consulting work, second career, reverse mortgage, etc.), that should be taken into account as well. Usually, the likelihood of revenue from such sources does not become apparent until you are approaching retirement age.

Adding It Up

You should now have enough information to do a preliminary estimate of your retirement income. Complete the following Retirement Income Projection, using the results you have obtained to this point.

For the tax calculation, refer to your latest tax return (and that of your spouse, if applicable). Divide the tax payable by the total income to determine your effective rate of tax. Admittedly, this is a very rough number, since it is impossible to know what the tax brackets will look like in 20 or 30 years. However, taxes as a percentage of your total income should decline after retirement, at least in theory. So using your current effective tax rate should produce a conservative result—your actual taxes due will likely be less than you will calculate here.

The end result may show your projected income to be less than your projected expenses. Not to worry. One of the purposes of this book is to show you how to bridge the gap. Once you see how large that gap is, you'll have a much better idea of how much work still has to be done.

Retirement Income Projection

CPP/QPP annual payments (current figures)	_____	(1)
Old Age Security payments (current figures)	_____	(2)
Pension income	_____	(3)
RRIF income	_____	(4)
Non-registered income	_____	(5)
Other income	_____	(6)
Total before taxes (add lines 1 through 6)	_____	(7)

Effective tax rate	_____	(8)
Taxes (line 7 x line 8)	_____	(9)
After-tax income (line 7 – line 9)	_____	(10)
Subtract estimated spending (from Expense Estimator in Chapter 3)	_____	(11)
Project surplus (shortfall) (line 10 – line 11)	_____	(12)

Key Points in Review

1. Aim for a retirement income that is at least 80 percent of your current income.

2. Both the Canada Pension Plan and Old Age Security are indexed for inflation. If that policy doesn't change, the benefits will have the same purchasing power when you retire as they do today.

3. Many Canadians overestimate the amount of income their employer pension plan will provide. Get an estimate of how much you will receive at retirement and update it annually.

4. If you don't have an employer pension plan, your RRSP will likely be your most important source of retirement income.

5. A non-registered investment portfolio will provide the extra income you need to maintain a comfortable living standard when you retire.

6. If your projected retirement expenses exceed your estimated income, don't panic. There is probably still time to fix matters.

5

Don't Discount Inflation

I've got all the money I'll ever need
if I die by four o'clock.

— Henny Youngman

IT WASN'T LONG AGO THAT INFLATION WAS THE NUMBER ONE bogeyman of retirees. Many were caught in a financial trap, living on a fixed income while the prices they paid for essentials were rising four, five, six percent a year—even more in some cases.

In the first edition of *Retiring Wealthy*, published in 1991, I told the story of a retired Goodyear worker named Alex Mansfield who had been interviewed shortly before on a television program with which I was associated. At that time he was 75 years old and president of the United Seniors of Ontario.

His story was typical of what we heard from retirees in the 1970s and 1980s.

"I thought I had planned the best I could for retirement," he said. "I bought a house and most of my money went into the mortgage. I got that paid off before retiring because I knew the first thing to do was to get rid of my debt. Then these RRSPs were available and I bought them a few years before my retirement. And I knew that I'd get a pension from the company."

So he did all the right things. But he revealed that, 13 years after stopping work, he was having a great deal of trouble making ends meet.

"I'm living on a fixed income and every year the property taxes go up 10 to 15 percent, and the telephone and electricity keep going up," he explained. "My wife died two years ago and that means her old age pension is gone. Occasionally I run short and have to dip into my savings.

"I don't mind paying property taxes, but older people on fixed incomes can't keep up. Everything is more expensive. I can hardly keep up with car insurance rates—no senior can.

"And I shouldn't complain too much. I was talking with two women recently who told me they weren't entitled to any pension because they had worked part-time. Now they're living on about $6000 a year!"

We aren't hearing many stories like that these days. As we move into the twenty-first century, inflation in Canada is almost a forgotten factor when it comes to retirement planning. The federal government and the Bank of Canada have set a target for inflation of 1 to 3 percent annually, but we haven't been near the upper end of that range for a long time. If anything, the concern of economists is that deflation—falling prices—is a greater threat at this time. Most seniors wouldn't complain about paying less at the supermarket, but in fact deflation is a dangerous condition that can lead to a serious economic slowdown. The last time we experienced it was during the Great Depression of the 1930s.

But how long will the current situation continue? Has inflation really been beaten into the ground? Or is it like a hibernating bear, waiting for the right conditions to emerge grumpily from its den?

No one can say with certainty. While it appears that inflation will not be a serious problem over the next few years, who knows what we can expect a decade or two down the road.

So smart investors should make some provision for inflation in their retirement plans. Even at very low levels, inflation will nibble away at purchasing power over time. The longer you live on a fixed income, the greater the cumulative effect will be.

Let's look at some illustrations.

Fred and Mary Jones. Fred and Mary are both aged 65 and expect to retire this year. They will each receive a modest pension, each has some RRSP savings, and both will draw CPP and OAS benefits. They expect their combined after-tax income to be $40 000 a year. Only the

CPP and OAS payments have built-in inflation protection. The rest of their income is relatively fixed.

Scenario: Inflation averages 1 percent a year. We'll first assume that inflation remains at very low levels throughout their retirement years, averaging just 1 percent annually. After 10 years, their after-tax income will have to rise to $44 200 in order for Fred and Mary to maintain their standard of living. That may not seem like a lot, but it represents an increase of more than 10 percent, which is not easy for retired people.

At the end of 20 years, when they are 85, their combined after-tax income will need to be $48 800 if Fred and Mary are to live in the same degree of comfort they enjoyed at age 65. If they both live to the ripe old age of 95, their after-tax income will have to reach almost $54 000 a year to enable them to stay even. And remember, we're only talking about 1 percent annual inflation here.

Bill and Arlene Wallace. They've been retired for some time. Bill is now 70 years old, and Arlene is three years younger. Bill worked in the construction industry, while Arlene was a stay-at-home mom. He has a small pension from a union plan and draws full CPP benefits as well as OAS. Arlene doesn't qualify for CPP but receives Old Age Security. Their combined after-tax income is $25 000 a year.

Scenario: Inflation averages 2 percent a year. An average increase in the cost-of-living index of 2 percent annually would fall exactly in the middle of the target inflation range set by Ottawa. This therefore seems like a more realistic figure to work with than the 1 percent scenario we looked at with Fred and Mary Jones.

Although Bill is now 70 years old, he's in good health so the odds are he will live at least another 10 years. By the time Bill is 80, this couple's after-tax income will need to increase by 34 percent, to $33 600, if they are to maintain their purchasing power. That is likely to be virtually impossible for people in this situation. They face the possibility of a significant deterioration in their standard of living over time.

Patrick and Susan Chong. This upwardly mobile couple have done very well for themselves. He's made a successful career as a stockbroker while she worked as a radiologist in a major hospital. They have saved their money carefully over the years and have decided to take early retirement. He's 55, she is 50. They aren't eligible for CPP or OAS yet, but their after-tax income from RRSPs, investments, and pension plans will be a tidy $90 000 annually.

Scenario: Inflation averages 3 percent a year. This time we'll look at a situation in which inflation runs at the upper level of Ottawa's target range. At the end of five years, their combined after-tax income will have to rise to more than $104 000 to maintain their purchasing power. At that point, Patrick will qualify for early CPP benefits, which will help. But even if he obtains the maximum level of payments (unlikely because of his early retirement), he'll only receive about $6300 a year. The rest of the money will have to come from elsewhere.

After 10 years, Patrick and Susan will need to push their after-tax income to almost $121 000 to maintain their standard of living. At this point, he will be 65, while she will be 60. Patrick will now be eligible to collect Old Age Security. But because of his high income, a portion of the payments will be subject to the social benefits repayment tax, or "claw-back." Susan can now begin to draw an early CPP pension, but it will be much reduced because she left the workforce at age 50.

The years pass. Another decade slips by. He is now 75, she is 70. It has been 20 years since they both took early retirement, and the financial strain is starting to tell on them. The $90 000 in after-tax income they took into early retirement, which seemed so comfortable at the time, must now have grown to $162 500 in after-tax income for Patrick and Susan to have the same purchasing power. It hasn't; nothing like it. They have long since realized that they made a terrible error in stopping work when they did. Early retirement means a much longer period of drawing on savings and investments, and a longer time for even relatively low levels of inflation to eat away at buying power.

It only gets worse. After another five years, their after-tax income needs are up to more than $188 000, more than double the level at which they started. The condo in Florida has long gone, as have many of the other luxuries they once enjoyed. While their income is modestly higher than it was when they took early retirement so long ago, inflation has run way ahead of them and their twilight years are nothing like they expected them to be.

The message from all these fictional case studies is clear. Your retirement plan must take inflation into account, even though it does not seem to be a major problem at this time.

The table that follows will help you do this. Select a target rate of inflation and then use it to determine how much your income will have to increase over time to maintain the same purchasing power.

For example, the inflation adjustor for 10 years at a 3 percent average annual rate is 1.34. That means for every $10 000 in after-tax income at the start of your retirement, you'll need $13 400 after a decade to maintain your standard of living.

The Inflation Effect

Years After Retirement	Inflation Adjustor at					
	1%	2%	3%	4%	5%	6%
1	1.01	1.02	1.03	1.04	1.05	1.06
2	1.02	1.04	1.06	1.08	1.10	1.12
3	1.03	1.06	1.09	1.13	1.16	1.19
4	1.04	1.08	1.13	1.17	1.22	1.26
5	1.05	1.10	1.16	1.22	1.28	1.34
6	1.06	1.13	1.19	1.27	1.34	1.42
7	1.07	1.15	1.23	1.32	.1.41	1.50
8	1.08	1.17	1.27	1.37	1.48	1.58
9	1.09	1.20	1.31	1.42	1.55	1.69
10	1.11	1.22	1.34	1.48	1.63	1.79
11	1.12	1.24	1.39	1.54	1.71	1.90
12	1.13	1.27	1.43	1.60	1.80	2.01
13	1.14	1.29	1.47	1.67	1.89	2.13

Years After Retirement	Inflation Adjustor at					
	1%	2%	3%	4%	5%	6%
14	1.15	1.32	1.51	1.73	1.98	2.26
15	1.16	1.35	1.56	1.80	2.08	2.40
16	1.17	1.37	1.61	1.87	2.19	2.54
17	1.18	1.40	1.65	1.95	2.29	2.69
18	1.20	1.43	1.70	2.03	2.41	2.85
19	1.21	1.46	1.75	2.11	2.53	3.03
20	1.22	1.49	1.81	2.19	2.65	3.21
21	1.23	1.52	1.86	2.28	2.79	3.40
22	1.25	1.55	1.92	2.37	2.93	3.60
23	1.26	1.58	1.97	2.47	3.07	3.82
24	1.27	1.61	2.03	2.56	3.23	4.05
25	1.28	1.64	2.09	2.67	3.39	4.29
26	1.29	1.66	2.16	2.77	3.56	4.55
27	1.31	1.67	2.22	2.88	3.73	4.82
28	1.32	1.69	2.29	3.00	3.92	5.11
29	1.33	1.71	2.36	3.12	4.12	5.42
30	1.35	1.72	2.43	3.24	4.32	5.74

There are a lot of numbers here, but don't pass by this table too quickly. The story it tells will have a profound effect on your retirement plan.

You can see at a glance that after 30 years of retirement, your income level will have to increase by more than one-third to maintain your purchasing power, even if inflation averages only 1 percent annually over that time.

At a 2 percent average inflation rate, you will need to increase your income by half again after 20 years.

At an average 3 percent, your income will need to double 24 years after stopping work.

If inflation averages 4 percent, it will take only about a decade for your buying power to be cut in half.

At 5 percent, you'll need to double your income in 15 years.

At 6 percent, you'd have to triple it after 19 years.

Pretty sobering numbers, aren't they? Especially with life expectancy increasing and more people talking about early retirement.

So what's the solution? How do you cope with this situation, especially since we don't know what will happen to the inflation level in the years to come? Here are some ways to deal with the problem.

Assume a Higher Inflation Rate

Assume that the rate of inflation will be higher than you actually expect. Let's go back to Ottawa's 1–3 percent range. In effect, the federal government is telling us it won't switch back into a strong anti-inflation mode until the consumer price index starts to move towards the upper end of that band. So it's reasonable to assume we won't see a lot of anti-inflation rhetoric until the level climbs back over 2 percent.

That 2 percent figure therefore looks like a decent average to work with, at least under present conditions. But the prudent planner will want to build in something of a cushion. So I recommend you use 3 percent as your average annual inflation target. If it comes in below that, it will simply mean you have some extra spending money available.

Calculate Your Inflation-Adjusted Needs

In the previous chapter, I explained how to use a worksheet to figure out your approximate retirement expenses in current dollars. Now it's time to apply an inflation adjustor to that number.

As a first step, estimate the number of years remaining until retirement. Then find the appropriate factor from the table. Let's say you have 25 years remaining. Using 3 percent average inflation, multiply your estimated retirement expenses by 2.09. In other words, you'll need a little more than twice as much money at retirement. Don't let that concern you; there are 25 years remaining during which your income will increase and your RRSP savings will be compounding tax-sheltered.

Make Sure You're Protected against Inflation

At this stage, you have an idea of your after-tax income needs when you stop work. But inflation won't end at that point. It will continue, so you have to make sure you're protected against it.

The first thing to do is to determine how much of your anticipated retirement income will be inflation-protected. At this time, both of the main government support programs have built-in inflation adjustors. If that policy is maintained, that part of your income will be secure in purchasing power terms.

Some pension plans also have a measure of inflation protection, especially for those working in the public sector. If you are a pension plan member, find out the policy in this regard. If your plan does not have inflation protection now, it's unlikely to be added in the future because of the potentially high cost involved.

RRSPs may also come with some inflation protection, although you have to set up your income programs to make it work out that way. If you design a RRIF or LIF (life income fund) to make payments under the government's minimum withdrawal formula, the amount you receive will increase each year, as long as the capital base isn't eroded (more on this in a later chapter). However, if inflation returns to higher levels, the annual payment increases may not be enough to compensate. There are also inflation-indexed annuities available, although they are expensive.

Once you are able to estimate how much of your retirement income will have built-in inflation protection, you will have an idea of what percentage is fixed and therefore vulnerable to rising prices.

Ensure Your Income will Increase

Develop plans to ensure your income will rise according to your needs. As long as you plan carefully, there are several possible ways to increase retirement income. They include:

Postpone CPP Payments. Although you become eligible for full payments at 65, you don't have to start collecting Canada Pension Plan benefits until age 70. Every year you wait increases the amount of your pension by 6 percent. So if you don't need your CPP immediately to make ends meet, put it off. When you do start to draw it, the extra income should more than compensate for inflation in the intervening years. In the case of a couple who both qualify for CPP, you may want to start drawing one pension first and keep the other in reserve as long as possible.

Postpone Converting RRSPs. You don't have to close your RRSP until the last day of the year in which you turn 69. If you don't need to draw on the money in your plan immediately, leave it alone. The longer the assets in your RRSP continue to grow tax-sheltered, the more capital you will have to draw on when it's needed.

If you need only some of the RRSP income immediately, arrange for a partial conversion. That is now permitted under the law. You'll obtain some immediate cash flow while the balance can continue to grow.

Manage Your RRSP/RRIF for Continued Growth. Just because you've retired it doesn't mean your RRSP savings need to stagnate. Although you should put a greater emphasis on safety at this stage, don't go overboard. Retain a significant growth component in your RRSP, and in your RRIF when you move on to that stage, so your capital base can increase. We'll look at ways to do this in subsequent chapters.

If Possible, Continue Investing. You may find yourself in the fortunate position of having more income than you really need in your early retirement years. Believe it or not, it does happen. Take advantage of such a situation by investing the surplus. You probably won't be able to contribute any more to RRSPs, but this is a good opportunity to continue to build your non-registered investment portfolio. This will increase the capital available for income generation later.

Look for New Sources of Income. You'd be amazed at the imaginative ways people can generate additional retirement income. Take our Florida friends, Lee and Dick, for example. They "retired" some 15 years ago. But Dick is a restless type who knows how to build things, while

Lee is a former real estate agent. They started by acquiring a somewhat run-down property in Fort Myers Beach, fixed it up, and resold it for a big profit. Then they acquired two buildings near the beach, also run down, which they turned into a very attractive hideaway motel, complete with swimming pool. That became a tidy business. Later, they sold off one of the buildings at a profit, but continue to operate the other one. Neither of them had ever been involved in the tourism industry. But they saw an opportunity and took it.

So there are many ways to beat the inflation problem. It's simply a matter of being aware of it, and planning accordingly.

Key Points in Review

1. Although inflation is not considered a serious problem these days, even modest price increases can erode the purchasing power of your retirement income over many years.

2. Even if inflation averages just 2 percent annually, your income will need to increase by 50 percent after 20 years to maintain buying power.

3. There are ways to protect yourself against the impact of inflation and ensure your standard of living won't be compromised. They include postponing CPP payments, allowing your RRSPs to compound after retirement, and finding new sources of income.

6

Let the Government Help You Save

Were I to define the State, I should prefer to think of it as the poor man's bank.

— Louis Blanc

NOW HERE'S A DEAL FOR YOU! OTTAWA IS GOING TO GIVE YOU MONEY! Lots of it! All you have to do is save a little bit yourself, and our federal government will shower its largesse upon you.

It's true. I kid you not. The registered retirement savings plan (RRSP) has to rank as one of the best tax shelters available to the ordinary person, not just in this country but throughout the world.

The government gives you a big tax write-off every time you contribute, plus you can shelter all the investment income earned inside the plan until the time comes to make use of it.

The result is a government contribution to a more comfortable retirement that could be worth tens, even hundreds, of thousands of dollars over your lifetime.

So why aren't more people taking advantage of it? You'd think with incentives like that, everyone in our heavily-taxed nation would be rushing to cash in.

But that's not the way it is. Every year, statistics and surveys confirm that most Canadians are not taking advantage of the tax-saving benefits offered by RRSPs. And those that do are, for the most part, falling well short of making their maximum contribution.

For the 1997 tax year, the last for which figures were available at the time of writing, Statistics Canada reported that only 13.5 percent of the total available RRSP contribution room was actually used. Canadians left on the table almost $200 billion worth of RRSP contributions they could have claimed but didn't.

Surveys done by major financial institutions consistently show that less than half the working population plans to make RRSP contributions in any given year.

The reasons vary, but in most cases it seems to be a matter of day-to-day financial needs taking precedence over saving for an event that won't take place until years into the future.

That's certainly understandable, especially if a family is struggling just to pay the rent and keep food on the table. But in many cases, the situation is nothing like that desperate. It comes down to a matter of priorities. Let's see, do I want to go to Nassau this winter or contribute to my RRSP? Which sounds like more fun: that red Firebird or the RRSP contribution? Hey, we can buy this terrific stereo system or we can contribute to our RRSPs. Which will it be?

It all boils down to personal decisions. But the fact you've read this far suggests you're at least thinking about a proper retirement plan. So if you aren't contributing regularly to an RRSP, it's either because you're too poor to so do or because you've decided other things are more important. If the latter is the case, it's time to reconsider.

I believe an RRSP should be one of your two top financial priorities, home ownership being the other. That view is widely, but not universally, accepted. There are a few financial experts who would argue differently; one school of thought, for example, contends you'll do better in the long run by putting after-tax dollars into a carefully-selected portfolio of securities with good capital gains potential.

That's all well and good—if you know how to pick such securities and are prepared to accept the risk. However, I suspect most Canadians would be more comfortable putting their savings into a conservatively-invested RRSP and taking the immediate tax benefits that result.

If you don't have an employer pension plan, your RRSP should be your largest single source of retirement income. Even if you have a pension, it should still form a considerable portion of your total retirement income package. But that will only happen if you do two things:

1. Contribute the maximum possible amount to your plan each year.
2. Manage your RRSP assets so as to obtain the highest possible return, consistent with the degree of risk you're prepared to accept.

In this and subsequent chapters, we'll deal with ways to achieve both these goals. But before we get into all that, let's run down some of the basic rules governing RRSPs. If you already know all this stuff, you can skip ahead. But if you're just starting out, you'll need this information to get off on the right foot.

Eligibility. Everyone aged 69 or less may contribute to an RRSP, as long as they have earned income. There is no minimum age for setting up an RRSP. Even a child can have a plan, as long as he or she has earned income.

Contribution Limits. The basic rule is that you can contribute up to 18 percent of last year's earned income, to a maximum of $13 500 a year. However, members of registered pension plans and deferred profit sharing plans have to deduct their pension adjustment (PA) from the amount they're allowed to put in. Your employer will supply that number.

Deadline. The last day for contributions for the previous tax year is 60 days from January 1 of the next year. That usually makes the deadline March 1, except in the case of a leap year or when that date falls on a Sunday.

Carry-Forwards. If you don't make your full contribution, you can carry forward any unused portion to a future date. Revenue Canada will track this for you and update your current RRSP status each year when you receive your notice of assessment.

Eligible Investments. You can invest your RRSP money in almost anything you can think of, including guaranteed investment certificates (GICs), term deposits, Treasury bills, Canada Savings Bonds, savings certificates, most types of bonds, Canadian stocks listed on recognized exchanges, shares of foreign companies listed on recognized exchanges (within limits), over-the-counter stocks traded on NASDAQ and the Canadian Dealing Network (CDN), some limited partnership units, units in labour-sponsored venture capital funds, shares of small businesses, mutual funds, mortgages (including your own), call options, warrants and rights issued by companies listed on Canadian exchanges, bankers' acceptances, and Canadian cash. Major exclusions from RRSPs include gold bullion, foreign currency, real property, and collectibles.

Foreign Property. The federal government wants you to keep most of your RRSP assets at home. As a result, foreign assets may not exceed 20 percent of the book value of each individual RRSP. However, there are many ways around this rule.

Number of Plans. You can open as many separate RRSPs as you like, in any number of financial institutions. This allows maximum flexibility, but it can also create problems. Too many plans may be difficult to keep track of. Also, they can be expensive, depending on what type of RRSPs you set up. Plus, it becomes more difficult to make full use of your foreign content when you're dealing with multiple plans. So even though there's no official limit on the number of RRSPs you can have, use some common sense.

Claiming Deductions. You must file an official receipt with your tax return to claim an RRSP deduction. If you've lost it, ask the financial institution to issue a duplicate.

Spousal Plans. You may set up an RRSP for your spouse and contribute to it as long as he/she is within the RRSP age limit. The total contributions you make to your own plan plus the spousal plan may not exceed your personal limit. Common law couples are also allowed to use spousal plans.

Transfers. You may transfer funds from one RRSP to another without penalty. Simply complete form T2033, which you can obtain from Revenue Canada or the financial institution to which you're transferring the money.

Withdrawals. Any withdrawals from an RRSP are taxable at your marginal rate, unless they are made under the Home Buyers' Plan or the education loan program. You are allowed to withdraw part of the assets from a plan without having the whole plan deregistered.

Now that you're caught up on the rules, let's consider some of the fundamentals that will get you off on the right foot.

Choose the Right Plan

It may be hard to believe, but such a basic decision as the type of RRSP you choose can make a huge difference in the amount of money that will be available to you at retirement.

Many people don't realize that an RRSP is not an investment in itself. They talk about "buying" an RRSP, when in fact all they are really doing is opening a shell which can be used to hold any type of qualified investment you wish. There are five basic types of RRSPs. They are:

- **Savings plans.** These are simply savings accounts dressed in RRSP garb to shelter the interest from taxes. They used to be quite common; today they're quite rare. The low interest rate environment that prevailed through most of the 1990s made such plans virtually obsolete. About the best you can say for them is that they're simple and protected by deposit insurance up to $60 000. But the returns will be very low until such time as interest rates turn around.

- **GIC plans.** This type of plan is what you're likely to get if you walk into a financial institution, plunk your money on the counter, and ask to open an RRSP. Your money will be invested in a term deposit/guaranteed investment certificate for the period you select (usually one to five years) and automatically rolled over when it matures unless you give other instructions. Until interest rates really hit the skids after the recession of the early 1990s, most RRSPs were of this type. They're still popular today, although not to the same degree. However, in the later years of the nineties, aggressive promotion of index-linked GICs, which offer the potential for higher payments based on the gains of major stock markets, gave these plans a new lease on life.

- **Mutual fund plans.** These RRSPs invest your contributions in mutual funds of your choice. They can range from ultra-conservative money market and mortgage funds to higher-risk stock funds, or any mix thereof. This type of plan has become extremely popular in recent years due to the good performance of the mutual funds industry.

- **Government of Canada plans.** A few years ago, the federal government decided it should more aggressively pursue some of the RRSP business that was flowing to the private sector. The result was the creation of a no-fee government RRSP. It was originally designed to hold Canada Savings Bonds but now can be used for other government investment products as well, such as Premium Bonds.

- **Self-directed plans.** These RRSP plans allow you to invest in anything you want, as long as it's considered an "eligible investment." A self-directed plan can be as conservatively or aggressively managed as you wish; you're in full control. The rate of return will vary depending on what you put in your plan, as will the risk level.

The bottom line is that the value of your RRSP can be increased significantly by selecting the right plan. The following table gives you an idea of what would have happened if you'd contributed $5000 to an RRSP on February 1, 1989 and left it untouched for 10 years, until January 31, 1999.

RRSP Returns*

Type of Plan	Average Annual Compound Rate of Return	Value after Ten Years
Canada Savings Bonds	6.6%	$9 474
5-year GICs	7.6%	10 401
Mutual Fund (Canadian Balanced)	9.2%	12 056
Mutual Fund (Self-directed: 80% Canadian equity funds, 20% U.S. equity funds)	9.4%	12 278
Mutual Fund (Canadian Bond)	9.6%	12 505

* Reprinted with permission from *The Globe and Mail*.

As you can see, the difference over that period between the best-performing and worst-performing RRSP was more than $3000, or about 25 percent. So choosing the right type of fund *does* make a difference.

Surprisingly, Canadian bond funds came out best in this comparison, which makes a couple of important points:

1. Stocks do not always outperform bonds over the long term, regardless of public perception.
2. Canadian stock markets have been very weak. If the government allowed you to invest your entire RRSP in U.S. equity funds, your average annual compound rate of return over the decade would have been 12.3 percent and your original $5000 would have grown to almost $16 000!

So what's the right type of RRSP for you? I recommend starting with a mutual fund plan with a company you have confidence in. You can begin with a single Canadian balanced fund and build from there. As your RRSP grows and you gain more investing confidence, you can move to a self-directed plan.

The important thing is to choose the right plan at the outset. I recently did a television interview about retirement planning. Afterwards, the cameraman proudly told me he'd been contributing to an RRSP for several years. When I asked him what type of plan, he hemmed and hawed. After more probing, it turned out his money was in a savings plan and he'd been earning a return of less than 3 percent a year. He'd done the right thing by starting his RRSP early. But by choosing the wrong type of plan—or having it chosen for him—he was leaving big dollars on the table in the form of unrealized returns. Don't make the same mistake.

Make the Maximum Possible Contribution

It's a proven statistical fact that most people do not make full use of their annual RRSP contribution limit. I don't want to start lecturing about the value of saving and all that good stuff. You've heard it all before. Let me simply say that the more money you can sock away in your RRSP, the better off you'll be at retirement.

Last year's notice of assessment from Revenue Canada will tell you how much room you have available, including any unused credits from prior years. Use it as your guideline and do the best you can.

If you want some encouragement to contribute more, take a look at the following table. It assumes an average annual compound rate of return of 6 percent in your RRSP.

Compounded RRSP Values

	Value After			
Annual Contribution	5 yrs.	10 yrs.	20 yrs.	30 yrs.
$1 000	$5 637	$13 181	$36 786	$79 058
2 000	11 274	26 362	73 571	158 116
5 000	28 186	65 904	183 928	395 291
10 000	56 371	131 808	367 856	790 582
13 500	76 101	177 941	496 606	1 067 286

As you can quickly see, the extra money goes a long way. If you contribute $1000 a year to your plan, it will grow to just over $79 000 after 30 years. But if you are able to increase the annual contribution to $2000, you'll end up with almost $160 000 in retirement capital upon which to draw.

The $13 500 line represents the maximum annual amount anyone can contribute to an RRSP. Of course, only people with very healthy incomes will be able to take advantage of it.

Don't Use the Carry-Forward if You Can Avoid It

If you don't make your full RRSP contribution in any given year, you don't lose the entitlement. It carries forward indefinitely, so as long as you have an RRSP you can always play catch-up. Your maximum allowable contribution will increase each year as the carry-forwards accumulate. The annual notice of assessment from Revenue Canada will show you exactly where you stand.

For example, suppose you were allowed to contribute $5000 to an RRSP last year but only put $3000 into the plan. You have a carry-forward credit of $2000, which is added to your regular entitlement for the current year. You can use it now, or carry it forward to next year or beyond.

The carry-forward rule can be useful in certain situations. People who have difficulty scraping together the money for a full RRSP contribution will at least be able to make it up in later years, instead of losing their entitlement completely, as was the case before this reform was introduced in 1991.

But the carry-forward concept can be dangerous to your financial health if not managed properly. It could cost your RRSP many thousands of dollars if you allow it to.

There are three basic problems to consider.

The first is psychological. When given an excuse to spend rather than save, people often grab it. The carry-forward rule provides just such an excuse. You might think of it as legitimized procrastination.

After all, it's much more fun to use the money you've earmarked for your RRSP to take a winter holiday in Florida. You'll just make it up next year, you promise yourself.

And what happens when next year rolls around? Your RRSP contribution limit has doubled, because of the carry-forward. Instead of being able to contribute, say, $6000, you're allowed $12 000. Ask yourself how likely it is that you'll have that kind of money available. And then ask yourself what's likely to happen after five or six years, when your carry-forward entitlement increases to $30 000 or $40 000. The chances are, you'll never catch up. Even though you technically have the carry-forward contribution room available, you may never take advantage of it.

The second disadvantage of the carry-forward is that you lose your tax deduction for the current year. I'm a firm believer in taking advantage of any tax benefits while you can; you never know what a future government is going to do.

For example, suppose you're in a 40 percent tax bracket and you're eligible for a $5000 RRSP contribution this year. You decide to use the carry-forward and defer contributing the money. You've given up a deduction which would have knocked $2000 off your income tax payable.

Now let's assume that the finance minister announces in the next budget that all future RRSP contributions will be treated as tax credits rather than deductions—an idea that has been kicked around in Ottawa in the past, although fortunately has never been acted on, at least to date. Your $5000 carry-forward will now be worth about $1275 in reduced taxes (the exact amount will vary, depending on your province of residence). You've just lost $725 in tax benefits.

The higher your tax bracket and the more money you carry forward, the greater your loss would be in this situation.

The third disadvantage of the carry-forward is the loss of years of compounding. Suppose you're 40 years old and you're entitled to make an RRSP contribution of $10,000 this year. You want to retire at 65.

At 6 percent a year, your $10 000 will grow to about $43 000 over that time.

But you don't make the contribution right away. Instead, you carry it forward for five years and finally get around to it when you're forty-five. You still want to retire at sixty-five. What happens?

Your contribution will now be worth only about $32 000 when you retire. By delaying five years and using the carry-forward, you've reduced the end value of your plan by about $11 000!

This is obviously better than never making the contribution at all. So if it would have been absolutely impossible for you to make the contribution any sooner, the carry-forward has been of value.

But if you've simply used it as an excuse for putting off contributing, it has cost you a lot of money. Think about that before using the carry-forward rule.

The table below illustrates how much the end value of an RRSP will be reduced for each dollar of contribution room you carry forward. I have assumed retirement age to be 65, and annual compound growth to be 6 percent.

What the Carry-Forward Costs You

| | Cost per Dollar of a Delay of | | |
Current Age	1 Year	3 Years	5 Years
20	$0.77	$2.20	$3.47
25	0.69	1.65	2.60
30	0.44	1.24	1.95
35	0.32	0.92	1.45
40	0.24	0.69	1.08
45	0.18	0.52	0.81
50	0.14	0.39	0.61
55	0.10	0.29	0.45
60	0.08	0.22	0.34

As you can see, the younger you are and the longer the delay, the greater the impact on the final value of your RRSP.

For example, if you are twenty-five years old and carry forward $2000 for three years, the loss to the end value of your plan will be $3300 ($2000 x $1.65). If you are forty-five years old and carry forward $12 000 for five years, the end value of your RRSP will be reduced by $9720 ($12 000 x $0.81).

The greater the average annual return you expect to earn in your RRSP, the higher the loss to the end value will be. For example, if our twenty-five year-old were to manage his money so as to earn 10 percent a year instead of 6 percent, the cost of a three-year delay to the end value of his plan would balloon to more than $22 000! The cost of a five-year delay for the forty-five year-old would be more than $30 000!

If you have a choice between carrying forward or not, calculate how much it will cost over the years before making a final decision. It may persuade you to postpone the Florida trip rather than the RRSP contribution.

Contribute Early

You've probably read this advice in the media so many times that you're sick of it: make your annual RRSP contribution early in the New Year. Every financial expert hammers away at this point. The result? Most Canadians still wait until the last minute, then rush frantically to beat the deadline.

Bad strategy! Playing the deadline game may not only result in a hurried, poorly considered investment decision; it will also cost you many dollars. Ideally, you should make your full RRSP contribution on January second of each year, not in January or February of the following year.

By waiting until the deadline each year to contribute, you lose up to 14 months of tax-sheltered compounding. Over many years, that can add up to a lot of money, as the following table shows.

I've assumed in each case that your money earns an average annual return of 6 percent, compounded semi-annually, and that no withdrawals are made from the RRSP before age 65.

The Value of Contributing Early

Age This Year	Accumulated Value of Early Deposit	Accumulated Value of Late Deposit	Cost of Delay
Annual Contribution: $1000			
35	$85 213	$80 322	$4 891
45	39 406	37 143	2 263
55	14 043	13 237	806
60	5 991	5 647	344
Annual Contribution: $2500			
35	213 034	200 805	12 229
45	98 514	92 859	5 655
55	35 107	33 092	2 015
60	14 978	14 118	860

Age This Year	Accumulated Value of Early Deposit	Accumulated Value of Late Deposit	Cost of Delay
Annual Contribution: $7500			
35	639 101	602 414	36 687
45	295 541	278 576	16 965
55	105 321	99 275	6 046
60	44 934	42 354	2 580
Annual Contribution: $13 500			
35	1 150 382	1 084 346	66 036
45	531 974	501 437	30 537
55	189 577	178 695	10 882
60	80 880	76 238	4 642

As you can see from the table, the younger you are and the more money you contribute to your RRSP each year, the greater the financial advantage of getting the cash into the plan at the start of the year. Even if you only contribute $1000 a year to an RRSP, a 35-year-old will end up almost $5000 ahead in terms of the plan's final value by getting the money in early. If you improve on the average annual growth rate of 6 percent (and you should!) the gains will be correspondingly higher.

Start Young

My final piece of advice for getting off on the right foot is very simple: if you can, start young. The more years your money can compound in the tax-sheltered environment of an RRSP, the more capital you will have accumulated at the end of the day.

The next table shows you what happens for people who contribute $1000 a year to an RRSP, based on their age when they open the plan. In all cases, we'll assume retirement at age 65, an average annual compound rate of return of 6 percent, and contributions made at the start of the year.

The Advantage of an Early Start

Starting Age	Total Contributions	Final Value
20	$45 000	$225 508
25	40 000	164 048
30	35 000	118 121
35	30 000	83 802
40	25 000	58 156
45	20 000	38 993
50	15 000	24 673
55	10 000	13 972
60	5 000	5 975

Take a look at the lines for the 20-year-old and the 40-year-old. The younger person contributes $45 000 to the RRSP over the years and ends up with a plan worth more than $225 000. The 40-year old contributes $20 000 less. But her plan is worth only $58 000 at retirement, a difference of $167 000. That's the price she pays for the late start.

Need I say more?

Key Points in Review

1. The RRSP is one of the world's most efficient tax shelters, but most Canadians are not making the best use of their plans.
2. Along with home ownership, contributing regularly to an RRSP should be among your top financial priorities.
3. Choosing the right type of RRSP from the outset can add many thousands of dollars to the final value of your plan.
4. Contribute as much as possible to your RRSP each year. If possible, get the maximum amount you're allowed into the plan.
5. Avoid using the carry-forward. Delaying contributions erodes the end value of an RRSP.

6. By contributing early in the year rather than waiting until the deadline, you benefit from an extra year of tax-sheltered growth.

7. If you can, start contributing to an RRSP while you're young. The more years the money grows in the plan, the richer you'll be when you retire.

7

Winning RRSP Strategies

*You can't expect to hit the jackpot if you
don't put a few nickels in the machine.*

— Flip Wilson

SETTING UP YOUR FIRST RRSP IS A MAJOR STEP TOWARD A SUCCESSFUL
retirement plan. Unhappily, many people seem to think it's the *only* step
they need to make.

It's not. It's only the beginning. Think of it as the equivalent of taking a bag of flour and a cup of sugar from the cupboard and some milk, eggs, and butter from the fridge. You have all the basic ingredients for a cake on the counter in front of you. But you're still a long way from having the cake itself.

When you open an RRSP, you should be making a mental commitment to a lifetime of careful money management. If that idea is too big for you, then forget the whole thing and leave your retirement dreams to the winds of fortune.

This doesn't mean you have to be some kind of financial whiz to build a high-performance RRSP. But it does mean that you should be prepared to devote some time to thinking about your investment strategies and selecting securities that best meet your objectives.

The starting point is to understand what an RRSP is, and what it is not.

It *is* a government-sanctioned plan for building retirement capital.

It is *not* an investment in and of itself.

Think of your RRSP as an empty box. Into that box you can put any type of security you wish, as long as it qualifies under the government's rules. It can be something as simple as a GIC or a Canada Savings Bond, or as complex as a covered call option. It's your call.

So managing your RRSP money doesn't have to be complicated. Keep it ultra-simple, if you prefer. However, by learning a little about the basics of good money management, you can broaden your range of investment opportunities and improve the return potential of your plan considerably.

If you need some added incentive, take a close look at the next table. It shows how much a slightly higher rate of return can add to the end value of an RRSP.

The Value of a Few Percentage Points

$2500/year over 20 years

Value @ 5%	$82 665
Value @ 7.5%	$108 262
Value @ 10%	$143 188

$5000/year over 25 years

Value @ 5%	$238 635
Value @ 7.5%	$339 890
Value @ 10%	$491 736

$13 500/year over 30 years

Value @ 5%	$896 924
Value @ 7.5%	$1 395 892
Value @ 10%	$2 220 669

By improving the average annual return by just two-and-a-half percentage points on a $5000 annual investment over 25 years, you add more than $100 000 to the end value of your RRSP. Think about that for a moment. You haven't contributed one extra cent, but you have more than $100 000 extra to retire on. If that isn't an incentive to manage your money well, I don't know what is!

So how do you go about it? The first step, as I explained in the last chapter, is to choose an RRSP that allows at least some flexibility in the type of securities you can hold. Assuming you've done that, let's move to the next stage—putting the pieces of the puzzle into place. We'll start with some of the basic rules of good money management.

Rule One: Use Asset Allocation Principles

The early 1990s were a rough time for stock markets. North America was in recession, and stocks wallowed. But bonds were a different story. Interest rates had spiked in the late eighties as central banks moved to head off what they saw as an inflationary danger. Instead, the high rates took the steam out of the economy and helped send it into a spiral. By the second half of 1990, it became clear that we were in trouble and the Bank of Canada started to aggressively cut rates. That was great news for bond investors because bond prices rise as interest rates fall. Anyone with positions in the bond market was sitting pretty, while stock investors were crying the blues.

Then came the recovery and for the rest of the decade the stock market went on a tear unlike any we'd seen before. There were some temporary setbacks along the way, of course. In 1994 the stock market lost some ground when interest rates temporarily jumped again. In 1997 an October crash caused by concerns over the Far East raised fears of a general meltdown. But the markets, especially in the U.S., shrugged off the worries and continued to roll forward. When the Dow finally broke through the psychological 10 000 barrier in March, 1999, it was widely seen as a fitting culmination to the most explosive stock market decade since the 1920s. It turns out it wasn't a culmination at all. Less than a month later, the Dow passed through 11 000, although it subsequently fell back from that level.

Unfortunately, the Canadian stock market didn't perform as well. Our market is heavily weighted toward the resource sector: gold, oil, and gas; mines and metals; and forestry products. When commodity prices sagged in the late nineties, our stock market—and our currency—

sagged too. As the decade and the century drew to a close, long-term investors in Canadian bonds had better returns to show than did long-term investors in Canadian stocks.

So what does it all mean? That you should have all your RRSP money in bonds? Or, if it were possible, in U.S. stocks? Or should you try to jump back and forth, depending on what the economy is doing?

None of the above. All this history is to show you that investing can be unpredictable. Things we expect to happen often don't and surprises abound.

The way to deal with all this in your RRSP and to sleep comfortably at night is to use a strategy known as asset allocation. Simply, this involves deciding how much of each class of investment you want to hold in your plan. This should be done before you actually purchase any securities.

Repeated studies have concluded that your asset allocation is more significant in the performance of an RRSP than the actual securities you select. In other words, it's more important to hold the correct proportion of stocks, bonds, and cash at any given time than it is to pick the top performers (although that certainly helps). Yet many people spend hours agonizing over which securities to buy and little or no time considering the make-up of their portfolio.

For asset allocation purposes, there are three basic types of securities:

1. *Cash.* Most people think of cash as bills and coins, but for investment purposes cash includes any liquid asset that can easily be converted to hard money at any time at full face value. This would include federal and provincial government Treasury bills, most money market mutual funds, deposit accounts, short term deposits, Canada Savings Bonds, short-term corporate notes, and bankers' acceptances.

2. *Fixed income securities.* These are investments that pay a fixed rate of return for a term of more than a year. Included are bonds, mortgages, preferred shares, mortgage-backed securities, guaranteed investment certificates, and various types of fixed income mutual funds.

3. *Growth investments.* These are holdings with the potential to produce capital gains. They include stocks, equity mutual funds, precious metals, real estate and real estate funds, and—in a more speculative vein—options, warrants, and futures.

If you're just starting an RRSP, the first thing you should do is to decide what asset allocation you want to work with. As a general rule, the higher the percentage of cash and fixed income securities in the plan, the more conservative it is. That means your risk will be less, but so will your return potential.

For readers who already have an RRSP, I strongly recommend that you take some time now to review the plan and determine your current asset allocation. Then decide whether it is appropriate for your situation, based on the comments that follow.

There are many different asset allocation formulas. There's no single magic one-size-fits-all approach; it depends on your age, risk tolerance level, growth objectives and, above all, what you feel comfortable with. What's important is to ensure that the use of asset allocation is a fundamental part of your RRSP management approach.

Here's one way to go about it, assuming retirement at age 65.

Asset Allocation by Age

	20–25	26–49	50–59	60–65	66+
Cash	5%	5%	5%	10%	15%
Fixed Income	45%	25%	35%	50%	60%
Growth	50%	70%	60%	40%	25%

Some words of explanation are in order here.

For the 20 to 25 age group, you'll see that the fixed income recommendation is higher than for later years, while the growth component is smaller. The reason is that I believe most young people should take a balanced approach to investing until they have learned more about how securities perform and better understand the ins and outs of portfolio management. There is a danger—and I have seen it happen—that young people may tend to be somewhat aggressive with their initial RRSP investments. If this results in a serious loss, it can have a long-time psychological impact on future decisions, which may be detrimental to good performance.

As a person becomes more comfortable with investing—and the ages shown here are only a broad guideline—the percentage of higher-risk growth securities in the plan can be increased. Someone in their late twenties, thirties, and even their forties can take a long-term view of stock markets and not be overly concerned by temporary setbacks. However, I recommend that a portion of all RRSPs be kept in fixed income securities, both to mitigate risk and to take advantage of those occasions when bonds outperform stocks.

As you approach your retirement years, you should gradually reduce the risk in your RRSP, since the time left to ride out any severe stock market setback is running short. Build your cash and fixed income reserves, which will be needed when the time comes to convert your savings to a revenue stream.

However, I suggest you always retain a portion of your RRSP (and later your RRIF) in growth securities as a protection against even modest rates of inflation. You don't want to outlive your money!

Rule Two: Select Your Investments with Care

Too many people treat their RRSP money carelessly. They give less thought to their investments than they do to buying a new TV set, even though the performance of their tax-sheltered securities will have a profound impact on the way they live for the final 20 or 30 years of their lives.

It's essential that you choose the investments for your RRSP with care. There are many choices available—so many, in fact, that the whole process can at times seem incredibly confusing. Here's a run-down of the types of investments I feel are most suitable for an RRSP. Some of these can only be held in self-directed plans.

Cash-Type Securities

Money Market Mutual Funds. These are the core cash holding for most RRSP investors. They may hold Treasury bills, short-term corporate notes, and bankers' acceptances. They are conservatively managed and the net asset value (NAV) is fixed, usually at $10. However, when interest rates are down, as they have been in recent years, returns are very low.

T-Bill Funds. These are money market funds that invest exclusively in Treasury bills. That makes them slightly safer in theory, but the returns are usually a little lower.

Treasury Bills. These are short-term debt securities issued by the federal and provincial governments, usually in maturities of three months, six months and one year. They're as safe an investment as you'll find and an excellent place to park cash in a self-directed plan if you're unsure where to invest or in the event short-term interest rates move up. You can buy Treasury bills through a stockbroker; however, you will find the maturities they offer will seem somewhat unusual—fifty-two days, four-and-a-half months, or some other odd time frame. That's because brokerage firms buy T-bills from governments and hold them in inventory for later resale to retail clients. You'll also find that the rate they quote you is a bit lower than the rates printed in the business pages; the difference is the firm's profit margin.

Remember that T-bills are short-term investments that have to be rolled over at maturity. So the rate you receive is guaranteed for only a minimal time. During periods when interest rates are declining, this means you will get a lower return on your money every time a T-bill matures and your money must be reinvested. When rates are on the rise, on the other hand, the shorter term works in your favour since you can take advantage of upward movements in yields every few months.

Short Term Deposits. Offered by financial institutions, these deposits are guaranteed and usually pay a higher return than you will receive from T-bills.

Canada Savings Bonds. Technically, they're misnamed. These aren't real bonds at all, but short-term savings certificates issued by the federal government. The interest rate reflects current short-term rates and CSBs can be cashed any time for full face value.

Fixed Income Securities

Guaranteed Investment Certificates (GICs). For many Canadians, these were the backbone of their RRSPs for many years. The classic GIC has a term of one to five years, during which time you are guaranteed a specific rate of return. Your principal is locked in for that period.

As interest rates dropped during the nineties, GICs lost their allure, however. Many people began to search for other alternatives in an effort to boost their returns. The response of the financial community was to resurrect an idea that had first been tried with limited success a decade before–the index-linked GIC. The idea was to tie the return of the GIC to the performance of a particular stock index, while guaranteeing the investor's principal if markets went south. The sales pitch was along the lines of: "Play the stock market without risk." The new incarnation of index-linked GICs became immensely popular during the market mania of the decade, spawning an ever-growing product range that includes international indexes.

The problem with this new breed of GIC is that the underlying terms and conditions vary greatly from one company to another. If you're tempted to invest in some of these for your RRSP, I recommend that you:

1. choose GICs linked to U.S. or international indexes. Surprisingly, they are fully RRSP eligible;
2. select a GIC that does not cap your potential rate of return;
3. choose one with an option that enables you to lock in your gain at any point along the way.

Like regular GICs, the index-linked variety is protected by deposit insurance to a maximum of $60 000.

Mortgage Mutual Funds. These funds invest in residential first mortgages, and their safety record is first rate. Even in recessionary times, Canadians are very conscientious about their mortgage payments, which means defaults are minimal. And some funds, such as the First Canadian Mortgage Fund offered by Bank of Montreal, go so far as to protect their investors from the effects of any defaults.

These funds hardly ever lose money over a calendar year. The one exception was 1994, when some funds suffered small losses when interest rates took a temporary jump.

There will be some movement in unit price as interest rates rise and fall. But it won't be as dramatic as with a bond fund, because the average term to maturity of the holdings in a mortgage fund is less (typically around three years). You can ignore these shifts, or take advantage of them to add more units at a reduced price.

Don't go into mortgage funds looking for big gains. When interest rates are low, so are the returns. But you'll usually earn somewhat more than from a money market fund, with only slightly higher risk.

Short-Term Bond Funds. When the first edition of *Retiring Wealthy* was published almost a decade ago, life for RRSP investors was much simpler. All you had to be concerned about was bond funds, pure and simple. Now bond funds come in a range of sizes, shapes, and colours, each designed to meet a specific need. The short-term bond fund is the conservative investor's delight. It invests in bonds with maturity dates no more than three (or sometimes five) years in the future. The short maturities protect you if bond prices slide. But they limit your return, so there's a trade-off involved. Usually, these funds will perform slightly better than a mortgage fund, but there is slightly more risk as well.

Standard Bond Funds. This is the most common type of bond fund. They invest in a range of bonds and debentures of varying maturities. Unless you're trying to implement a specific strategy in your RRSP, they're the best type of bond fund to hold.

Long-Term Bond Funds. This type of bond fund is at the opposite end of the scale from the short-term fund. In this case, the managers load up with long-term bonds (those with maturities of more than 10 years). The idea is to take maximum advantage of any price increases resulting from interest rate declines. Some fund managers, such as Robert Marcus of Altamira, were very successful with this strategy in the late nineties. However, these funds contain a much higher degree of risk, which must be offset against their return potential. You do not want to hold long-term bond funds when interest rates are on the rise.

High-Yield Bond Funds. Now you're into real risk. These funds invest in low-grade corporate bonds, commonly known as junk bonds. They can pay off in a big way if conditions are right, but should only be used in RRSPs in very specific circumstances.

International Bond Funds. These funds actually come in two types. One is fully eligible for RRSPs, because it invests in Canadian debt securities denominated in foreign currencies. The other invests directly in foreign bonds and comes under the foreign content rule.

International bond funds perform best when two conditions prevail: world interest rates are falling and the Canadian dollar is weak. That combination occurred in 1998 and many of these funds turned in double-digit returns as a result.

If the Canadian dollar is rising strongly, international bond funds are not a good choice for your RRSP.

Bonds (Regular). Bonds are debt instruments issued by governments, municipalities, and corporations. When you purchase a bond, you are simply lending money to the issuer at an agreed interest rate (the coupon rate) for a specific period of time (the term to maturity).

On the surface, bonds appear to be a fairly straightforward investment. But they're more complicated than it appears, which is why for most people a bond fund may be the better choice for an RRSP. Some financial advisors recommend direct bond investment instead, however, in order to eliminate the annual management fees charged by mutual funds. You'll need a self-directed plan to do that, plus some basic bond knowledge.

As I pointed out in the discussion of bond funds, the market price of bonds will fluctuate, largely in response to developments in the economy and interest rate movements. So timing can be an important factor in deciding when to invest in bonds for your RRSP. As a general rule, you should add to your bond holdings when interest rates are high and take some profits when rates drop and bond prices rise accordingly.

There's something else to consider, however—safety. You'll sometimes come across bonds that appear to offer great yields. Usually, these wonderful values are issued by shaky corporations. When you encounter such situations, be extremely wary. No one gets something for nothing in the bond world. If a bond is offering an unusually high return, there's probably something wrong with it.

That something is usually risk. The greater the chance that the issuer will default on payment, the higher the interest rate must be to attract investors—a danger premium, if you like. We've seen situations where issues of such bonds have defaulted, leaving investors with little or nothing. That's the last thing you want to happen to your RRSP. So make inquiries about the safety of a bond issue before you decide to buy.

There are two agencies in Canada that rate most bonds issued in the country for safety: the Dominion Bond Rating Service (DBRS) and the Canadian Bond Rating Service (CBRS). They use slightly different symbols in their ratings, but they're usually in close agreement. Here's how to interpret their ratings. The first notation is used by DBRS for all types of bonds and long-term debt, and by CBRS for long-term government bonds. The notation in brackets is used by CBRS for corporate long-term bonds.

AAA (A++) Top of the line. These are the Rolls-Royces of bonds. This rating is usually reserved for the issues of senior governments and their crown corporations, plus, in the case of CBRS, a few rich and powerful companies. A default on any bond with this rating would be a financial shock of tremendous magnitude. Buy with confidence.

AA (A+) Excellent prospects. These bonds don't quite make it to the top rank but they aren't far off in safety terms. Many provincial governments have this rating. Given the slightly higher return these bonds usually pay, they're well worth considering.

A (A) Solid citizens. They aren't Government of Canada or Province of Alberta, but the issuers are stable and well-respected. Should be okay for your retirement plan.

BBB (B++) Worth considering. Bonds with this rating are more susceptible to changing economic conditions, but should be all right for RRSPs. I wouldn't go any farther down the scale, though.

BB (B+)	Some risk. Now we're starting to move into what the rating companies consider to be speculative territory. These bonds shouldn't carry a high degree of risk—but they do have some.
B (B)	Risky. This is the point at which yields can sometimes start looking very seductive. After all, these companies have to do something to raise money. But you must understand the risks involved. DBRS calls this category "highly speculative." CBRS describes it as "poor quality."
CCC	Very highly speculative. This rating is only used by DBRS. When you get down to this level on the bond scale, you're really inviting trouble.
CC	Extremely speculative. Again, this rating is only used by DBRS. Be very wary of bonds with this rating.
C (C)	Roll the dice. DBRS labels this category "extremely speculative"—which is what they also call CC. So this level is presumably even more dangerous. CBRS refers to these bonds as being of "speculative quality." My advice: save your gambling instincts for the crap tables.
D (D)	In default. If your bond slips into this category, the issuer has stopped making payments on principal or interest or both. You'll be lucky if you ever get your money back. Don't say you weren't warned!
Suspended	CBRS uses this designation in cases where "the issuer is experiencing severe financial or operating difficulties of which the outcome is uncertain."

Most categories are subdivided into high and low groups to provide greater precision for the financial community, but you generally don't need to be concerned about that.

Any time you're considering a bond purchase, especially in a case when you're not familiar with the issuer, ask your broker to supply you with current rating information. Also ask if the issuer has been put on watch, which means the rating services are reassessing its position as a result of recent developments.

The easiest way to buy bonds for an RRSP is to use a "bond ladder" approach. This is a carefully selected portfolio of bonds with varying maturities. Many brokerage firms offer packaged bond ladder portfolios specifically designed for this purpose.

Bonds (Foreign Currency). Some Canadian governments and corporations occasionally issue bonds denominated in foreign currencies. U.S. dollars, Japanese yen, British pounds sterling and, now, Euros are the most common. Although these are mainly intended for the international financial markets, some RRSP investors search them out for their self-directed retirement plans.

That's because, although these bonds are denominated in foreign currencies, they're considered Canadian content for RRSP purposes. This means people who are nervous about the value of the Canadian dollar can protect themselves by investing part of their RRSP assets in more stable currencies.

I only recommend these bonds in very special circumstances. If you strongly believe our dollar is about to plunge, however, you may want to consider them.

Stripped Bonds. Some investors use stripped bonds as the backbone of their self-directed RRSPs. "Strips," as they're called in the investment community, have been available in Canada since the mid-1980s. The concept was imported from the U.S., where "zero coupon bonds," as they're known in that country, had been popular for many years.

Strips have a sort of Jekyll and Hyde personality, appealing to both ultra-conservative investors and fast buck artists. Conservative investors see them as one of the most effective ways to lock in guaranteed returns for a long period—10, 20, even 30 years! Speculators buy them with the idea of scoring big capital gains in a short time—a strategy I don't recommend for your RRSP.

To understand how one security can appeal to investors so far apart on the risk spectrum, you need to know something about how strips work.

When a bond is issued by a government or corporation, semi-annual interest coupons are usually attached to it. These used to be real coupons that were clipped by the bondholder and cashed as the interest came due. Now the process is done electronically in most cases.

Somewhere along the way, a smart financial dealer figured out that by separating the coupons from the bonds—hence, "stripping" the bond—he could sell two securities instead of one: the couponless bond and the coupons themselves.

A bond without coupons doesn't produce any interest for its owner. The only time it will generate a return will be at maturity, when it can be redeemed for full face value.

Now, no one is going to pay a thousand dollars today for a bond with a thousand dollar face value that doesn't mature for several years and pays no interest. So stripped bonds are sold at a discounted price. The more time that remains until maturity, the less you'll pay. The difference between your purchase price today and the value at maturity is expressed as an annual yield.

The big attraction of strips to conservative investors is that the yield is locked in for many years. There is no other way to ensure an annual compound rate of return over such a lengthy period of time. GICs rarely run more than five years. Ordinary bonds provide a predictable return, but you may not be able to reinvest the interest at the same rate, especially if rates were high when you bought in.

With strips, there are no surprises. If you're planning to retire in 15 years, you simply buy 15-year strips when interest rates are high, tuck them away in your RRSP, and forget them. The money will be there when you need it. And since financial dealers normally select only the highest quality bonds to strip—government or government-guaranteed, or high-quality corporates like BCE—the chance of the issuer defaulting is very low. Since strips are not covered by deposit insurance, this is an important consideration.

However, strips are much more volatile than regular bonds. They can experience some significant price swings as interest rates move up or down. If you intend to hold them for the long term, that's not a problem. But if you think you might sell before maturity, it's something to consider.

This volatility is why bond speculators like strips. Some nice capital gains can be made by buying when interest rates are high (and the price of the strips is therefore depressed), and selling out when rates drop and the price jumps. But this is a game only for experienced bond traders;

guess wrong and you can get whipsawed. For most people, the conservative approach is preferable.

If strips interest you, there are certain points to keep in mind when you buy.

1. Only buy them for registered investments. Revenue Canada takes the position that you're earning annual interest on your investment, even though you won't actually receive any cash for many years. This imputed interest is subject to tax at your marginal rate. So unless you're keen on paying tax on money you haven't received, make sure the strip is in a tax-sheltered environment such as an RRSP or registered retirement income fund (RRIF).

2. Buy when interest rates are high. This enables you to lock in higher rates for a lengthy period, and it minimizes the risk of loss if for any reason you have to sell before maturity. This explains why strips were not as popular in the late nineties as they were in the early part of the decade–interest rates were just too low.

3. Shop around for your strips. Brokerage houses, the main source for strips, usually maintain their own inventories of these bonds. So you'll find that the offerings, and the prices, vary from one house to another. Check to see who has the best deal before making a commitment. Also inquire about what commission is being charged. It's buried in the price you pay for the strip so you'll have to ask. Some brokers have taken to charging unconscionably high commissions for these bonds; you can often negotiate them down to more reasonable levels, especially if you are making a large purchase.

Canada Premium Bonds. These are included in the fixed income category because, unlike the companion Canada Savings Bonds, they cannot be redeemed at any time. Instead, they can only be cashed in once a year, at the anniversary date or 30 days thereafter. This makes them more like one-year GICs in nature. Premium Bonds offer a higher rate of return than CSBs as compensation for this relative illiquidity, as well as three-year rate guarantees.

Preferred Shares. There's a lot of confusion about preferred shares, which is understandable because they come in several forms. At its most basic level, a preferred share is another type of debt security issued by a corporation. Investors receive dividends which are paid at a fixed rate, and the shares are usually redeemable after a certain time. However, preferred shares rank behind bonds in terms of priority in the event a company runs into trouble, so they could be higher risk. Also, one of their main attractions is the eligibility of their payments for the dividend tax credit. That benefit is lost inside an RRSP.

Growth Securities

Canadian Equity Funds. For most people, equity (stock) mutual funds are the entry point to growth securities. That's because they're readily available, affordable, and offer professional money management. Canadian equity funds are the most common type sold in this country for two reasons: familiarity and the 20 percent foreign content rule that limits international holdings in registered plans. However, the Canadian stock market has historically not performed as well as that of the United States, so you may wish to consider other options for your RRSP.

International Equity Funds. These cover a huge range, from U.S. stock funds to those specializing in emerging markets, from Rio to Russia. The risk level can also vary greatly, so you'll need to do some careful research or obtain professional advice before deciding which funds are best suited for your plan.

Sector Funds. These mutual funds specialize in specific areas of the economy, such as technology, telecommunications, natural resources, and health care. When the target sector is doing well, a fund can produce enormous gains. But when things are going badly, as they were for the natural resources sector through the middle and late nineties, returns can be dismal.

Stocks. If you have a self-directed RRSP, you may invest directly in the stock markets, either Canadian, U.S., or international. This can be good or bad, depending on your stock-picking skills and your timing. Generally, I suggest that only seasoned investors go this route with their RRSP.

There are several types of securities that don't fit neatly into any specific category. These include dividend income funds, royalty income trusts, real estate investment trusts, balanced mutual funds, and asset allocation funds. Each can be useful in special situations, some of which will be discussed later in this book.

Rule Three: Don't Speculate

Your RRSP is not a place for high-risk investments. If you want to gamble, go to Vegas. This money is earmarked for your retirement. If you lose a large chunk of it, you'll pay the price where it hurts most—in the type of home you live in and the kind of food you eat.

When I was just beginning to learn the art of investing, I set up a self-directed RRSP through a stockbroker. Now, this fellow had a wonderful talent for storytelling—an ability which, I have since learned, is shared by many of his colleagues. He could spin gold out of straw. Companies with no product, no revenues, and no profits looked like the next IBM or General Motors by the time he finished praising their prospects. His favourite opening line whenever he called me with one of these fairy tales was, "Have I got one for you!"

The only problem was that, in most cases, it was all smoke and mirrors. The companies were built on a good idea and a prayer. Usually, that's not enough to guarantee success.

In one particular case, this broker was touting an Ontario firm that had supposedly developed a leading-edge technology for outdoor advertising. Contracts with a number of major North American firms were about to be signed. The stock was going to double or triple overnight. Grab it while you can.

This was for my RRSP, remember?

The story sounded great. I bought a thousand shares at $3.50 each.

The stock began to drift down. Then an article appeared in one of the financial papers, describing the activities of a well-known stock promoter. One of his clients had been my outdoor advertising company.

The stock sank like a stone, while my broker kept assuring me it was only a temporary setback.

Then came the news that the company had been completely reorganized, most of the senior managers had been replaced, and the contracts they had thought were solid were anything but.

The share price submerged at somewhere below 20 cents.

I still have an RRSP with the brokerage firm although, need I say it, not with the same advisor. It still shows this worthless stock as part of my portfolio with the notation, "market price not available." I don't ask them to delete it because it serves as a constant reminder to me of the foolhardiness of buying speculative stocks in an RRSP. Let it do the same for you.

Rule Four: Keep Your Costs Low

Managing an RRSP doesn't have to be expensive. Some types of plans cost nothing at all; others charge only a small annual administration fee. But if you're not careful, you can run up some fairly hefty bills, which will not be tax-deductible and will be paid from the proceeds of your plan. Here are some examples:

- **Mutual fund commissions.** Many mutual funds charge a front-end load when you buy. While you shouldn't pay more than 4 percent (and 2 percent is a better target to shoot for), this can still add up to a lot of money over time. One way to avoid having commissions drained out of your RRSP is to buy the funds outside your plan and then make a contribution in kind.

- **Mutual fund redemption fees.** If you buy a back-end load (also called a deferred sales charge) fund for your RRSP and then decide to cash in your units, you may be assessed a redemption charge depending on how long you've held it. This will be paid from within your plan.

- **Mutual fund switching fees.** Some companies and their sales representatives will charge you for moving your money from one fund in their group to another (for example, from a bond fund to an equity fund). This can get expensive if you're an avid switcher. If you're in this situation, I suggest moving your money around only when absolutely necessary.

- **Broker's commissions.** Every time you trade a stock, you'll pay your broker a commission. You'll also pay when you buy Treasury bills, stripped bonds, and regular bonds. These charges won't be as obvious because they're built into the price you pay for the security, but they're a drain on your RRSP money nevertheless.

- **Transfer fees.** If you switch your RRSP elsewhere, you'll probably have to pay a fee to the transferring institution.

- **Self-directed RRSP fees.** Annual administration fees typically run between $100 and $150.

- **Trustee and administration fees.** Many RRSPs charge a trustee fee in some form or another. However, in recent years some organizations have abandoned these charges as a competitive move.

Rule Five: Monitor Your Plan

I'm always amazed at the number of people who admit to never looking closely at their RRSP statements. They toss them in a drawer or, worse, in the waste basket, as if they were so much junk mail. Such indifference can be costly. RRSP trustees make mistakes—and far too often for my peace of mind. Think about it for a moment. Every day, hundreds of thousands of RRSP transactions are taking place in financial institutions across the country. During the peak season, in January and February, the number may run into the millions. Do you really believe all those data entries are taking place error-free? If you do, I have a very tall, free-standing building with a terrific view across Lake Ontario you might want to buy!

The reality is that mistakes are made far too often in RRSP accounts. I know because it's happened to me—not once, but several times. Since I somehow doubt that the financial industry has singled me out as the sole recipient in Canada of its errors, I strongly suggest you be alert for mistakes in your RRSP statements.

Here are some of the things that can happen.

Securities Disappear from Your Plan

A data entry person inadvertently hits a "Delete" key and thousands of dollars worth of assets disappear from your RRSP. It has happened to my wife and me on a number of occasions, the worst involving the disappearance of five securities with a total value of over $18 000! Remember, you don't have any certificates that prove ownership of your RRSP assets—your stocks, bonds, mutual funds, GICs, or what have you. The trust company has them in safekeeping somewhere. Your only proofs of ownership are your original purchase receipts (assuming you still have them) and the records of the trustee.

If those records are incorrect, you could be in for trouble down the road. Suppose, for example, your RRSP statement failed to show some of your assets because of a computer error and you didn't notice it. Five or ten years from now, it may occur to you that all is not well. The trustee may be able to locate your misplaced securities, if you have your purchase receipts. But be prepared for a long, arduous, time-wasting process.

Nor will an ordinary audit turn up the discrepancy. Auditors don't review each plan individually; instead they send you a form with your year-end statement asking you to report any difference with your own personal records. If you don't keep personal records, you'll have no way of knowing whether the statement is correct.

So protect your RRSP assets by making sure they don't vanish into some computer limbo.

You Receive Incorrect Income Credits

I've had some other Pape's dividends incorrectly credited to my RRSP account. I don't mind receiving other people's money, except that they're liable to discover the error and want it back. On the other hand, I've seen bond interest income that should have been paid to me credited to someone else.

The message is to make sure you receive all the credits you should, including reinvestment of mutual fund dividends in your plan. Failure to do so could be costly.

You Are Charged Unnecessary Expenses

RRSP administrators are sometimes too quick to grab money from your plan. The payment of annual trustee fees or self-directed charges are good examples. You should have a choice whether to pay such costs from inside or outside your plan. But some companies don't bother to send you an invoice; they simply deduct the money from your RRSP.

This is a drain on your tax-sheltered savings—I always prefer to use non-RRSP money for such expenses.

So review your statements carefully. Never take anything for granted. Finally, to conclude this chapter, here's a little self-test to see what type of RRSP manager you are. I've identified eight varieties of RRSP people. See which group you fall into—and which you'd like to be in.

- **The slacker.** This person puts money into an RRSP for the tax break and then forgets about it. He has no idea what his funds are invested in, what rate of return is being earned, or whether his investments are safe. He never reads the statements he receives periodically. After all, he's done the right thing by making a contribution; why should he worry about it any more?

- **The speculator.** To her, RRSP money is the key to instant riches. She's received her tax refund; now she can try to pyramid a few thousand dollars into a million by taking a flier on every penny stock with a good story that comes along. Hey, it's tax sheltered and you can't spend it for years. Why not take a chance that you'll strike it big? She also likes buying lottery tickets.

- **The scholar.** He carefully researches every investment before taking action and can tell you the rate of return of each individual security in his plan off the top of his head. He knows exactly where his money is and the current asset allocation of his plan to the nearest hundredth of a percentage point. He's also willing to provide detailed computer projections of what his RRSP funds will be worth at retirement, if you really want to see them.

- **The stoic.** She believes there's really very little she can do to improve her RRSP returns. She knows little about investing and dislikes making financial decisions. Her attitude is one of *Que sera, sera* when it comes to her retirement money. Whatever happens will happen. She's like that about life, too.

- **The shuttlecock.** He changes his ideas on RRSP investing almost daily, depending on who last whispered in his ear. He has no clearly defined objectives of his own and moves his money around frequently on the slightest whim. Brokers love him. Why not, he makes them rich.

- **The sophisticate.** She loves to be on the leading edge of RRSP investing strategies. GICs and mutual funds are too mundane for her. But foreign currency bonds? She's got them. Corporate strips? Perfect. Covered call options? Sure. Her returns may be below average, but who cares? She's RRSP chic.

- **The struggler.** He wants to do a good job with his RRSP, but somehow can't pull it off. His investment decisions are ill-timed, he buys the wrong mutual funds, he sells at the low. Nothing ever seems to go right. His returns are not only below average—they're negative!

- **The success.** She manages her RRSP investments prudently. Her investments are chosen with an eye to both safety and above-average return. She keeps track of her portfolio and checks her statements with care to ensure nothing is amiss. When indicated, she adjusts her asset mix to take advantage of changing economic conditions. She contributes regularly throughout the year, to her maximum limit. She's destined to retire a millionaire!

Key Points in Review

1. Improving your annual RRSP return by a few percentage points can add tens of thousands of dollars to the end value of your plan, with no extra contributions.

2. The asset allocation you select for your RRSP will have a greater impact on your return then the actual securities you buy.

3. Mutual funds are an easier way to invest than trying to build a stock and bond portfolio within your RRSP.

4. Stripped bonds are an excellent way to build the fixed income side of an RRSP, but it's best to buy them when interest rates are high.

5. Avoid speculating in an RRSP. Lost money can never be replaced, and any capital losses are not tax-deductible.

6. Keep RRSP costs to a minimum. Where possible, pay fees and other expenses from money outside the plan.

7. Review your RRSP statements carefully. Mistakes are not common but they do occur occasionally. Missing one could be expensive.

8

Advanced RRSP Strategies

Folks are serious about three things—
their religion, their family and, most of all,
their money.

— Bert Lance

IF YOU'VE BEEN MANAGING YOUR OWN RRSP FOR SOME TIME, YOU'RE probably already aware of the basic rules outlined in the last chapter. However, it never hurts to review them periodically–you'd be surprised how easy it is to fall into bad habits. Even I find myself occasionally filing my monthly statements after just a cursory glance, despite having been stung by serious errors in the past. Never get complacent!

When you feel comfortable that you have all the fundamentals in place and that your RRSP is ticking along well, it's time to start looking at implementing some advanced strategies. These can provide the extra edge you need to pump up your returns or provide some other benefits, without adding significantly to your risk.

In some cases, such as the first advanced strategy we'll look at, you can actually put several thousand dollars into your own pocket while increasing your RRSP returns at the same time. How can you work such magic? Well, let's take a look.

The Advanced Strategies

Using Other People's Money

Normally, I am not a big fan of "leveraging," the technical term for borrowing to invest. Proponents of this strategy always stress the upside rewards, but the risks can be great and the potential for personal distress and family discord if things go wrong is very real.

However, there is one situation in which I make an exception: borrowing to invest in an RRSP. I do so because the math is compelling. It is almost impossible for you to lose money on this kind of transaction. Rather, the likelihood is that you'll end up several thousand dollars on the plus side.

RRSP borrowing has become a hot topic in recent years because of the carry-forward rules. Many people now have thousands of dollars in unused contribution room available and are beginning to wonder if they are ever going to use it. As a result, some financial institutions, taking a lead from Scotiabank, are aggressively marketing RRSP catch-up loans. These allow you to borrow several thousand dollars at sometimes (but not always) favourable rates to top up your RRSP and take advantage of all that carry-forward room.

These catch-up loans differ in term and in conditions from the standard RRSP loans which have been around for many years. The traditional RRSP loan is offered at prime rate or slightly above and is typically repayable over one or two years. It is normally used to maximize the current year's contribution when adequate cash is not available.

That's a common problem. After all, it *is* a lousy time of year to come up with a big chunk of money. The Christmas bills are arriving and your savings program just hasn't done the job.

This is where a standard RRSP loan can come to the rescue. It is one of the most effective ways to use other people's money to provide for your future, even though the interest is not tax-deductible.

Let's assume you're allowed to make a $7000 contribution to an RRSP this year. You haven't saved any money and the deadline is fast approaching. Your marginal tax rate is 45 percent and you can borrow the money at 7 percent, with the loan repayable over the next year in monthly installments. You can invest the contribution for a guaranteed 5 percent return inside the RRSP. Here's what happens over the first year.

Standard RRSP Loan	
Amount of loan	$7 000
Tax refund generated	3 150
Investment income inside plan	350
Gross benefit	3 500
Interest cost	269
Net benefit	3 231

It will cost you $605.71 a month to repay this loan over a year, of which only $269 is interest (that's correct!). You can reduce the interest charge even more by applying your tax refund to paying off the loan as soon as the government cheque arrives.

Your net bottom line benefit from this transaction in the first year is over $3200. That's a return of 46 percent on your contribution! But it doesn't end there. The $7000 in your plan—which would not have been there had you not borrowed to make the investment—will continue to grow in value each year. The following table shows you how much that single contribution will be worth over time, assuming various rates of return.

Astounding, isn't it? If you average a 10 percent annual return in your RRSP, which is quite feasible in a well-run mutual fund portfolio, the value of your original $7000 contribution grows to almost $200 000 in 35 years. If you manage a 12 percent average annual return, your single contribution grows to almost $370 000 over that time. Even at a modest 6 percent, your $7000 is worth more than $53 000 at the end.

If there ever was a good reason for borrowing to invest, this has to be it! You get a great immediate return on your investment, plus tax-free compounding of your interest for years into the future.

How Your $7000 Contribution Will Grow

	Value at Annual Growth Rate of			
Years	6%	8%	10%	12%
5	$9 397	$10 285	$11 274	$12 336
10	12 536	15 112	18 156	21 741
15	16 776	22 205	29 240	38 315
20	22 450	32 627	47 093	67 524
25	30 043	47 940	75 843	119 001
30	40 205	70 439	122 146	209 719
35	53 803	103 497	196 717	369 597

One word of caution, however. Do plan to repay the loan within a year. If you don't, the non-deductible interest cost of carrying it may exceed the tax-sheltered return on your RRSP investment in subsequent years.

Catch-up loans require a more complicated analysis before you proceed. Because these loans are usually for larger amounts of money, it may not be practical to repay them in a year or even two. Also, the interest rate after year one may be higher than with short-term RRSP loans.

You should explore all the details before entering into a longer-term agreement. If you own a home, you may be better off applying for a home owner's line of credit to finance an RRSP catch-up loan. Draws against these secured lines of credit are usually charged interest at prime or prime plus a quarter point, which may be less expensive than the terms available for a long-term RRSP loan.

Making Contributions in Kind

This is an alternative way to get money into your RRSP and claim a tax deduction even though you don't have the ready cash available. It's one of those little-known RRSP tricks that can get you through a financial squeeze.

You need two things to make it work. One is a self-directed RRSP. The other is some qualifying investments not currently held in a tax shelter. These can be anything from Canada Savings Bonds to stocks; as long as they're RRSP-eligible, they'll do.

Revenue Canada allows you to contribute any qualifying investment directly into your self-directed plan and claim a corresponding deduction at fair market value.

If you contribute a fixed-value security, such as a Canada Savings Bond or GIC, you'll receive credit for the principal plus accrued interest to the date of the contribution. Be sure to get an up-to-date valuation of any compound-interest investments you've owned for some time before depositing them; the accrued interest could be more than you expect and push you over your contribution limit.

Securities such as stocks, bonds, and mutual funds will be assessed on the basis of their market value on the day they go into the plan. In this case, some tax implications will come into play that should be considered before the securities are contributed.

The government takes the position that when a marketable security is contributed to an RRSP, it has been sold for tax purposes. If its value has increased since acquisition, a capital gain is deemed to have been realized. So you'll have to decide before contributing whether you wish to incur the tax liability at this stage. Unhappily, this is a single-sided coin. Revenue Canada will not recognize any capital loss if you contribute a money-losing asset to your RRSP. That this is unfair is obvious, but those are the rules. You can't stick your dogs into your retirement plan and get a tax break for them. In that case, your best bet is to sell the security, which triggers a deductible loss, and then contribute the proceeds to your plan.

Using Substitutions

A strategy that's closely related to the contribution in kind is the substitution. In this case, you swap an asset inside the RRSP for one of comparable value outside the plan.

This can be useful in several ways. One is to provide yourself with an interest-free loan. Suppose you have some spare cash inside your RRSP and a GIC outside the plan that is locked in for another four years. Instead of asking a bank to take the GIC as security against a loan, simply swap it into your plan for an offsetting amount of cash. Now you have the money you need, without it costing you a penny in interest.

Another benefit of the substitution is tax efficiency. Suppose you have ended up with some stock in your RRSP that pays a good dividend. You don't want to sell, but you don't like the fact that you are losing out on the benefit of the dividend tax credit. Meanwhile, outside the plan you have a GIC that pays interest, taxed at your top marginal rate. Assuming the two securities are of equal value, you arrange with your plan trustee to put the GIC into the RRSP in exchange for the stock. If there is a difference in value–say the stock is worth $200 more– you can make up the balance in cash. Remember, the value going in must always equal the value coming out. Also keep in mind that the same tax rules apply for substitutions as for contributions in kind.

Substitutions such as this do not affect your normal RRSP contribution entitlement, nor do they give rise to any tax deduction. It's simply a swap of one security for another. Just make sure the asset you're moving into the RRSP is a qualified investment under the tax laws. If you have any doubt, consult an officer of the financial institution that holds your plan before going ahead. Ensure that it's someone fairly senior; most junior employees will not be aware of the complexities of the tax regulations in this area.

Developing Tax-Efficient Portfolios

The comments about substitutions bring us to our next advanced strategy: make sure your registered and non-registered investment portfolios are structured for maximum tax efficiency.

One measure of the complexity of our Canadian tax system is the fact that every type of investment income is taxed in a different way. You'll pay more tax for a hundred dollars of interest income than you will for a hundred dollars in dividends. Your tax liability on capital gains will be at a rate somewhat in excess of that assessed on dividend income.

Given this situation (which perhaps some future government will address in a new round of tax reform), your objective should be to use your RRSP to shield your most highly-taxed assets from Revenue Canada. In practical terms, this means any security that pays interest income.

In the best of all possible worlds, your RRSP would be made up entirely of interest-bearing securities, while all those paying dividends, capital gains or any other type of tax-advantaged income would be held outside your plan. However, that's not always feasible. Many people have enough trouble just scraping up the money they need to make an RRSP contribution and to keep up the mortgage payments on the house. There's nothing left over to build a non-registered investment portfolio, at least in the early years. This situation is especially common when people are in their twenties and thirties and raising a family. As they grow older, income increases and expenses decline as the mortgage is paid off and children leave home. That's the point at which more money becomes available to invest outside an RRSP.

But if you wait until then to start investing in growth securities, you'll miss out on years of potentially above-average returns. That's why I recommend including stocks and equity mutual funds in an RRSP if you're not able to afford a non-registered portfolio. These securities can provide the engine that enables your plan to produce above-average returns.

The time may come, however, when you can afford both registered and non-registered portfolios. It's at that point that you want to take steps to maximize the tax efficiency, through the use of the substitution rule.

There's another situation in which tax efficiency needs to be carefully reviewed. That's when your portfolio is being managed by a professional organization. Believe it or not, they can screw up badly. I know this from personal experience.

A friend had been contributing to her RRSP for many years. She then inherited a large amount of money. She decided to put everything into the hands of a professional money manager in her home town of Edmonton.

The manager reorganized the portfolios and everything seemed fine. Until she asked me to take a look at them, that is. A quick glance revealed a serious flaw that at first I could not believe. But on closer inspection, there was no doubt. The money manager had constructed both her RRSP and her non-registered portfolio in exactly the same way. No attempt had been made at tax efficiency. The two portfolios held exactly the same securities in the same proportions; the only difference was that one was larger than the other. I estimated that this approach was costing her approximately $2000 a year in extra taxes.

Needless to say, her money has been moved elsewhere. The moral is obvious: never assume anything, even if you have a professional money manager advising you. If you have both an RRSP and a non-registered investment portfolio, make sure they are as tax-effective as possible.

Maximizing Overcontributions

Technically, you're not allowed to put more money into your RRSP than the total of your current contribution limit and any unused deductions or carry-forward credits. However, the government allows a little leeway before they begin to penalize you. You can take advantage of that leeway to add a bit more juice to your RRSP.

The magic number is $2000. You can exceed your contribution limit by that amount before the penalty (1 percent interest per month) cuts in. That figure is lifetime cumulative, not an annual extra allowance.

Two thousand dollars may not seem like very much. But, compounded over many years, it can add up to a fair amount of extra capital. That's why this particular strategy works best for younger people—you need a lot of time for it to pay off in any meaningful way.

It's very simple to implement. Simply add $2000 to your RRSP over and above your allowed contribution limit and don't claim a deduction for the amount. Invest the money as you normally would and then sit back and let the laws of compounding take their natural course. Here's what will happen over various time periods at different average annual rates of return.

How $2000 Will Grow

Years in Plan	Average Annual Return		
	6%	8%	10%
20	$6 414	$9 322	$13 455
25	8 584	13 697	21 669
30	11 487	20 125	34 899
35	15 372	29 571	56 205
40	20 571	43 449	90 519

As you can see, the original $2000 can grow to as much as $90 000 if you make the overcontribution at age 25 and retire at 65. Those numbers are hard to believe, but they're true.

To wring a few more dollars out of the overcontribution, claim it as a deduction in your final year of RRSP eligibility. Just remember that it is there to be claimed, or better still put a written reminder in your RRSP file.

Redirecting Contributions to Spousal Plans

There's no immediate benefit in setting up an RRSP for your spouse and directing your contributions to it. You do not receive any additional tax deduction; you're just redirecting your contribution entitlement to your spouse. So this is one strategy that requires a long-range view.

The payoff from a spousal RRSP comes if one spouse is likely to have less income than the other after retirement. In that case, making contributions to a spousal plan today can save you many tax dollars down the road.

Here's how it works.

Let's take a couple in which the husband, Bill, works full time. He has no pension plan but has managed his money well. Between his registered and non-registered investments, his CPP, and some part-time consulting, he will have an income in the $60 000–plus range when he retires in five years.

His wife, Sarah, worked part time for several years, but only has a small amount of money put aside. Her annual income in retirement is not expected to exceed $15 000.

Bill expects to be able to contribute an average of $12 000 a year to his RRSP over the next five years. He makes his contributions at the start of each year, to maximize his return. If those contributions are invested to yield 10 percent a year, they'll add about $80 000 to his plan by the time he stops work. Let's assume that will translate into about $5000 more a year in post-retirement income. His marginal tax rate at that time (the rate he pays on his last dollar of income) is expected to be about 47 percent. Here's what will happen:

Bill's additional income	$5000
Tax @ 47%	$2350
After-tax return	$2650

Looking at these numbers, Bill decides he can do better. Instead of contributing more to his RRSP, he opens a plan for Sarah and makes a spousal contribution to it each year. The effect of this is to switch $5000 a year worth of post-retirement income from his hands to hers.

What's the advantage? Sarah will pay tax at a much lower rate—probably around 27 percent. Here's what happens when the money comes to her instead:

Sarah's additional income	$5000
Tax @ 27%	$1350
After-tax return	$3650

The bottom line: this simple maneuver has increased their after-tax income by $1000 a year. Multiply that by the number of years they'll be living in retirement, and the value of a spousal RRSP for income-splitting becomes obvious.

Another advantage will be to reduce the impact of the Old Age Security claw-back on this couple. Bill will be over the income threshold, so he'll have some of his payment taxed away. But by shifting $5000 a year to Sarah, he'll reduce the amount of OAS he'd otherwise have to pay back. Since Sarah is well below the claw-back threshold, her OAS will not be affected.

Just one caution. The less the difference between the tax brackets of two spouses, the less the advantage of a spousal plan. If both spouses are in the same tax bracket, there is probably no advantage at all, unless reducing or eliminating the claw-back comes into play.

Making Use of Retiring Allowances

This strategy isn't available to everyone. Only those who receive a lump-sum payment upon leaving a job may make use of it. But if the opportunity arises, don't miss it.

Typically, the retiring allowance strategy comes into play when someone is laid off and receives a severance package as a result. You are allowed to contribute $2000 of that payment to an RRSP for every year or part-year you worked for the employer prior to 1996. No credit is allowed for 1996 and beyond. As well, you may contribute an extra $1500 for each year or part year prior to 1989 for which you did not earn pension plan credits.

For long-service employees, the amount available for direct transfer to an RRSP can be substantial. If at all possible, take maximum advantage of it. Not only will it dramatically increase the size of your tax-sheltered investment portfolio, but it will also reduce the taxes you would have to pay if you took the money into income. If the severance payment is sizeable, you end up handing half of it back to Revenue Canada unless you use this escape clause.

Maximizing Your Foreign Content

You're allowed to hold 20 percent of your RRSP in foreign content. If you go over that amount, a penalty tax of 1 percent a month on the excess is applied.

That rule has become a thorn in investors' sides in recent years, and many organizations have asked the federal government to change it. However, as of mid-1999, nothing has been done.

The reason behind the growing pressure was the weak performance of Canadian stock markets in the latter part of the nineties. With commodity prices hitting their lowest point in two decades, most Canadian resource companies struggled, dragging the broad indexes down with them. RRSP investors watched with envy as American stock markets soared while their own Canadian equity funds bumbled along by comparison.

However, the foreign content limit (which will inevitably be raised or eliminated in due course) really does not have to be a problem. You can have as much foreign content in your plan as you wish. It's simply a case of understanding all the options and making use of those that best suit your needs.

For starters, you should of course make use of the 20 percent that you're allowed. The best way to do this is with a combination of U.S. and international equity funds, or balanced funds if you want to take a more conservative approach.

The next step is to choose Canadian equity funds that maximize their own allowable foreign content. Mutual funds can also invest up to 20 percent of their assets abroad without compromising their RRSP eligibility. Their foreign content does not count against your personal limit—consider it to be a bonus, if you like. So, in theory, you could add another 16 percent foreign content to your RRSP in this way (20 percent of 80 percent).

But this is just the start. There are many perfectly legal ways to add more foreign content to your plan. Here are some worth considering.

International Bond Funds. Some international bond funds are designed to retain full RRSP eligibility by limiting their investments to Canadian bonds denominated in foreign currencies, or bonds of international agencies approved for RRSPs by the Department of Finance. These include issues from organizations such as the World Bank.

You have to be careful, however. Not all international bond funds qualify as domestic content for RRSPs. Ask before you invest.

U.S. Dollar Money Market Funds. By using the same technique described above, some U.S. dollar money market funds are 100 percent eligible for your RRSP. This creates the unusual situation where you can hold the equivalent of American cash without it being considered foreign content.

Pseudo-Canadian Funds. A subset of the mutual funds industry has been created to cater to the needs of investors who have maximized their foreign content under the rules and wish to add more. I call these "pseudo-Canadian funds" because they masquerade as Canadian content while in fact increasing the foreign exposure of an RRSP. The usual way this is done is by buying Treasury bills to cover 80 percent of the fund's assets. This provides the required Canadian content. The T-bills are then used as security for the purchase of index futures on whatever stock exchange(s) the fund is targeting. For example, most U.S. pseudo-Canadian funds base their returns on the Standard and Poor's 500 Index, known for short as the S&P 500. There are variations on this theme, but you get the idea. In essence, these are index funds on foreign exchanges that have been structured in such a way so as to circumvent the RRSP rules.

Clone Funds. A variation on the pseudo-Canadian idea that first appeared in mid-1999. Clone funds replicate existing funds that would normally be considered foreign content in an RRSP—the Ivy RSP Foreign Equity Fund offered by Mackenzie Financial is an example. The technique for achieving this is highly technical and these funds appear to fly in the face of the foreign content rule, but more companies are rushing to offer them. As long as the costs are not excessive, these are a very effective way of adding more U.S. and international content to your plan.

Index-Linked GICs. GICs issued by a Canadian financial institution are fully RRSP eligible no matter how their returns are calculated. So an index-linked GIC that is tied to the performance of the S&P 500 or the Tokyo Nikkei Index is every bit as qualified for your plan as one based on the TSE 35. Strange, but true.

Using these various instruments, there is no reason why you should feel shackled by the 20 percent foreign content rule. I recommend you hold at least 40 percent of your plan in non-Canadian securities to increase profit potential and reduce risk.

Investing in Labour-Sponsored Funds

Labour-sponsored venture capital funds receive all kinds of perks because the federal government, as well as many provinces, sees them as a capital conduit for small business and a potential stimulant for new jobs. Whether the funds are meeting those expectations is a subject for some debate, but there is no doubt that they offer some important strategic advantages for RRSP investors.

These advantages include the following:

More Foreign Content. I just outlined a number of ways around the 20 percent foreign content rule. Well, here's another one. As a result of tax rulings approved in late 1998, you can now obtain extra RRSP room by investing some money in a labour-sponsored fund. The formula is three dollars worth of extra foreign content room for every one dollar invested, as long as the total foreign content in your plan does not exceed 40 percent. So if you buy $5000 worth of a labour-sponsored fund for your self-directed RRSP, you get an additional $15 000 worth of foreign content.

Extra Tax Credits. If you buy a labour-sponsored fund with money you're contributing to an RRSP, you naturally get the usual RRSP deduction. But you get a bonus as well. The federal government will give you a tax credit of 15 percent of the amount of your purchase, up to $5000 a year. So the maximum annual amount of the federal credit, which is deducted directly from your tax payable, is $750. Most provinces (exceptions are Alberta, Prince Edward Island and Newfoundland) offer a matching credit. However, in some cases the provincial credit is only available on a limited number of funds. Ontario is the most wide-open province when it comes to matching credits, which helps explain why residents there have a much greater choice than is available anywhere else in Canada.

Tax Credits for "Old" Money. In some provinces, including Ontario, you can buy labour-sponsored fund units with money already in your RRSP—"old" RRSP money if you like—and receive the tax credits outside your plan. Some people, including me, use this technique regularly to get more tax mileage out of money contributed to an RRSP years ago.

There are some negatives to consider before you decide to make use of labour-sponsored funds. The most serious is the holding period—you may not dispose of your units for a minimum of eight years. If you do, you'll have to refund your tax credits, which could be expensive. So be sure you won't need to draw on the money in the meantime.

Also, be aware that most labour-sponsored funds have not been impressive performers. It was known from the outset that these funds would likely be high-risk because they invest in start-up businesses. But most have been around for several years now, and it is somewhat surprising to see that investors haven't received better returns as some of the fledgling companies have grown into big winners. This underperformance may change in the future, but as we enter the twenty-first century it continues to be a problem for many of these funds.

Creditor-Proofing Your Plan

Most Canadians don't realize that, if they run into financial trouble, creditors can seize their RRSPs (and RRIFs as well) in many cases. In this respect, RRSPs are unlike pension plans, which are protected by law from the long arms of bill collectors.

Although the rules are changing, the process is very slow. That's one of the reasons why segregated funds have become so popular in recent years.

"Seg funds," as they're known, are the life insurance industry's equivalent of mutual funds. The difference is that they form part of some type of insurance contract (typically as a variable annuity contract) and so come under insurance laws, which provide for creditor protection in most situations. Seg funds also offer other popular benefits, including capital guarantees.

For years, the life insurance industry slept on these marketing advantages. It was only in the late nineties that Manulife began to vigorously exploit them. That led to many mutual fund companies, including C.I., BPI, Trimark, Mackenzie, and Templeton, introducing their own brand-name line of seg funds, in cooperation with insurance companies. Some industry experts believe that seg funds will eventually account for a quarter of the total fund market.

The guarantees are what draw most investors to these funds. But creditor-proofing might actually be more important to you if you're in a high-risk occupation for lawsuits (such as medicine), or if you run an unincorporated business that might conceivably go bankrupt and expose your personal assets to seizure.

Seg funds are also worth considering if you're older or in poor health and want to protect the value of your RRSP or RRIF against the possibility of a stock market crash. However, you will pay a premium for this protection in the form of higher annual fees, so I don't advise that younger people use seg funds for this purpose.

Key Points in Review

1. A one-year RRSP loan to allow you to make the maximum contribution to your plan is one of the best ways to use other people's money.
2. Long-term RRSP catch-up loans should be carefully assessed and the interest rate terms fully understood before proceeding. A home equity line of credit may work better.
3. A contribution in kind enables you to deposit a security directly into your RRSP and receive a tax credit.
4. Substitutions, or swaps, can be used to give yourself an interest-free loan or to improve the tax efficiency of your total portfolio.

5. A one-time overcontribution of $2000 to your RRSP can increase the end value of your plan by tens of thousands. However, the strategy only works for younger people.

6. Spousal plans allow you to split income after retirement, which may lower your family's total tax bill.

7. If you receive a severance payment as a result of a layoff, you may be able to tax shelter a large portion of it in your RRSP.

8. The foreign content rule has come under increased fire in recent years, but there are many ways of getting around it. You should aim for at least 40 percent foreign content in your RRSP.

9. Labour-sponsored venture capital funds offer special tax credits plus a foreign content bonus. But they must be held for at least eight years and their performance as a group has been underwhelming.

10. Segregated funds can be used to creditor-proof your RRSP. They also offer a form of loss insurance that may be of interest to older people.

9

Diversionary Tactics

The principle of spending money to be paid by posterity, under the name of funding, is but swindling futurity on a large scale.

— Thomas Jefferson

THERE WAS A TIME WHEN RRSPS WERE MEANT FOR RETIREMENT saving. Period. Full stop. End of story.

No more. Now you can use your RRSP money to buy a home, to go back to school, or to help your spouse get a university degree. And who knows what other diversions the federal government will allow in years to come.

Don't mistake my meaning. There is nothing wrong with home ownership or with furthering your education. Both are highly desirable goals and if RRSP money is the only way to finance them, the option must certainly be considered.

The Hazards of Borrowing from Your RRSP

But there's a cost involved, and it's a significant one. Unless you make some offsetting moves, the end value of your RRSP will be considerably diminished if you use the interest-free loan provisions of the Home Buyers' Plan or the education program known as the Lifelong Learning Plan.

The younger you are, the greater the impact of borrowing from your RRSP. Take a look at the following scenarios.

Scenario 1: Ted Morgan is 30 years old. He has been putting money into his RRSP since he graduated from college at 22. His plan is now worth $20 000. He wants to buy a first house and considers dipping into his RRSP to help with the cost. However, in the end he decides against it and takes a conventional bank mortgage instead. Here's what happens to the money currently in his RRSP, assuming retirement at 65.

Ted Morgan's RRSP

Value today (age 30)	$20 000
Average annual compound rate of return	8%
Value of current investment at 65	
(future contributions not considered)	$295 707

By leaving the money untouched in his RRSP, Ted sees it grow almost 15 times by age 65.

Scenario 2: Jane Miller is also 30 years old, and she also has $20 000 in her RRSP. She too is looking at buying a home. In her case, she decides to take the $20 000 interest-free loan that is allowed under the Home Buyers' Plan. She repays the loan in 15 equal annual instalments, starting in the first year after she makes the withdrawal. For simplicity, we'll assume that the loan and the repayments are all made on the first business day in January of each year.

Jane's RRSP assets will be reduced to zero in the first year (we won't take any new contributions into consideration in this illustration). After that, the repayments begin and continue until Jane is 46, at which time the original $20 000 has been repaid. Jane also aims to retire at 65. Here's how it all works out.

Jane Miller's RRSP

Value today (age 30)	$20 000
Average annual compound rate of return	8%
Amount of loan	$20 000
Annual repayments	$1 333.33
Value of original $20 000 when repayment	
complete, including gains	$39 099
Value of original $20 000 at 65	
(future contributions not considered)	$168 739

Look carefully at the bottom line of each scenario. By using the Home Buyers' Plan, even with dutiful repayments, Jane Miller's $20 000 has a final value at retirement that is almost $127 000 less than the amount Ted Morgan's money has grown to.

That extra money will add almost $5300 to Ted's RRIF income at age 66, using the minimum withdrawal formula.

That is the real but hidden cost of using the Home Buyers' Plan or the education loan program, which also has a $20 000 ceiling. You don't even think about it at the time, and there is nothing in the federal government's information material that warns you of the consequences of using these plans.

I could make a case for incorporating a prominent warning into all applications for these loans, along the lines of those required on cigarette packages. Can't you just see it?

> WARNING: USE OF THIS LOAN MAY BE HAZARDOUS TO YOUR FUTURE FINANCIAL HEALTH AND RESULT IN A DIMINISHED STANDARD OF LIVING IN RETIREMENT!

Somehow, I doubt it will ever happen. So if you're considering the use of either of these programs, consider yourself warned. If you want to mitigate, or even eliminate, the negative impact on your RRSP, read on.

How to Control the Damage

The key to RRSP damage control, as far as the Home Buyers' Plan is concerned, lies in reinvesting the money you save by taking the interest-free loan. Let's go back to the example of Jane Miller. By borrowing $20 000 from her RRSP, she reduces the amount she will have to finance through a mortgage by a like amount. Let's take a closer look at that $20 000 mortgage reduction and its implications.

Let's say she takes an $80 000 mortgage amortized over 25 years at an interest rate of 7 percent. Had she not borrowed from her RRSP, the mortgage would have been for $100 000.

Here's what she saves as a result.

Jane Miller's Mortgage Savings

Annual payment (principal and interest) @ $100 000	$8 405
Annual payment (principal and interest) @ $80 000	$6 724
Saving	$1 681
RRSP annual repayment	$1 333
Net saving	$348

By using the interest-free money from her RRSP, Jane has saved herself almost $1700 a year in mortgage payments. However, she has to make annual payments to her plan over 15 years. When all is said and done, she ends up with a net cash saving of $348 a year.

She has a choice. She can either spend that money, or she can use it to help offset the effects of the borrowing from her RRSP.

Let's assume that, after reading this book, she decides to invest that money. She is already maximizing her RRSP contributions so she begins a non-registered investment portfolio and puts the money into mutual funds. Let's assume her after-tax return on her funds averages 6 percent a year. She continues this pattern of investment for 15 years, until the loan has been repaid. She then adds the equivalent amount that had been going toward the RRSP to her annual non-registered investment, and keeps putting in money at the same rate until she retires at 65. Here's how it all turns out.

Jane Miller's Non-Registered Portfolio

Final value after 15 years @ $348	$27 537
Final value after 20 years @ $1 681	$65 547
Total	$93 084

By using this approach, Jane ends up with a non-registered portfolio worth $93 000. At first glance, this appears to fall short of the $127 000 the RRSP lost because of the loan. However, we have to look at the impact of taxes.

The value of Jane's non-registered portfolio is after-tax. Any money inside an RRSP is taxed as it is withdrawn. If we assume that Jane has a marginal tax rate of 40 percent once she retires, the after-tax value of $127 000 is just over $76 000.

115

In other words, by using this investment strategy Jane actually comes out ahead of the game, even though she took a $20 000 loan from her RRSP.

So it is possible to eat your cake and have it too. Unfortunately, there has been virtually no publicity on the subject of how to deal with the impact of borrowing from an RRSP, so very few people are even aware that it's a problem. It is, and it's a potentially big one. Don't let it catch you.

If your loan is for education purposes, you won't see the direct cash savings that you will with a mortgage. So your approach will have to be slightly different.

In this case, decide from the outset that you will commit a percentage of any income increase that results from your enhanced education level toward additional retirement investing.

Let's use a target figure of 20 percent of your higher pay scale.

A college degree or a significant upgrading of your qualifications should be worth at least $5000 a year in extra income. Devote $1000 of that to building a non-registered portfolio (assuming you are maximizing your RRSP contribution).

Let's say you go back to college for two years at age 28 to earn your degree. At age 30, you reenter the work force and begin saving that extra thousand a year, all the while repaying the money you borrowed from your RRSP and making a regular contribution to your plan. Again, we'll assume the after-tax return on your non-registered investments works out to 6 percent.

At age 65, your non-registered portfolio will be valued at just over $118 000. On an after-tax basis, that should more than offset the loss within your RRSP.

The key is not to let the loan from your RRSP manage you. If *you* manage *it*, your retirement lifestyle does not have to be compromised.

Key Points in Review

1. First-time home buyers and those wishing to upgrade their education are now permitted to borrow from their RRSPs. However, the cost of these loans on the end value of your RRSP, and on your ultimate retirement income, can be high.

2. There are strategies that enable you to mitigate or eliminate the negative impact of RRSP loans on your retirement plans. But most people don't know about them and they get minimal publicity.

3. One such strategy is to direct mortgage payment savings into building a non-registered investment portfolio. You'll end up with a tax-paid sum of money that may actually be worth more than the amount lost to your RRSP.

4. Students using RRSP education loans should commit a percentage of any increase in income that results to building a non-registered portfolio. Twenty percent is a reasonable target.

10

Strategies for
Late Starters

*While there's snow on the roof, it doesn't mean
the fire has gone out in the furnace.*

— John G. Diefenbaker

EVERYTHING YOU READ–INCLUDING EVERYTHING SO FAR IN THIS book–emphasizes the importance of starting your retirement program early. But what if you can't? What if you're already in your forties and just getting around to thinking about it now? It's not an unusual situation. Despite repeated urgings, many people just can't get serious about retirement planning until the target date for stopping work starts to show up on their personal radar scopes. Often, that happens when the mortgage is paid off, the kids have left home, and the month-to-month financial pressures start to ease. Suddenly, there's extra money to be put toward some new project. What might that be? Well, gosh, maybe we should start thinking about retirement!

If that sounds like you, then this is your chapter. We'll look at some strategies you can use to make up some of the ground you've lost by waiting this long. But some words of warning at the outset. First, you can never fully compensate for the lost years. All you can do is mitigate the damage. Second, you'll have to sacrifice more. Because you have so few years remaining until retirement, you'll need to commit a greater percentage of your income to your savings program. Third, you'll need self-discipline and a lot of it if you are going to succeed. Finally, don't kid yourself. It won't be easy.

On that sombre note, here goes.

Essentials for Late Starters

Open an RRSP Now. If you don't have an RRSP at this stage, open one immediately. That's the first step, and it's an essential one.

Make Your Maximum Allowable Contribution. You've lost enough time already. Contribute the maximum to which you're entitled. This year and every year.

Save, Save, Save. You're going to have to put away a lot more of your income than you ever thought possible, if you hope to have a comfortable lifestyle in retirement. Some experts contend that people in their forties should aim at saving at least 20 percent of everything they earn—and that's 20 percent of gross income, not after-tax income. If you don't start until your fifties, 30 percent is your target.

Let's look at some numbers that will quickly show why such high savings rates are necessary for late starters. In all cases, we'll assume the target retirement age is 65 and that the target is to retire on 75 percent of gross income. We'll aim for a gross income at retirement of $66 000 a year, so the retirement income goal will be $49 500. We will assume annual increments of 2 percent in salary, RRSP contributions, and Canada Pension Plan/Old Age Security payments. In all cases, the only sources of retirement income will be OAS/CPP and a RRIF. The retirement income figures are for the first year (age 65 at the start of the year) and are based on the federal government's minimum withdrawal formula.

Let's start with the story of Susie Smith. Susie is 25 years old and earns $30 000 a year. She has taken to heart all the admonitions to start saving for retirement early and intends to put 10 percent of her gross income into her RRSP each year. So she will start with $3000 a year, and that will increase by 2 percent annually in line with her income growth.

Here is what her situation will be in the first full year of retirement, at age 65, at various average annual compound rates of return on her invested money.

Susie Smith's Retirement Income

	Compound return of				
	6%	8%	10%	12%	15%
Total capital	$642 175	$1 053 890	$1 775 863	$3 052 322	$7 050 088
RRIF income	25 687	42 156	71 035	122 093	282 004
CPP/OAS	30 802	30 802	30 802	30 802	30 802
Total income	56 489	72 958	101 837	152 895	312 806

Susie ends up sitting pretty. Remember, the target retirement income is $49 500. Even if her RRSP money earns only a modest 6 percent a year on average, she will easily exceed that goal once her CPP/OAS payments are included. If her investments do better than 6 percent, she can look forward to a life of luxury when she retires. Her main worry may be the OAS claw-back, which will almost certainly affect her.

Now to the case of Brian Shaw. He is 40 years old and has just come to the realization that, yes, he'd better start to put some money away for the future. He's done zip until now, so he's starting from scratch. He's currently making about $40 000 a year, on track for close to $66 000 at age 65. So his retirement income target is the same as Susie's. Since he's starting later, he realizes he must put more aside, so he commits himself to put 20 percent of his income, or $8000 a year, into his RRSP for the next 25 years. The amount will increase by 2 percent a year as his salary rises. That's slightly more than the 18 percent of earned income normally allowed, but he's got plenty of carry-forward credits so he foresees no problem. Here's how he will end up.

Brian Shaw's Retirement Income

	Compound return of				
	6%	8%	10%	12%	15%
Total capital	$562 068	$749 933	$1 011 351	$1 376 207	$2 213 545
RRIF income	22 483	29 997	40 454	55 048	88 542
CPP/OAS	22 886	22 886	22 886	22 886	22 886
Total income	45 369	52 883	63 340	77 934	111 428

Brian comes out looking pretty good, despite the late start. At a 6 percent annual return, he comes up a bit short of his target of $49 500. But if he manages his money to yield 8 percent annually, he achieves his goal with plenty to spare. But remember, he's saving 20 percent of his income every year. Otherwise, he'd never make it.

Finally, we'll consider the situation of Matt Jones. He's 50 now, and has suddenly become aware of the fact that retirement is just 15 years away. He's done nothing to this point and knows he must start immediately. His current income is $49 000 a year, and he expects to be earning about $66 000 when he retires, assuming increments of 2 percent a year. So his retirement income target is also $49 500. Matt swallows hard and makes a big commitment. He will put 30 percent of his annual income–$14 700 a year–into his newly opened RRSP. Like Brian, he has many years of unused carry-forward credits to call on, and he anticipates that the contribution limits may be raised in the future. So he operates on the assumption that his total savings can go into his plan. If not, he'll put the balance into a tax-advantaged non-registered portfolio. Here's his situation as he enters the first year of his retirement at age 65.

Matt Jones's Retirement Income

	Compound return of				
	6%	8%	10%	12%	15%
Total capital	$409 296	$483 239	$572 293	$679 584	$883 116
RRIF income	16 372	19 330	22 892	27 183	35 325
CPP/OAS	18 775	18 775	18 775	18 775	18 775
Total income	35 147	38 105	41 667	45 958	54 100

Oh boy! Matt is in trouble! Even saving 30 percent of his gross income every year and investing for a 12 percent average annual return doesn't generate quite the revenue he needs to live on comfortably in his old age. Either he must put aside even more, or learn to be a super-successful investor.

It doesn't matter what your income level is, or what assumptions you make about annual salary increases. The end result is going to end up more or less the same, assuming you're starting from the same age.

So there's the bottom line. The older you are when you begin, the more you need to save, save, save. There just isn't any way around it, short of winning the lottery.

Take More Risk. It's ironic, isn't it? Normally, younger people are told it's okay to take more risk because they have lots of time to recover from any losses. Older people, on the other hand, are urged to be more cautious.

But in this case, we have to stand things on their heads. The older you are when you begin your retirement planning process, the *more* risk you are going to have to take in your effort to make up lost ground.

We've just seen why in the case of Matt Jones. He has to earn at least 12 percent a year on his invested money just to come close to reaching his target retirement income. That's tough to do—not impossible, but tough. Any time you have to achieve an average annual return of more than 10 percent over a period of several years, you know you have your work cut out for you.

Essentially, this means that an older person cannot afford the safety of putting GICs or stripped bonds into a retirement plan the way the person who starts young can. Equities, especially U.S. and international stocks, will be the key to success for the 50-plus starter. If world stock markets do well during the first part of the new century, you should end up all right. If they don't, be prepared to cut back on your lifestyle after you retire or make plans to work until age 70.

Consider a Catch-Up Loan. One way to make up some of the lost time is to apply for a catch-up loan that will enable you to use all your RRSP carry-forward credits immediately. Let's say you're 40 years old and you now have 10 years of back credits available (the carry-forward became effective in 1991, so the year 2000 will mark the tenth anniversary). To remain consistent with the examples we looked at previously, we'll assume you are earning $40 000 a year now, and that your income increased by 2 percent a year over the past decade. So 10 years ago, you were earning $32 750 a year. You had no pension plan, so your unused RRSP carry-forward in that year was 18 percent of that amount, or about $5900. Your carry-forward allowance went up two percentage points each year as your salary increased. You are now sitting on almost $72 000 worth of unused RRSP credits.

If you can swing it, take out a loan for the full amount and put it in your RRSP immediately. Space out your deductions over several years to maximize the refund you receive from Revenue Canada. Assuming a ten-year repayment schedule at an average interest rate of 8 percent, it will cost you about $874 a month to pay off the loan. That's somewhat more than the 20 percent of salary that you originally targeted, but you bite the bullet and go ahead. Until the loan is paid off, you don't make any more RRSP contributions.

At an annual growth rate of 8 percent, that $72 000 will be worth $493 000 at age 65. Add to that the accumulated value of the last 15 years of regular RRSP contributions as per the Brian Shaw example (about $320 000 at 8 percent), and you end up with a nest egg worth about $813 000. That's about $63 000 better than by simply making an annual contribution equivalent to 20 percent of salary over a 25-year period.

Forget Early Retirement. This may come as a shock to baby boomers, but if you haven't seriously begun to save for retirement by the time you're 40, early retirement will never be anything more than a dream. There is no way you can accumulate enough capital to retire comfortably at 55 or 60. Unless your employer comes through with a golden handshake as an incentive for you to depart early, count on staying at your job, or one like it, until at least 65.

The financial reality of early retirement is that it gives you fewer years to save money and more years to spend it. Unless you plan extremely carefully, you run the risk of finding yourself in difficulty before you hit 70.

I've seen it happen to people I know. They quit their jobs in their fifties, believing they were in a reasonably good financial position. Within five years, they were back at work, sometimes full time, earning enough to make ends meet.

The earlier you stop work, the greater the impact of even modest rates of inflation on your post-retirement income. A 55-year-old man has a life expectancy of about 23 years; a woman of the same age can expect to live about 27 years.

Consider the position of a man who retires at 55 on $50 000 a year. To maintain his purchasing power, he'll have to arrange his financial affairs in such a way that his annual income in 23 years will be in the $80 000 range, assuming an average annual inflation rate of 2 percent. That's not impossible, considering he will be able to draw on his Canada Pension Plan and Old Age Security in the future (although much of the OAS will likely be taxed back). But it will take very careful planning.

A woman, with her longer life expectancy, will need about $85 000 a year after 27 years to stay even in buying power terms.

These large amounts of money will have to be generated from a smaller pool of savings than would be accumulated if work continued until age 65. As well, early retirees lose years of compounding, assuming they have to use their registered and non-registered savings to help finance their leisure time.

The table below shows the difference in the amount of money available in an RRSP at ages 55 and 65, assuming contributions of $5000 a year and an average annual growth rate of 10 percent.

The Effect of Early Retirement on an RRSP

Starting Age	Annual Contribution	Value at 55	Value at 65
25	$5 000	$822 470	$2 212 963
30	5 000	491 736	1 355 122
35	5 000	286 375	822 470
40	5 000	158 863	491 736
45	5 000	79 687	286 375

Even when you begin young, the value of the RRSP fund at 55 is only slightly more than a third of what it will be a decade later. The older you are when you start, the greater the difference in percentage terms between the value of your plan at age 55 and the value at 65, which is why early retirement is so difficult in that kind of situation.

Other Strategies

Sell Your House

It's not as radical a step as it may sound. If the kids have left home, you may no longer need that large four-bedroom house in the 'burbs. A two-bedroom condo might be better suited to your current lifestyle.

Many people in their forties and fifties have a lot of equity tied up in their homes. If you've owned the house for 20 years or more and you live in an area where prices have escalated (e.g., Vancouver, Calgary, Toronto), you may have a lot of money tied up that could be used to give a kick-start to your retirement savings program.

Remember that capital gains on the sale of a personal residence are not taxed in this country—so your home is actually a form of tax shelter. You can turn those paper profits into real money by selling your home and either renting or purchasing smaller accommodation at a lower price.

Suppose, for example, you bought a four-bedroom house in Toronto 25 years ago, as we did. We paid about $130 000 at that time. Today, the house is easily worth at least $350 000 and probably more like $400 000. That's a large amount of money that could be put towards a retirement plan. I know that many people in the 50-plus age group are in a similar situation.

So give it some thought. If you could clear, say, $50 000 out of a sale and downsized new purchase and invest the proceeds in an RRSP using your carry-forward entitlements, that amount would grow to almost $160 000 after 15 years at an 8 percent average annual return.

Cut Costs

If you need to find more money to direct to your retirement plan, you may have to bite the bullet and cut some of your living expenses. You should realize some savings as the children leave home to start independent lives. But further sacrifices may be needed. Among the possibilities to consider:

- **Cars.** If you have two, think about whether you really need both. Also, plan to make your car last longer. Don't automatically trade it in every three or four years. Instead, the next time you need to replace your car, choose a model that has established a reputation for longevity and plan to keep it for the next five to seven years. A top-rated car, like a Honda Accord or Toyota Camry, that's a couple of years old will be the best buy.

- **Vacation home.** If you have a summer cottage and the kids are grown up, ask yourself how much use you'll continue to make of it. Cottages can be very expensive in terms of the capital they tie up and the maintenance costs.

- **Leisure expenses.** Do you belong to an expensive club? If so, are you getting enough use out of it to justify the cost? Or could you better use the annual fees for your retirement savings plan? What about vacations? If you tend to overspend on them, look for ways to cut back. Do you really need as many cable outlets in your home? Are you dining out more than is necessary? Do you need a $15 bottle of wine when a $10 bottle will do just fine? In short, look at all the ways in which you spend your leisure money, and resolve to cut back by at least 25 percent if you need to boost your savings.

There may be several other kinds of money-saving opportunities available to you. Review the total family budget carefully and see what you can find.

Get a Second Job

If cutting spending seems too harsh to you, explore the possibility of getting a second part-time job or becoming a mini-entrepreneur from your own home. Many people are discovering that a small Internet marketing venture geared to a personal hobby or skill (anything from selling home-made quilts to offering consulting advice) can provide some welcome extra income. You can also get some valuable tax breaks, such as deducting the cost of a home office, in this way.

Exercise Self-Discipline

When it comes right down to it, the only way late starters can be successful is if they genuinely want to build a good retirement plan and are prepared to exercise the self-discipline and make whatever sacrifices are needed. It won't be easy, but if you have the determination it can be done.

Key Points in Review

1. If you've reached your forties or fifties and have still not started a comprehensive retirement plan, do it now! You can't make up for the lost years completely, but you can go a long way toward ensuring a comfortable lifestyle when you stop work.

2. Open an RRSP and make your maximum possible contribution every year.

3. Save, save, save. If you're in your forties, your target should be 20 percent of gross income. If you don't start until your fifties, make it 30 percent.

4. Usually, older people are told to take less risk with their RRSP investments. But late starters may have to take *more* risk in an effort to compensate for the lost years of compounding.

5. A catch-up RRSP loan can give your retirement plan a head start.

6. Forget about early retirement. Most late starters will have to work until at least 65.

7. Consider selling your house, moving to smaller accommodation, and investing your net profit in your RRSP.

8. Find extra savings dollars by cutting expenses or moonlighting.

9. It won't be easy. You'll need self-discipline and high motivation to build a decent retirement plan if you start late.

11

The Vanishing Pension

At a job interview, a Canadian will
ask about the pension plan before inquiring
about the starting salary.

— Richard Stengel

DO YOU HAVE AN EMPLOYER PENSION PLAN? IF SO, COUNT YOURSELF
lucky. According to Statistics Canada, only about one-third of our
labour force has any kind of employer or union plan that will help to
support them when they retire. And that percentage has been declining
in recent years.

The reality is that if you work in the public sector, you probably have
a pension plan and likely a very good one. If you're in the private sector, however, you probably don't, unless you have a very strong union
working on your behalf.

There's no getting away from the fact that employer pension plans
seem to be going the way of the dinosaurs. There are two reasons for
this: they've become too expensive and they are over-regulated.

In these times of "lean and mean," one of the casualties has been the
perks normally associated with a job in years past. There was a time
when a pension plan was taken for granted when you began work with
a company. But no more. They have become a luxury, not only because
of the high contributions an employer must make, but also because of
the ever-escalating administration costs.

One of the main reasons for these expenses is shared jurisdiction. The federal government puts basic pension legislation in place, which is then overlaid with provincial laws and regulations. The result is a complex administrative stew that discourages the introduction of new pension plans.

Over the years, the provinces and the federal government have introduced new rules that have imposed tighter controls on the use and ownership of pension surpluses, increased the portability of private plans, required earlier vesting, and demanded more detailed reporting. All these may be laudable ideas from the point of view of pension plan members. But they have increased costs and added to the paperwork, to the point where many employers are unwilling to undertake the responsibility, especially if they operate in more than one province and have to meet varying standards. In the first edition of *Retiring Wealthy*, I wrote, "Unless there's a change of heart by someone, the odds are that fewer Canadians will be covered by employer pension plans in the years to come." That is exactly what has happened.

Those people that do obtain employer benefits may find they are less generous than expected. Even a top-notch pension plan is unlikely to provide more than 50 percent of your income after retirement, including Canada Pension Plan and Old Age Security. And that level will only be achieved after many years of service. Many plans pay much less.

Types of Pension Plans

Defined Benefit Plans

Originally, most private pension plans in Canada were of the defined benefit type. These plans guarantee the employee a specific income at retirement, according to a set formula. Typically, this formula is based on the number of years of service plus your income level. More generous plans will use the average of your best three or five years' earnings to determine your pension. Less generous plans may base the pension on average earnings over your time with the employer. These are known as average career earnings plans, and are less desirable from the pensioner's point of view because the final payout will be based in part on your early years with the employer, when your salary was lower.

A typical formula for calculating a pension in a plan based on your best earnings years would be:

(2% x years of service) x average of best five years of income

So if you had been with your employer for twenty-five years and your best five years averaged out to $40 000 annually, your pension entitlement would be:

$$(2\% \times 25) \times \$40\ 000$$
$$= 50\% \times \$40\ 000$$
$$= \$20\ 000$$

That amount would be guaranteed, assuming the pension fund remained solvent.

However, rising costs and bureaucratic interference have encouraged employers to move to other types of pension arrangements. Some of these are discussed below.

Money Purchase Plans

Also known as defined contribution plans, these programs do not carry any income guarantee. Instead, contributions made by you and your employer are invested on your behalf, and the final pension is based on the total value of your pension credits when you retire.

Increasingly, individual plan members are asked to select the type of investments they prefer from a predetermined list supplied by the fund managers. This puts a greater onus for maximizing returns on the employees. They're required to make decisions on the amount of risk they're prepared to accept, the asset mix they want, and the rate of return they'd like. If they know nothing about investing, they'd better learn fast or there'll be trouble ahead.

The pension that's eventually paid will be based on the end value of your account at retirement. The greater the value, the more money you'll have to live on when you stop work. Conversely, if the fund doesn't do well, you'll suffer the financial consequences.

Failure of a money purchase plan to maximize returns can lead to a serious reduction in your retirement standard of living. The accompanying table illustrates the end value of a plan, based on annual combined contribution of $5000 from employer and employee.

Value of Money Purchase Plan

	Average Annual Rate of Return			
Years	6%	8%	10%	12%
10	$65 904	$72 433	$79 687	$87 744
20	183 928	228 810	286 375	360 262
30	395 291	566 416	822 470	1 206 664

As you can see, the end value of the plan varies greatly with the annual rate of return. Translating those numbers into retirement income produces even more dramatic results. Let's assume your money purchase plan averaged a 6 percent annual return and you contributed to it for 30 years. You retire at age 65 and the money goes into a life income fund (LIF). If you begin withdrawals the next year (age 66), your first year payment at the minimum rate would be about $16 500. But if the plan's return had averaged 10 percent a year instead, the first year's payout would be more than $34 000! That's more than double the payment at 6 percent. You can imagine what a huge difference that would make to your retirement lifestyle.

Clearly, the rewards of good financial management are very high in these situations. But there are no guarantees. This makes it more difficult to project the likely retirement income from a money purchase plan, especially in the early years.

Group RRSPs

As an alternative to money purchase plans, many employers are making use of group RRSPs (sometimes abbreviated as GRSPs). They are similar to money purchase plans in the way they're funded and managed. Again, the end value of the plan will depend on a combination of contributions and growth rate, and the actual pension that will be paid cannot be predicted with accuracy until you're close to retirement.

However, there are some important differences between a money purchase pension plan and a group RRSP. In fact, technically, there is no such thing as a group RRSP. Every RRSP is registered in the name of a single individual. A group plan simply involves bundling many individual plans together under the same set of rules.

For most people, the group RRSP is a better choice than a money purchase plan because it provides greater flexibility. For example, you can withdraw money from a group RRSP if you need it for a cash emergency. You can't do that with a money purchase plan, which is owned collectively by all the participants. Also, you have more options at retirement. With a money purchase plan, you can only choose between an annuity and a life income fund (LIF). A group RRSP allows you to open a RRIF, which has fewer constraints than a LIF, or buy an annuity, or even take the money in a lump-sum payment if you prefer.

Employers also prefer the group RRSP approach because it doesn't fall under the pension regulations, which means they aren't obliged to file all sorts of returns. Less paperwork means more efficiency.

The differences in the definition of contribution limits can be important in certain circumstances. For example, alimony and maintenance payments are deducted from earned income for purposes of determining your RRSP contribution limit. A person with large annual alimony/maintenance obligations might find more retirement contribution room in a money purchase plan, which is based strictly on salary.

Deferred Profit Sharing Plans

These programs are designed to allow employees to participate in the profits of a company for retirement purposes. They operate in a similar way to money purchase plans, but the employer contribution limit is only half as much. No employee contributions are allowed.

Obviously, the type of plan will have an important bearing on your retirement income projections. In most cases, you won't have any choice; however, a few companies offer employees a selection of retirement programs. Also, the retirement plan of a company might be the difference in deciding which of two job offers to accept.

If you find yourself faced with this kind of decision, you'll have to weigh several factors.

There's no doubt the defined benefit plan offers the greatest level of security. Your pension is guaranteed and is predictable, based on your income level and years of service. On the other hand, money purchase plans and group RRSPs may be more portable. And if the investments perform well, the pay-out could be higher than from a defined benefit plan.

Your Pension: Factors to Consider

The Pension Gap

If you're in a higher income category, you'll need to consider the pension cap. This is one of those little-known pension rules that can reach out and grab you when you least expect it.

Years ago, the federal government decided it would limit the amount of tax assistance it would provide for private pension plans. Otherwise, a company might be tempted to use tax-deductible contributions to fund outrageously high benefits for some of its employees. As a result, the pension cap concept was introduced. This imposes a limit on the amount of money a pensioner may receive from a private plan.

The cap is calculated by multiplying $1722.22 by your years of service in the plan. Based on this formula, the accompanying table shows the maximum pension you can receive in the first year after retirement.

The Effect of the Pension Cap

Years of Service	Maximum Pension
10	$17 222
15	25 833
20	34 444
25	43 056
30	51 667
35	60 278
40	68 889

Your pension may exceed these limits in subsequent years if your plan provides for indexing. Government rules allowed for indexing up to 4 percent a year or the increase in the consumer price index (CPI), whichever is greater, for most plans. Individual pension plans may only be indexed to the CPI if the beneficiary is receiving the maximum allowable payment.

Although the pension cap was modified slightly in the 1991 pension reform, it is essentially the same formula that has been used since 1977. Since the pension cap is not indexed to inflation, this has meant that more retiring Canadians find they are bumping up against the ceiling each year. When the first edition of this book was published, I noted that the federal government had announced plans to index the pension cap to the average wage in 1995. It never happened. Indexing has now been delayed three times and is currently not scheduled to start until 2005 at the earliest. As a result, Ottawa is depriving a growing number of people of full, tax-assisted benefits.

If the pension cap becomes a problem, there are ways around it. However, Ottawa won't help fund additional benefits with tax deductions. Some companies have set up supplementary retirement plans for higher income employees, for example. These are paid for with after-tax dollars, sometimes totally by the employer, sometimes with joint contributions, and the income they earn is taxed. They're known as retirement compensation arrangements (RCAs) for tax purposes.

Another device some larger companies are using is the matching savings plan. These programs are designed to encourage employees to put money aside for retirement over and above their normal pension contributions. A typical matching plan allows employees to contribute a certain percentage of income. The employer adds a company contribution that is a percentage of the employee's amount, usually between 25 and 50 percent. The funds are directed into an RRSP until the employee's limit is reached; after that they go into a non-registered managed securities portfolio. Over many years, such plans can boost employer retirement benefits considerably.

The Pension Adjustment

One of the technical aspects of pensions you'll have to be aware of is the pension adjustment (PA). This figure is supposed to reflect the value of the future retirement benefits you receive from your plan each year.

For money purchase plans and deferred profit sharing plans, the PA is simply the total amount of money contributed on your behalf annually. The calculation for defined benefit plans is more complicated, and takes into account the formula under which benefits will eventually be paid.

Your PA is extremely important because it determines how much room you have left to contribute to an RRSP each year. You'll find it in box 52 on the T4 slip you receive from your employer at tax time. To calculate your RRSP limit, multiply your earned income for the previous year by 18 percent (maximum $13 500). Subtract the PA from the result. The difference is your RRSP entitlement.

To illustrate, suppose your earned income was $40 000 and your PA for the year was $6000. The following calculation shows your RRSP limit:

$$\$40\ 000 \times 18\%$$
$$= \$7200 \text{ (retirement savings limit)}$$
$$- \$6000 \text{ (pension adjustment)}$$
$$= \$1200 \text{ (RRSP limit)}$$

In determining the PA, there is an "offset" of $600 that is used in the calculation. This can have the effect of increasing your RRSP limit in some cases. The offset is to help compensate for any inequities that may occur over the years, such as frequent job changes. However, it does not apply to money purchase or deferred profit sharing plans.

Understanding Your Plan

If you have an employer pension plan, it is absolutely essential that you understand it thoroughly and have a good idea (updated regularly) of how much it will pay when you retire. Most people know surprisingly little about their pension plans; the more information you have, the better position you'll be in to plan your retirement. Here are some questions to ask your plan's administrator.

What Is Our Benefits Formula? If career average is used, probe more deeply. Some companies will upgrade career earnings to reflect inflation. The answer you'd prefer, however, is a formula based on your best three years of earnings.

When Am I Vested in the Plan? Vesting simply means you gain entitlement to the contributions the employer has made on your behalf. If you leave the company before you're vested, all you're likely to receive is a refund of your premiums plus some modest interest. If you're vested, you're guaranteed some retirement benefits, although they may be very modest. In most provinces, an RPP is considered to be vested after two years.

If you're vested and leave to go elsewhere, you're usually given three choices.

1. You may leave the money in the plan and draw a benefit at retirement. In this case, ask some hard questions about how the benefit will be calculated and how much it is likely to be. Compare that with the income that will likely be generated by the other two options.

2. Switch the money into a locked-in RRSP, also known as a locked-in retirement account, or LIRA. These plans function in most respects like an ordinary RRSP. However, you cannot withdraw the money before retirement, and your income option when you stop work is restricted to an annuity or a life income fund. This means you can't invest funds from a locked-in RRSP in a registered retirement income fund.

3. Have the money transferred to the pension plan at your new place of employment–if there is a plan and if such a transfer is permitted.

If you leave your job, you may be entitled to a pension adjustment reversal (PAR). This concept was introduced in the 1997 budget as a way of restoring lost RRSP contribution room to people who lose pension plan benefits because they leave their employment, or for other reasons. If you think you may be eligible for a PAR, get hold of a copy of Revenue Canada's booklet titled *Pension Adjustment Reversal Guide*. You can obtain it from your local taxation office or download it from the Revenue Canada Web site at **http://www.rc.gc.ca**.

What Is My Plan Invested In, and What Return Is It Earning? This is a "nice to know" piece of information if you're in a plan over which you have no control. It's essential information if you're required to make decisions on what type of securities your pension money is invested in, as is increasingly the case with money purchase plans and group RRSPs. If the returns are not meeting your expectations, find out why—and consider alternatives.

Is the Plan Fully Funded? It's nice to know your pension plan has adequate resources to meet its obligations. If it doesn't, ask for an explanation. It may be perfectly valid but, on the other hand, it may not. Actuaries warn that some defined benefit pension plans, particularly those run by smaller companies, could face financial shortfalls in the future because of the current low interest rate environment. Multi-employer plans that cover a specific industry such as construction also may be at risk—in fact, a couple have been forced to reduce benefits to retirees.

Is My Plan Integrated with the CPP? This means the benefits paid by the plan will be adjusted to reflect payments you receive under the Canada Pension Plan. The argument is that the employer also contributed to the CPP and this should be recognized in the payments made to you. Most private pension plans are integrated with the CPP.

When Can I Retire? Provisions for retiring on a full pension can vary widely. Some plans allow for retirement after a certain number of years of service, others on reaching a specific age. A formula now being used more often involves adding age to years of service; if the total is equal to or greater than a target number (for example, 90), you may retire with full benefits.

Can I Retire Early? Find out if the plan has a set formula for early retirement and, if so, how it works. Ask especially about bridging arrangements, which provide for extra benefits until your CPP and OAS payments kick in.

What Happens if I Die? This book is about retiring wealthy, not dying. Nonetheless, you should know what benefits your spouse and children can expect to receive from your pension plan if you're not around to collect. Make sure you understand the difference between survivor benefits if you should die before retirement and the amounts payable after you begin drawing a pension.

Am I Allowed to Make Past Service Contributions and, If I Do, What Effect Will They Have on My Pension? If you're allowed to make contributions for previous years of service (for example, you were with the company but hadn't joined the pension plan), it may be in your interest to do so. But find out how much your benefits will increase as a result. Also, the government has tightened up in recent years on the tax deductibility of past service contributions, so find out what you're allowed to claim before going ahead. For a full explanation of the current rules, obtain a copy of the current edition of Revenue Canada's guide titled *RRSPs and Other Registered Plans for Retirement.*

What Happens to Any Pension Surplus? Surpluses can build over time if the pension fund investments perform better than the actuaries allowed for. Some employers use any surpluses to improve benefits, but this is certainly not a universal practice. A great debate continues to rage over who owns pension surpluses, the employees or the employer. If your company has a firm policy in this regard, or if your province has passed legislation on this question, you should know about it.

Are Benefits Indexed and, If So, Are There Any Limits? This is one of the most important questions you can ask. An unindexed pension plan (which most of them are) can put you in a vulnerable financial position as you grow older and the buying power of your pension cheque erodes. It's better to find out the bad news up front and plan accordingly than to be hit with it at retirement. If the plan is indexed, count yourself lucky; very few Canadian pension plans offer this desirable but very expensive feature, and they are mainly in the public sector.

How Often Are Benefits Improved? Some employers upgrade their pension plans every two or three years to keep pace with changes in salaries, economic conditions, inflation, etc. Others keep their plans in what amounts to the Dark Ages. Find out about the track record of your employer.

Who Pays What? The employee's contribution to the pension plan is usually clearly defined. The employer's may be more ambiguous. Find out whether the company is on the hook for a certain percentage of salaries each year, or whether the only obligation is to contribute just enough to bring the plan's assets into line with the anticipated future benefits.

What Kind of Reports Do I Get? A well-managed pension plan will provide a benefits report at least once a year that will detail your current status and outline your entitlements. If you're not receiving such a report, ask why.

When you know as much as possible about your pension plan, you'll be in a better position to assess how significant the income it produces will be in your total retirement financial plan. You'll also have a better fix on how much additional income you'll have to generate from sources over which you have more control—your RRSPs and non-registered investments.

Key Points in Review

1. High costs and excessive regulation have made pension plans much less desirable for employers.
2. Group RRSPs offer greater flexibility than money purchase pension plans, and don't carry the heavy administrative burden.
3. The federal government's pension cap places a ceiling on the amount that can be paid out of an RPP to any individual.
4. Most people overestimate the amount of income they will eventually receive from their pension plan.
5. It is essential to know all the terms of your pension plan, if you have one. Get an estimate of how much income you can expect to receive from it when you retire, and find out about survivor benefits if you should die.

12

Managing Group Pension Money

*In investing money, the amount of interest
you want should depend on whether you want
to eat well or sleep well.*

— J. Kenfield Morley

THERE WAS A TIME WHEN NO ONE WORRIED ABOUT HOW THE MONEY in their pension plan was invested. A professional organization was hired to handle those details, and every so often plan members received an unintelligible report that was supposed to keep them up-to-date on their plan's progress.

Members of defined benefit pension plans are still in this kind of situation today. But if you are part of a money purchase plan or a group RRSP, it's a different story. Increasingly, you're being asked to direct the placement of your retirement savings yourself–in other words, to assume responsibility for managing your investment portfolio.

Many people are ill-equipped to do that. They've never been taught about investing, and they become nervous when anything more complicated than a GIC is mentioned. Suddenly they are being asked to construct their own investment portfolio from a number of available options. If they get it wrong, the cost will be high in terms of lost retirement income.

Since every plan has its own investment options, it is impossible to draw up an ideal portfolio mix that can be applied across the board. However, here are some basic guidelines to use if you're required to make this kind of decision.

Rule 1: **Understand all the choices.** Typically, you'll be offered several types of securities from which to choose. These may include several mutual funds and some GIC options. If you don't understand any of them, insist on a detailed explanation before you make any decisions. Some employers offer special seminars so that employees can get answers quickly and easily. But if your organization doesn't, ask for a meeting with the plan administrator and don't leave until you're satisfied.

Rule 2: **Check the performance history of any funds being offered.** Chances are you'll be asked to choose from a number of "pooled" funds. These are mutual funds that are limited to a specific group (such as your company's employees). So you may not find any performance figures for them in the business press. Ask for numbers. You want to see both short- and long-term figures. Then compare the results with those of publicly available mutual funds in the same category. See which ones are out-performing the averages. Those should be among your leading candidates.

Rule 3: **Decide on an asset allocation.** Before you invest a penny, work out how you want to allocate your money. If you prefer to be aggressive and you're relatively young, put more emphasis on the equity side. If you're older and/or more conservative, beef up the fixed income side of the portfolio.

Rule 4: **Check out the foreign content.** See if any of the funds you're offered fall into the foreign content category. It would be nice if one or two do, as this will allow a degree of geographic diversification. Just remember that your foreign content limit cannot exceed 20 percent.

Rule 5: **Consider the investment climate.** If times are good and there is no sign of inflation on the horizon, you can afford to be a little bolder in your equity weighting. If we're heading into a recession, fixed income securities, such as bond funds, will probably do better because interest rates tend to fall in bad economic times.

Rule 6: **Consider a balanced fund.** If you don't want to spend a lot of time figuring everything out, put your money into a balanced fund. It will give you exposure to both stocks and bonds, and carries less risk.

Rule 7: **Review your portfolio periodically.** You need to keep on top of what's happening with your money. Read each statement carefully. If there are any discrepancies, report them to the plan administrator immediately.

That's it. If you follow these seven rules, you'll find that managing your retirement savings program isn't all that difficult. Plus, you'll be in a much better position when it comes to calling the shots on your personal RRSP or non-registered plan.

Key Points in Review

1. Increasingly, people are being called upon to make their own investment decisions for a group RRSP or money purchase pension plan.
2. Before you invest, understand all the available choices.
3. Asset allocation principles should be applied in the same way as with a private RRSP.
4. A balanced fund is usually the best choice for an individual who knows nothing about investing and doesn't particularly want to learn.

13

Individual Pension Plans

Once you are original, you are different; once you
are different, you are an individualist; once you
are an individualist, you are alone.

— Stewart James

IN THE FIRST EDITION OF *RETIRING WEALTHY*, I WROTE GLOWINGLY
about a then-recent initiative of the federal government, the creation of
individual pension plans (IPPs).

The idea was to provide a method by which owner-managers and
high-income executives could plan for their retirement years in situations where an ordinary pension plan did not exist and it was impractical to create one.

By setting up an IPP, a person could create a defined-benefit pension
plan specifically tailored to his or her needs. The level of retirement
income would be guaranteed, indexing could be included and, if
desired, the company could pick up all the (tax deductible) contributions. The plan beneficiary didn't need to put in one cent.

IPPs also carried another advantage—you could contribute more to
them than to an RRSP. That was because the rules allowed for additional funding of the pension plan to ensure that the benefits could be
paid. So the company could get a larger tax deduction than the owner-
manager could claim as an individual. In cases where the corporate and
the personal entity were, in effect, one and the same, the advantages
were obvious: more tax relief, plus a larger pool of tax-sheltered assets.
Who wouldn't want that?

After these plans were legalized in 1991, the accounting firm of Price Waterhouse (now PricewaterhouseCoopers) did an analysis of IPP projections using as their model a 45-year-old man who earned $86 000 a year (the income required at that time to produce the maximum private pension allowed by Revenue Canada). They found that, at the outset, the company and the employee would be able to contribute about $4700 a year more to an IPP than to an RRSP. By age 55, the IPP's contribution advantage increased to about $11 000 annually—a huge differential.

The pot was made even sweeter because, under the rules that prevailed at that time, the employee could also contribute up to $1000 a year to an RRSP under what is known as the "offset" provision.

Assuming an average annual return on invested money of 9 percent, the accounting firm calculated that the total value of the RRSP/IPP combination when the employee reached age 65 would be over $1.4 million. Without the IPP, contributing only to an RRSP at the maximum limit, the employee would end up with about $1 million in retirement capital. The upside of the IPP in this case was about 40 percent!

Not surprisingly, some accounting firms and brokerage houses began aggressively marketing the concept to qualified people. What is surprising, however, is that the response was underwhelming. Some plans were established, of course, but the IPP business never became as popular or as lucrative as some companies expected, given the obvious financial advantages.

Despite the tepid response, the idea of providing such benefits for people perceived as being well-to-do apparently stuck in the craw of the Liberal party when it was returned to office. In his 1995 and 1996 budgets, Finance Minister Paul Martin launched a frontal attack on IPPs, slashing the benefits of the plans in a way that shocked the accounting community. By the time he was finished, the maximum annual funding for an IPP had been reduced by more than 38 percent out to the year 2005. The amount of pension income the plans could pay out was frozen until that year, and who knows what will happen beyond that. The offset disappeared and, if it ever does come back, it will be reduced to $600.

In short, the advantage of an IPP over an RRSP was significantly reduced in many situations, and accounting firms were so spooked by the government's blitz that some virtually stopped recommending the plans, even when they still made some sense, because of concerns about yet more restrictive measures.

Existing IPPs were subjected to a complete reevaluation in the 1997 tax year. In many cases the recommendation was to wind up the plan, or to suspend contributions to it for a period of time. Although in absolute terms not a lot of people were affected, those that were had to rebuild their retirement savings program from scratch—and this after complying fully with the rules that had been put into place only a few years before. And politicians wonder why their actions are sometimes so resented!

You can still set up an IPP today, but the real question is: does it make any sense to do so? In some cases, it does. But the applications are limited. PricewaterhouseCoopers only recommends such plans now to people who are 56 or older and have incomes of at least $70 000. Even then, the advisability of a plan will depend on whether the company has adequate cash flow to fund it comfortably. The maximum income an individual can have that qualifies for a pension benefit is $86 111 a year, and this amount is frozen. Any income beyond that cannot be funded from a tax-assisted pension plan (in other words, contributions to fund a pension beyond that level are not deductible). The best advice I can offer, if you think an IPP may be right for you despite all the changes, is to discuss the pros and cons with an accounting firm or pension consultant who is knowledgeable about these plans.

An IPP does offer a few advantages that are not available in an ordinary RRSP. Creditor protection is the most important of these. If the company or the individual ends up in financial difficulty, the assets in the IPP are protected, as they are in any other pension plan. Creditors may seize your house and your car, but they can't take away your pension. Indexing is another benefit. Your pension payments can be increased in line with changes in the Consumer Price Index, which ensures that you'll retain your purchasing power. Another advantage is that, because contributions to the plan are tax deductible, they make it easier for companies to qualify for the small business tax rate if profits are under $200 000.

Also, if the investments in the plan lose money, the company can make extra contributions (tax deductible) to cover the losses and ensure the benefit level will be met. This is obviously something you cannot do in an RRSP.

What about the disadvantages? For starters, an IPP is expensive. You'll pay a set up charge, which could be several thousand dollars. Then your company will be hit with an annual administration fee, unless you're prepared to handle all the paperwork yourself. There is a charge every three years for an actuary to revalue the plan, which is required by pension legislation. Then there are the fees that have to be paid annually to pension commissions, which are really nothing more than taxes in disguise.

Even if you employ an accounting firm to file all your returns, you'll still have to contend with some bureaucratic red tape each year. You, or the plan administrator if it is someone else, will have to review and sign all the documents before they can be filed. And you will not believe all the levels of officialdom that want reports about your plan, from Revenue Canada to your provincial pension commission.

Of course, someone has to make the investment decisions for the money that goes into the plan. If you are not comfortable with this job, you'll have to find someone who is. You may decide to give the responsibility to an investment counsellor, who will charge a fee for the service.

If the invested money performs well, you could end up in a situation where the plan is considered to be over-funded. In that case, the surplus will be paid out to the plan's beneficiary in a lump sum and treated as income in the year it is received.

Another disadvantage of an IPP is the loss of income splitting. Staying with an RRSP enables you to make use of a spousal plan, which directs some of your retirement income into the hands of your wife or husband. This can be a valuable tax planning strategy if one spouse is likely to be in a much higher tax bracket than the other, and may also enable you to escape the Old Age Security claw-back.

An IPP does not provide this flexibility. The pension income that is paid out will go to the plan's beneficiary.

Yet another potential problem is the solvency of your company. These plans are best suited for owners of small businesses, but what happens if financial problems emerge and there's no money available to make the required contributions? Obviously, that would create difficulties. But it's not the end of the world. In the event of a cash crunch, the owner-manager would have several alternatives. The terms of the IPP could be amended to greatly reduce the benefits, thereby reducing the annual contribution required. Or the plan could be temporarily suspended until the company's financial condition improved. As a last resort, your IPP would have to be wound up. However, the money that had built up in the plan over time would be rolled into a locked-in RRSP, which means it would still be available to provide a reduced level of retirement benefits.

Finally, if you are in a situation where you think you might be eligible for the $500 000 small business capital gains exemption, you'll need to review that situation thoroughly before setting up an IPP. There are situations, too complex to detail here, in which assets invested in an IPP could impair a company's qualification for that exemption. If you think you may wish to use it at some point, be sure your accountant is aware of the fact.

If, after all this, you do set up an IPP, you can begin to draw a pension from it as early as age 55. By age 69, the plan must be converted to an income stream. This can be done by purchasing a life annuity, shifting the assets into a life income fund (LIF), or self-annuitizing the plan. If you choose a LIF, be careful—there's yet another potential pitfall to be reckoned with. When the assets of a pension plan are moved to a LIF, a "maximum transfer value" rule applies that is age-related. This cap is designed to ensure the benefits paid out do not exceed the amount that would be permitted under pension plan rules. As a result, there could be an "excess amount" left over that would be immediately taxable. That would happen if the pension plan contained more money than was needed to fund the LIF to the maximum permissible amount. Again, discuss the consequences with an accounting professional before acting.

(It should be noted that these transfer rules apply to any money moved out of a defined benefit pension plan to a RRIF or LIF, not just in this specific case.)

The route most often recommended for drawing income from an IPP is to self-annuitize the plan. This means the pension plan continues to exist, but now starts to pay out income to the beneficiary. If you die, payments from the plan can continue to your spouse. Any money that is left after both spouses die is an asset of the plan. The IPP is then wound up after all pension liabilities have been satisfied, and the money that remains is returned to the company. This is treated as taxable income at that time. So whoever is the owner of the company at that point—which could be your children or other heirs—would effectively end up with the after-tax balance.

Clearly, IPPs aren't for everyone. They're expensive and only make sense to those in very specific situations. But if the money is available and you think you might be among those who can use such a plan, talk to an accounting firm. They should be able to tell you pretty quickly if you're a candidate.

Key Points in Review

1. When IPPs were introduced in 1991, they were seen as highly bene-ficial for owner-managers and key executives. However, budget changes in 1995 and 1996 greatly reduced the value of these plans.
2. IPPs should now only be considered by high-income people aged 56 or more.
3. The advantages of IPPs include creditor protection and indexing of payments. The plans can also be used for estate planning in certain situations.
4. If the investments in the plan lose money, additional contributions can be made to ensure the plan is solvent and can meet the benefit obligations.
5. Disadvantages include high costs, bureaucratic red tape, and the possible loss of access to the $500 000 capital gains exemption for small businesses.

14

Building a Non-Registered Portfolio

Take calculated risks. That is quite different from being rash.

— General George Patton

SO FAR, I'VE SPENT A LOT OF TIME EXPLAINING HOW TO PUT TOGETHER a sound RRSP and what to do about your pension plan, if you have one. But that's only part of the story. By the time you retire, you should also have a healthy non-registered portfolio to provide the supplementary income you'll probably need to ensure a comfortable lifestyle, and to provide a cushion in the event that inflation reemerges as a serious problem.

Don't feel you have to rush into this segment of your Retiring Wealthy program, however. There's not the same pressure to get started early on a non-registered portfolio as there is with RRSPs. Since income from your non-registered portfolio will be taxed, your assets won't build as quickly as they will in a tax-sheltered environment. So you should ensure that other, more tax-efficient, financial priorities are met first. These include paying off all non-deductible debt, buying a home, paying off your mortgage, and maximizing your RRSP and pension contributions. When these goals have been satisfied, you can start building your non-registered portfolio. For most people, that will be in their middle forties.

Here are some guidelines to help you set up a portfolio that will provide maximum growth potential outside your RRSP with a limited amount of risk.

Look for a Risk/Return Advantage

There's a textbook relationship between the risk and return elements of any investment. In its simplest terms, it's this: the greater the potential return, the higher the potential risk. You'll see this illustrated in the accompanying chart, which was produced by Royal Trust.

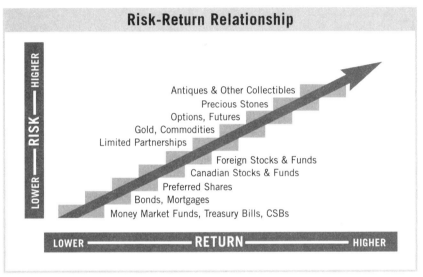

Source: Royal Trust

As you can see, the farther out a particular investment falls on the scale, the greater the risk—but also, the greater the potential return. The safest investments—savings accounts, Treasury bills, Canada Savings Bonds and the like—have the lowest return potential. Stocks, on the other hand, contain more risk but offer more profit potential. For most people, I recommend sticking with the lower half of the chart when making investment decisions.

But you should be aware that situations can arise that short-circuit the classic risk/return relationships. If you're alert to them, you can score big profits with minimal risk.

For example, Treasury bills and money market funds usually rank at the bottom end of the scale for both risk and return. Your money is safe, but you don't get a great yield for it. The exception is times when short-term interest rates are artificially high, as they were in the early nineties. Then you can get the best of all possible worlds—maximum security, plus an excellent return.

In 1990, three-month Treasury bills produced a return of more than 13 percent. The only time since the end of the Second World War when you could have done better was in 1980–82 (in 1981, T-bills returned an astounding 18 percent plus). However, we're living in a different era today. Interest rates have been in broad decline for several years and the chances of seeing double-digit T-bill returns any time soon are very remote.

You can see the downward pattern in the returns of money market mutual funds. Over the decade to the end of March 1999, the average Canadian money market fund returned just over 6 percent a year, according to the *Globe and Mail Report on Business*. But shorter-term results are much lower. Average five-year return was slightly more than 4 percent, while the three-year average was a meagre 3.4 percent.

Your Strategy: If short-term interest rates should rise significantly, weight your portfolio towards the bottom of the scale. Your risk will be very low, and your rewards will be out of proportion to what you might normally expect from conservative interest-bearing securities. You will also be reducing stock market exposure, usually a good move when interest rates are on the rise.

Buy Stocks when They Are Cheap

The stock market is usually seen as a risky place for your money. Under normal conditions, that can be true, although your degree of risk will be determined in part by the quality of the securities you select.

But there are times when your stock market risk can be reduced considerably and your potential returns greatly increased. Again, it happens because of a shift in the normal risk/return relationship.

Profiting from this situation requires more intestinal fortitude than buying T-bills when interest rates are high, however. You have to be prepared to invest in the stock market when the rest of the world is crying doom and gloom and the Henny-Pennies are everywhere.

Most people lose money in the stock market because they buy and sell at exactly the wrong time. They invest money when stocks are riding a bull market crest and the business pages are full of stories of great profits and new highs–the exact scenario we saw in the late nineties. Of course, that means they're buying when prices are inflated. When a bear market arrives on the scene, as inevitably happens, they panic on the bad news of falling profits and plunging prices, and sell. Then they turn around and complain about how risky the market is and how no one ever makes money but the professionals.

Well, come on! What do you expect? The secret to making money is to buy low, sell high, not the reverse. That means buying good stocks when they are out of favour and selling when everyone wants to take them off your hands at a nice profit.

The table that follows makes the point dramatically. It shows how the TSE 300 index performed in the years immediately following a calendar year loss, from the mid-fifties to 1998. As you can see, the Total Return Index (which takes price advances and declines plus dividends into account) fell on a year-over-year basis (January 1 to December 31) on 11 occasions during that period. Eight times, the market rebounded strongly in the two years immediately following. Twice it rose in one of the two years, with a net double-digit gain over that time. Only once, in 1969–70, did the Index fall two years running.

In virtually every case, had you invested in a broad selection of TSE stocks (or an index mutual fund) during periods when the market was in the dumps, you would have walked away with some spectacular profits. For example, $10 000 invested in early January, 1995 in stocks which followed the index in performance would have grown to $12 618 just two years later. And your profits would have been in tax-advantaged dividends and capital gains.

That's using a special situation to stand the risk/return chart on its ear.

Your Strategy: Add to your stock or equity fund holdings during periods when the stock market is out of favour and prices are cheap. Reduce your holdings and take profits when the market is roaring ahead and everyone is buying.

Stock Market Rebounds

Year	Decline	1st Year Following	2nd Year Following
1957	−20.6%	+31.3%	+4.6%
1962	−7.1%	+15.6%	+25.4%
1966	−7.1%	+18.1%	+22.5%
1969	−0.8%	−3.6%	+8.0%
1970	−3.6%	+8.0%	+27.4%
1974	−25.9%	+18.5%	+11.0%
1981	−10.3%	+5.5%	+35.5%
1984	−2.4%	+25.1%	+9.0%
1990	−14.8%	+12.0%	−1.4%
1992	−1.4%	+32.6%	−0.2%
1994	−0.2%	+14.5%	+28.3%

Source: Scotia Capital Markets

Buy Bonds When Rates Are High

Bonds are one of the lowest rungs on the risk/return ladder. They're considered to be relatively safe, but their return potential is generally limited.

However, situations can arise which increase the returns from bonds enormously. When interest rates hit high levels, you know they can't stay there very long because the economy will be stifled. That's the time to load up with bonds. The longer the terms you select, the greater the profit you'll make.

In 1994, for example, bond prices, which rise when interest rates fall and vice versa, took a tumble when rates temporarily jumped. But then rates went into a long-term decline and bond prices moved up steadily over the next several years. As a result, Canadian bond funds as a group actually outperformed Canadian equity funds over the decade to the end of March 1999.

The longer the maturity of a bond, the greater the potential capital gain (after all, a bond which will pay 6 percent for 20 years is worth more than one that pays 6 percent for 10 years at a time when rates are falling).

Your Strategy: Watch for situations when interest rates are pushed up to unrealistic levels, especially on long-term bonds. That's a signal to start building the bond section of your portfolio. When interest rates drop to more normal levels, reduce your holdings to lock in your gains.

Warning: Do not hold strip bonds in your non-registered portfolio. You will have to pay tax on the deemed interest each year, even though you won't actually receive a cent until the bonds mature. Keep strips for your RRSP.

Make Sure Your Non-Registered Portfolio Complements Your Registered Investments

Although your non-registered portfolio will be separate from your RRSP money, don't isolate the two. Your two investment plans should work together in harmony, not at cross-purposes.

For starters, that means holding your most tax-efficient investments outside your RRSP. You can use the substitution rule to achieve that.

Guaranteed investment certificates are one common type of security that should be held inside an RRSP whenever possible. Using GICs for your non-registered portfolio is a poor idea because of the twin hits these investments take from taxes and inflation.

Look at it this way. If I were to recommend a stock that would provide an average dividend return, after tax, of about 4 percent but which would drop in value by over 20 percent over the next five years, would you make the investment? Probably not.

Now consider a five-year GIC that pays 5 percent a year. If you invest $10 000, you'll receive $500 a year in interest. But you'll pay tax on that at your top rate. If you're in a 40 percent tax bracket, you'll be left with a 3 percent after-tax return on your GIC. If inflation is averaging 1.5 percent a year, you will have a positive real return, but not by much.

In the meantime, the purchasing power of your original investment is falling. At maturity, again assuming 1.5 percent annual inflation, your original $10 000 will only buy $9272 worth of goods. Reinvest it for another five years and your principal will have $8600 in buying power at the second maturity date.

Of course, if inflation rises, the erosion of the real value of your investment will accelerate.

Not particularly attractive, right? Yet millions of dollars are invested in this way every year! This doesn't mean GICs are bad. It does mean that if you're holding them outside an RRSP, you should make every effort to substitute them for a more tax-efficient security in your registered plan.

Your Strategy: Take a close look at all your assets, registered and non-registered, and see if they are deployed in the best possible way.

Maintain a Balanced Approach

Greed is often the motivating force behind many of our worst investment decisions. It drives us to buy stocks when markets are unrealistically high. It tempts us to take flyers on get-rich-quick schemes which, in our heart of hearts, we know have little chance of success. It leads us into shoddy tax shelter deals which end up being more expensive than simply handing the money over to Revenue Canada.

Your Strategy: No matter what markets are doing, always keep your perspective. A well-balanced portfolio will greatly reduce your risk, while still providing a decent rate of return on your money. In a non-registered plan, substitute preferred shares for bonds on the fixed income side to benefit from the dividend tax credit.

Adjust Your Portfolio to Your Age

The younger you are, the more risk you can afford to take with your money because there's more time to recover from temporary setbacks, like a stock market correction. That's one reason my asset mix formula becomes more conservative as you age. The older you are, the lower the growth component of your total portfolio should be. Unfortunately, even many investment professionals don't follow this approach. I've seen more cases than I can count of older people, some in their late sixties or early seventies, whose portfolios, both registered and non-registered, were almost entirely in stocks and equity funds, usually on the advice of a broker or other investment specialist. This is entirely too much risk for most older people, who are at a point in their lives when safety and income should be a priority.

That doesn't mean you should have no growth investments when you get older. Reducing growth holdings to zero would leave you vulnerable to inflation. It's a matter of finding the right balance.

Your Strategy: As you approach and enter your retirement years, your non-registered portfolio should increasingly be weighted toward securities that generate tax-advantaged income. In this way, you'll build a steady cash flow that will supplement your RRSP/pension-generated income, and you'll give the government a smaller percentage of it than if you rely on bonds or GICs outside the registered plan.

Base Your Investment Decisions on After-Tax Return

All that counts with any investment is how much money ends up in your pocket after Revenue Canada gets through with you. When you're building a non-registered portfolio, the impact of taxes is therefore one of the most important factors to take into account.

Our tax system doesn't make life easy for you in this regard. There are several types of investment income in Canada and each, predictably, is taxed in a different way.

Here's how it works.

Interest Income

Interest is taxed at your top marginal rate. That makes it the most inefficient form of investment income from a tax perspective, so try to shelter your interest-bearing securities inside an RRSP or other registered plan whenever possible.

Your Strategy: Compare the after-tax return of interest and dividends before buying. As a general rule of thumb, multiply your dividend return by 1.3 to find how much interest is required to produce the same after-tax result (this ratio will vary somewhat depending on your province). For example, if the dividend yield on an investment such as a preferred share is 5 percent, you'll receive $50 before tax per year for every thousand dollars you invest. The equivalent before-tax interest income will be:

$$\$50 \times 1.3 = \$65$$

So you'd need an interest rate of 6.5 percent to match the 5 percent dividend in after-tax terms. Usually, when interest rates are high, interest-bearing securities are a better choice despite their tax disadvantage. But when interest rates are low, as they were through the middle and late nineties, you may do better with dividends on an after-tax basis.

Dividends

You get a tax break on dividends from taxable Canadian corporations through the dividend tax credit. It's a cumbersome piece of tax legislation and it's not as advantageous as it was before the former Progressive Conservative government of Brian Mulroney hacked away at it, but it's still a valuable investment tool. The tax credit—which is deducted directly from your tax payable—is calculated by multiplying the actual dividends you receive by 125 percent to obtain an artificial number called the grossed-up amount. You then take 13.33 percent of that amount as your credit (I know this sounds unnecessarily convoluted, but that's the way it works). So for every hundred dollars you receive in dividends, your dividend tax credit would be calculated as follows:

$$\text{Gross-up} = \$100 \times 125\% = \$125$$
$$\text{Dividend Tax Credit} = \$125 \times 13.33\% = \$16.66$$

This tax credit makes dividends an extremely tax-effective way to receive investment income, all else being equal. In fact, if you had no other income and no deductions or tax credits apart from the basic personal credit and the dividend tax credit, you could earn about $22 000 in dividends (before gross-up) and not have to pay any tax at all.

There are several ways to earn dividend income in your portfolio. You can invest in preferred shares, which pay a higher rate of return than common stock but have little growth potential. You can put your money into the common stock of companies which traditionally pay high dividends–banks and utilities, for example. (Your dividend yield will be less, but you'll have some capital gains potential to offset that.) Or you can invest in mutual funds that specialize in dividend-paying stocks.

If you choose the mutual fund route, be very careful. Many so-called "dividend" funds are in reality blue chip common stock funds, and the amount of dividends they pay out is small. The most blatant example of this is the AGF Dividend Fund, which pays virtually no dividends at all. The company admits the name is misleading–this is really a common stock fund–but they have made no move to change it as yet.

Three funds that fall into the true dividend category are the BPI Dividend Income Fund, the Spectrum United Dividend Income Fund and the Strategic Value Dividend Fund.

Your Strategy: Ask some hard questions before investing in a dividend fund. Find out what the portfolio consists of (a large percentage of preferred shares is a good sign). Also, inquire about the fund's distribution record–how much it has paid out annually in the past and what percentage of that amount was dividends.

Rental Income

Net income from rents is taxed at your marginal rate, in the same way as interest income. That's where the similarity ends. There is a host of eligible deductions that can be made from rental income that do not come into play when you receive interest. They include mortgage interest, maintenance, utilities, advertising, and a range of other expenses associated with owning and operating an income property. You are also permitted to make a claim for the annual depreciation of a rental building and any furnishings, as long as the amount does not create or increase a rental loss. This claim is known as capital cost allowance (CCA).

However, you don't have to actually own an income property in order to receive tax-advantaged rental income. You can also do so by investing in a real estate mutual fund or a real estate investment trust (REIT). REITs in particular have become quite popular, and there are several available that trade on the Toronto Stock Exchange. Most invest in a portfolio of commercial properties, such as shopping centres and office buildings. But a few are more focused, building their real estate portfolios around hotels, nursing homes, and other such specialized properties.

REIT investors enjoy tax-advantaged cash flow because CCA can be used to shelter part of their distributions. The amount of tax-sheltering will vary from year to year, but it is not unusual to receive half or more of the distributed income on a tax-deferred basis. Be aware, however, that all distributions that are untaxed have the effect of reducing your "adjusted cost base" for capital gains purposes when you sell. For example, suppose you bought units in a REIT for $10 each. In the first year, you receive a distribution of $1 per unit, half of which is tax sheltered. You then decide to sell at $11. Here's what happens:

Purchase price	$10.00
Tax-sheltered portion of distribution	$0.50
Adjusted cost base	$9.50
Sale price	$11.00
Capital gain for tax purposes	$1.50

So instead of a $1-per-unit capital gain as you might expect, the effect of the tax-sheltered distribution is to add an extra 50 cents per unit to the amount subject to tax. But remember, this only comes into play if you sell your units. Otherwise, you can continue to benefit from tax-deferred distributions until your adjusted cost base falls below zero.

As you can see, rental income is a tax-efficient way to receive investment income. And any capital gains made on the sale of a rental property are also given favourable tax treatment.

Your Strategy: Buy some REITs for your non-registered plan as you come up to retirement. They will provide steady cash flow and a good tax break.

Royalty Income Trusts

In the latter part of the nineties, a new investment concept appeared, known as the royalty income trust. These trusts are designed to turn cash flow from an underlying asset into an income stream for investors. Many of the trusts are based on resources, such as coal mines and oil wells. Others focus on utilities—power generating stations and pipelines. Still others draw their revenue from manufacturing (e.g., Simmons mattresses). And some, such as the North West Company Fund, are involved in retailing. Whatever the business, the attraction is good cash flow and, in most cases, some tax advantages.

The problem with royalty trusts is that they are vulnerable to changing economic conditions. For example, when oil prices fell in late 1998 and early 1999, the money available for distributions from petroleum-based trusts dropped too—and so did the market price of the shares. So you must be careful if you plan to put any money in this type of security.

Your Strategy: Like REITs, to which they are close cousins, royalty trusts are most useful after retirement because of strong cash flow and the tax breaks most (but not all) offer. Be sure you understand the risks involved before plunging in.

Capital Gains

At the present time, capital gains get two breaks from Revenue Canada. For starters, the first 25 percent of net gains are tax free, which lowers the effective rate that you pay considerably.

As well, there are a couple of exemptions that may shelter capital gains from taxes entirely. These are:

1. The principal residence exemption. Any profit made on the sale of your home is tax free. That is a tremendous tax advantage which has made some people quite wealthy.

2. A special $500 000 small business and farm exemption. Subject to some strict rules, business owners and farmers can avoid tax on the first half-million dollars in profit from the sale of their business or farm.

Many people fail to pursue capital gains because they are concerned about risk. But there's no need to take a big chance. You can limit risk by taking advantage of aberrations in the risk/return scale to increase the capital gains potential of stocks. A program of regular investing in high-quality stocks or equity funds with good capital gains potential is another route to go—it's known as dollar-cost averaging.

Also, investing money in a conservatively managed global equity fund can reduce risk considerably, since the manager can roam the world looking for the best values while avoiding regions that are experiencing economic problems. Funds like Templeton Growth and Fidelity International Portfolio fall into this group.

The fact is that stock markets were on the rise throughout most of the twentieth century and, as we enter the twenty-first, there is no reason to expect things will be different. Of course, markets don't move up in a straight line, and there is always a "wall of worry" to conquer. But we're talking long-term trends here and, in the case of stock markets, the trend is up.

For example, when he spoke at the annual meeting of the Templeton Growth Fund in Toronto in 1990, investment guru Sir John Templeton predicted the Dow Jones Industrial Average would reach the six thousand mark by the turn of the century. At the time of his speech, that represented growth of about 100 percent over the decade and, with the world in the midst of a recession, many people scoffed.

In fact, the Dow cracked through the six thousand level in 1996 and kept going from there, except for a couple of hiccups along the way in October 1997 and late summer 1998. In early 1999, the Dow broke the magical ten thousand barrier and was still moving up.

Your Strategy: Don't be frightened to go after capital gains by investing in stocks and/or equity funds. Mitigate the risk by adding a good percentage of U.S. and international stocks to your mix. Cut back on the percentage of stocks in your portfolio as you near retirement.

Key Points in Review

1. Unless you have a generous pension plan, you will probably need cash flow from a non-registered portfolio to supplement your retirement income and ensure that you are able to maintain your standard of living.

2. Don't start your non-registered portfolio until you have taken care of other financial priorities, such as paying off debt and maximizing RRSP contributions.

3. Always assess your investments on a risk-versus-return basis. Watch for opportunities when normally higher-risk securities become bargains, such as the stock market after a crash.

4. Invest in bonds during periods when interest rates are unusually high.

5. Do not hold stripped bonds outside a registered plan.

6. Rationalize your registered and non-registered portfolios for maximum tax efficiency.

7. Don't let greed cloud your investment judgement. Maintain a balanced perspective at all times.

8. Adjust your non-registered portfolio to your age. As you come up to retirement, a larger portion of your assets should be held in securities that offer tax-advantaged distributions.

9. Don't be afraid to invest a portion of your assets in stocks and/or equity mutual funds. The fear that keeps some people on the sidelines ends up costing them a lot of money.

15

The Big CPP Bet

The worth of a state, in the long run, is the worth of the individuals composing it.

— John Stuart Mill

I HAVEN'T THE FAINTEST IDEA WHO JO BINGHAM WAS, BUT I LOVE THE definition of "subsidy" that she (or he?) left behind: "A formula for handing you back your own money with a flourish that makes you think it's a gift."

If you look at the support programs that governments provide for older Canadians, you'll understand what I mean.

Take the Canada Pension Plan (CPP) or its counterpart, the Quebec Pension Plan (QPP). They are both designed to pay you a pension out of the proceeds of your own money, and your employer's, which has been contributed over many years. This is not money the government has kicked in. It's yours, invested on your behalf over the years in securities (mainly provincial bonds) that paid below-average returns. (Part of the CPP money is now being invested in the stock market. We'll see how that develops in terms of returns.)

But apart from the fact that the CPP's investments have been poor performers until recently, there is a more serious issue: collectively, we have not invested enough to properly fund the plan since the CPP was created in 1966. As a result, we're now being asked to shell out more each year.

There is no doubt in my mind that the money that pours into the CPP would be put to better use and provide higher returns in a well-managed self-directed RRSP. But this is the system our governments have chosen, and it looks like we're stuck with it. Given that fact, it's important to understand just how the CPP and other support programs operate, so you can use them most effectively.

The CPP has now been in place for well over 30 years, and Canadians have come to take it for granted. We dutifully pay into it each year with a minimum of grumbling, assuming that our contributions will be returned to us down the road, when we retire.

They probably will be, given the higher contribution levels now in place. But the CPP remains a dangerously underfunded program. And the recent move into the stock market in an effort to boost returns could have serious consequences for the plan if we should ever again experience a major crash, such as occurred in 1929.

When the CPP was originally conceived by the Liberal government of Lester B. Pearson, politicians pooh-poohed critics who warned the plan was too rich for the country.

Twenty years later, in December, 1986, the federal government had to convene a meeting with the provinces to take drastic action to prevent the CPP from going bankrupt. They put together a 25-year program that was designed to increase the contributions paid by employees and their employers each year until 2011. Under this plan, employer/employee contributions would increase at a rate of one-fifth of one percent a year from 1987 to 1991. After that, contributions would rise by fifteen 100ths of a percent until 2011. At that point, the total amount paid by both employer and employee would total 7.6 percent of contributory earnings (self-employed people pay the whole lot themselves). That figure was more than double the level originally established and, we were assured at the time, would be adequate to do the job.

Five years passed. Then, in 1991, we learned that the proposed increases still weren't enough to keep the CPP solvent. After a federal-provincial conference in Toronto in late January, it was announced that premiums would have to go up still more if there was going to be money available to pay pensioners in the twenty-first century. It was decided that annual increases would continue at the one-fifth of one percent rate until 1996, after which they would increase to one-quarter of a percent until the year 2006. From 2007 to 2016, the annual increase would revert to one-fifth of a percent.

Commenting on the revised 1991 plan, I wrote in the first edition of *Retiring Wealthy*, "The provinces and the federal government will review the projections again in 1996. Don't be surprised if at that time they decide the current schedule of premium escalations still isn't high enough and raise the ante yet again."

As I predicted, the 1991 fix still didn't do the job. The CPP continued to slide toward insolvency, pushed along that slippery road by higher-than-expected disability claims and by more people retiring earlier and choosing to start drawing a pension at age 60.

So, once again, it was back to the drawing board. In 1997, a new federal-provincial agreement was reached that was supposed to ensure the survival of the CPP forever. It involved accelerating the increase in contributions required from employers and employees so that by 2003, they will amount to 9.9 percent of pensionable earnings.

To illustrate what this means to your wallet, in 1999 the maximum contribution, based on pensionable earnings of $37 400, was just under $1200 for an employed person and almost $2400 for someone who is self-employed. Even if the pensionable earnings figure remains unchanged—which it won't—by 2003 an employed person will be paying in about $1850 a year at the top level. A self-employed individual could be looking at a total charge of more than $3700 a year! That's a lot of money!

In a report on this latest plan, the federal government promised no more premium hikes. "This level—the steady state rate—is projected to be sufficient to sustain the CPP with no further rate increases," we were told.

Maybe. But previous history tells us that every plan revision that has gone before has had to be scrapped. Perhaps this time it will be different but, based on all that has happened to date, I doubt it.

No matter how you look at it, we're going to be paying a lot of money into the CPP in the years to come, even if it turns out that the new contribution levels are enough to fend off any more contribution increases.

So be warned. There's a good possibility that the CPP we know now may not be the same CPP when you retire, especially if you are still under 50. Don't take it for granted that you'll receive benefits at the same level as today.

What could happen? There are several possibilities. One suggestion is to raise the qualifying age for full CPP benefits in line with increases in life expectancy (currently it's age 65). Another is to curtail the flexibility to take a reduced pension at an earlier age (currently you can begin to draw payments at age 60 if you are fully retired). Or it might be decided that full indexing to inflation is too expensive and that a partial indexing formula should be substituted.

I expect this debate to heat up as we move into the twenty-first century, as Canadians hand over an ever-increasing proportion of their pay cheques to fund these retirement benefits. However, it's impossible at this stage to know how the issue will be resolved. All the information and strategies that follow are therefore based on the rules as they stood in mid-1999. If any changes to CPP benefits are announced in the future, you'll have to adjust your retirement income projections accordingly.

While the Canada Pension Plan is generally thought of in the context of retirement, the benefits it offers are actually more extensive. In all cases, however, eligibility for these benefits will depend on how long contributions have been made to the plan. (The QPP functions in a similar way but there are some differences.)

Survivor Benefits

Besides providing a pension, the CPP also offers three types of survivor benefits.

The first is a lump-sum payment to your estate. The maximum amount is $2500, which will be paid, in order of priority, to the person responsible for funeral costs, or the surviving spouse, or next of kin.

Next, your spouse (including a common law spouse) is entitled to a regular income, even if you die before retirement. A number of factors are taken into account in calculating how much this income will be, including the amount the pensioner was receiving (or would have received at the time of death), the age of the surviving spouse, and whether the survivor is disabled. The maximum survivor's benefit payable under the CPP to a spouse under 65 was $414.46 a month in 1999. At 65 and older, the maximum is equal to 60 percent of the retirement pension, which worked out to $451 a month in 1999. (The QPP calculates these benefits differently; check with your local office if you think you are eligible.)

Finally, your dependent children may receive a special orphan's benefit. This was $171.33 a month in 1999 (the QPP rate was $54.40 a month).

To obtain CPP survivor benefits, you must apply to Human Resources Development Canada (HRDC). You'll need to provide a number of documents; check with a local office for details. You should apply as soon as possible after the contributor's death. Don't delay or you may lose benefits, because the CPP will only make back payments for up to 12 months.

Disability Benefits

CPP contributors who become disabled have their own benefits program. However, the criteria for eligibility are quite strict. You must be certified by a physician as having a physical or mental disability that is "severe and prolonged," and that does not allow you to work. You must also have contributed to the CPP for at least four of the last six years.

Disability benefits provide an income for you until age 65, when they are replaced by regular CPP payments (you can't collect both at the same time). Payments are also provided for any dependent children you may have. The maximum CPP disability payment in 1999 was $903.55 a month, plus an additional $171.33 per child.

To get a disability pension, you have to apply in writing. You can get an application kit by calling 1-800-277-9914.

Retirement Benefits

The first point to remember is that you must apply to get any pension money. Payments do not begin automatically at any point; you have to make it happen.

Your pension begins the month after you apply, and cannot be made retroactive, unless you're over 70. So if you want to collect, don't put it off.

The amount you receive will be determined by how long you contributed to the CPP and your income level over the years. This is a point most people aren't aware of, and it could have a significant impact on the amount of pension money you receive.

Your CPP benefit is based on career average earnings, with the lowest 15 percent of your qualifying years dropped off. So if you retire having contributed to the CPP for thirty-five years, the lowest five years of your earnings would be dropped from the calculation of your pension income. Special provisions are made for women who leave the workforce to raise children, for people over 65 who are still working, and for periods of disability.

If you have several years of low earned income, they will reduce your CPP benefit, even if you reached the maximum pensionable level years ago. For example, if you retire early you may have a number of years with no pensionable earnings for CPP purposes (employer pension and investment income doesn't count). Those zeros on your record will reduce the benefit you'll be able to draw.

This is one reason why many people start collecting CPP as soon as they become eligible. They don't want to accumulate zero income years after age 60, thereby reducing their pension benefits.

Even if you qualify for the maximum pension, your CPP payments will not exceed 25 percent of your pre-retirement income. If your income is higher than the maximum pensionable earnings, the percentage of your income replaced by the CPP at retirement will be even lower.

If you're over 40, you should be receiving a periodic Statement of Contributions from HRDC. It spells out in detail the CPP contributions you've made to date and your pension entitlement if you were eligible to make a claim now. If you are receiving these reports, consult the latest one to see what your CPP benefit would be. If not, check with a local office for your current status (be sure to have your Social Insurance Number ready when you call).

To receive a full pension, the rules state you must contribute for at least 85 percent of the years from the time you start work (or from the beginning of 1966, when the plan was launched) until you retire. That's only the first step in estimating your CPP income, however. When you retire, there are two important decisions you must make regarding how you'll receive your CPP payments.

The first is the age at which you'll apply. Full CPP benefits are payable at age 65. However, you can begin collecting as early as age 60, as long as you are "substantially retired." That means either that you've completely stopped working, or that any employment income you receive during the first year won't exceed the CPP benefit to which you're entitled (after the first year, employment income restrictions don't apply). The QPP is somewhat stricter on this point, requiring that you be fully retired before an early pension is allowed.

If you choose to start early, your pension entitlement will be reduced by half a per cent for each month you collect before your sixty-fifth birthday (6 percent a year). So if you started drawing CPP payments as soon as you turned 60, your payments would be 70 percent of your entitlement at 65. Remember, however, that your pension entitlement may also be reduced if you postpone applying, as this will add several years with no pensionable earnings to your career total.

In 1999, the maximum CPP benefit was $751.67 a month, or slightly more than $9000 a year. Therefore, if you started collecting at age 60, the most you could receive would be $526.17 a month ($751.67 x 70%), or $6314 a year.

Alternatively, you can wait until as late as age 70 to have your payments begin. For every month after your 65th birthday that you delay, your pension will increase by half a percent. So if you put off drawing your CPP benefit until the last possible moment, you'll be allowed 130 percent of your normal entitlement.

Based on the 1999 maximum payment, the most you could draw from the CPP if you waited until age 70 to start would be $977.17 a month, or $11 726 a year.

So which is the better course—to start drawing as soon as possible, even though the payments will be less, or to wait until you're 70?

For most people, starting as soon as they're eligible is a better choice. You begin receiving money immediately, and you protect your pension against being eroded by several years of non-pensionable earnings (once you apply, the book is closed on your career earnings).

The other side of this coin is that the longer you live, the greater the advantage in waiting to draw your CPP. The problem, of course, is that we can't predict our own lifespan. The average 60-year-old woman can expect to live another 23 years. However, specialized studies done by pension consultants have found that people who buy annuities tend to live longer than the general population.

If general life expectancy were the sole criterion in deciding when to start drawing CPP, it would suggest that men should probably start no later than age 65, while women would do better waiting until 70.

However, for most people, other considerations will come into play. These include:

- **Income needs.** Clearly, if you're short of money and need CPP payments to make ends meet, it makes no sense to delay your application. Start drawing your pension as soon as possible.

- **Pensionable earnings.** As I've already explained, if you have no pensionable earnings while you're waiting, you may reduce the ultimate benefit you receive. Do your calculations (or ask Human Resources Development Canada to help you do them) before making a decision.

- **Inflation protection.** If you don't need your CPP money in order to live comfortably, you could hold it in reserve for a few years, especially if you feel you may have some difficulty keeping up with inflation down the road. The CPP will give your buying power a boost when you do start to collect it, and the longer you delay before age 70, the higher your pension will be.

- **Lifestyle priorities.** Some retirees want more money in their early years, while they're still healthy and relatively young, so they can travel or fulfill other lifelong objectives. Your CPP payments may be enough to give you the extra spending power to achieve those dreams.

- **Taxes.** CPP payments are taxed at your full marginal rate. If you expect your tax bracket to be lower in the future, you may wish to postpone applying until that time, to give you a greater after-tax return.

Splitting Payments

When you've made up your mind when to start collecting CPP, there's another decision to make—whether or not to split your payments with your spouse.

If you're both 60 or older, CPP payments can be divided between spouses, on the basis of a set formula. If both spouses are eligible for CPP payments, both must apply for benefits and the income from both their pensions must be divided between them. The division is based on the years they have been married compared to the total number of contributory years.

HRDC offers a couple of examples of how this works on its Web site.

Example 1: Betty and John have been married since 1962. Betty has never been employed outside of the home. John's Canada Pension Plan retirement pension is $700 per month. Betty completed an application for an assignment. Once the assignment application is approved, Betty and John will each receive $350 per month. Early each year, Betty and John will receive T4 slips indicating the amount that each received in the previous year and which they will use when calculating their income tax.

Example 2: Mary and Peter have been living together since 1984. Peter receives a monthly retirement pension of $400. He earned $100 of pension before he and Mary began living together and the other $300 after their relationship began. Mary's monthly retirement pension is $550. She was not in the paid labour force prior to her relationship with Peter. During their lives together, Mary and Peter earned a total pension amount of $850. One half of this amount is $425. Peter submitted an assignment application. Once the application is approved, Peter will receive $100 which he earned prior to his relationship with Mary plus $425 for a total of $525. Mary will receive $425 each month. Again, T4 slips will show the amount each received during the previous year and which they will use when calculating their income tax.

CPP splitting works best if one spouse has a much lower pension than the other. In that case, it could be advantageous from a tax point of view. For example, suppose a husband qualifies for the maximum CPP benefit and has an employer pension that pays $40 000 a year. He'll be required to pay tax on his CPP payments at his top marginal rate, which will be in the 40 percent range (the exact figure depending on his province of residence). If his annual payment in 1999 was $7000, he'd have to fork over $2800 of that in taxes.

However, suppose his wife had never worked, had very little income, and no CPP entitlement. He could direct a portion of his CPP payment to her and, in effect, shelter most or all of it from tax.

CPP splitting may also be useful as a strategy to reduce the impact of the Old Age Security claw-back—more on this later.

If you want to apply for an assignment of this type, be prepared to gather up a lot of information for the government. They'll want to see your original birth or baptismal certificate or a certified true copy, your original marriage certificate or a certified true copy or proof of your common-law relationship, and your spouse's birth certificate or a certified true copy (if he or she is not already receiving a CPP retirement pension).

The Quebec Pension Plan used to forbid this kind of income splitting, which was one of the major points of difference between it and the CPP. That has now changed, although the formula Quebec uses for allocating the money is somewhat different.

One major advantage of the CPP/QPP is that you never lose the right to collect it, no matter where you live after you retire. Your entitlement is based on the contributions you made to the plan over many years, not on your country of residence. In fact, if you retire to the States, Human Resources Development Canada will even arrange to have your cheques deposited directly into your account at a U.S. bank. Now that's service!

So if you're considering retiring abroad, perhaps to the sun belt, don't forget to apply for your CPP anyway. After all, you and your employers have paid enough into it; you might as well get the benefits.

Key Points in Review

1. The CPP has been chronically underfunded, resulting in three major revisions to the premium schedule since it was launched. Despite soothing words from the federal government, there is no guarantee that premium rates won't rise again.

2. There appears to be a better-than-even chance that CPP benefits will have to be scaled back in the future. Possibilities include eliminating full indexing and raising the minimum age for starting to draw a pension.

3. CPP (and QPP) benefits go beyond providing retirement income. You can also receive money from the plan if you become disabled and can't work. As well, provision is made for survivor benefits if you should die.

4. CPP payments are not automatic. You must apply for them.

5. You can begin drawing a pension as early as age 60 if you are retired. However, the amount you receive will be discounted.

6. Full benefits are payable at age 65.

7. You may postpone receiving CPP until age 70. Every month you wait beyond 65 increases the amount of your pension cheque.

8. CPP benefits are fully taxable.

9. Payments may be split between spouses according to a special formula. This may help some people reduce the tax payable on their benefits.

10. You can live your retirement years outside Canada and still collect CPP.

16

OAS–The Cheshire Cat Program

*It vanished quite slowly, beginning with the end of
the tail, and ending with the grin, which remained
some time after the rest of it had gone.*

— Lewis Carroll

Old Age Security

THE FEDERAL GOVERNMENT DOESN'T LIKE OLD AGE SECURITY (OAS).
In fact, it would dearly love to be rid of it, despite the fact it has come to
be regarded as one of the pillars of our much-vaunted welfare safety net.

It's not just a political party thing. Every government in the past
decade has done their best to emasculate it. But, like the villain in an
Arnold Schwarzenegger movie, it keeps coming back to life—at least so
far. However, its days may be numbered, even if no further frontal
assaults are launched.

The Progressive Conservative government of Brian Mulroney was
the first to take a shot—to date, the only successful one—at this increasingly expensive millstone.

They did it by planting a virus in the system that over time would
ensure that a diminishing number of Canadians would be able to collect OAS payments and keep the money.

It's officially called the social benefits repayments tax, but most people know it simply as "the claw-back." It has already saved the federal
government a lot of money, and will continue to do so in the future.

The claw-back has also ensured that tens of thousands of people who would otherwise have kept their OAS money must repay some or all of the benefit.

But that wasn't good enough for the Liberal government that succeeded the PCs in office. They wanted to scrap the plan entirely, and moved to do so by introducing a new concept called the Seniors' Benefit. Canadians weren't biting, however. After more than a year of sniping and criticism, Finance Minister Paul Martin took it off the table in 1998.

But the claw-back remained, as it does to this day.

When the bill creating this special tax was introduced in 1989, the finance minister of the day, Michael Wilson, promised that only the rich would be affected. Anyone with retirement income of less than $50 000 a year would continue to receive full benefits. That represented the overwhelming majority of the population. What's to get excited about?

The Budget Papers tabled at the time estimated that only about 4 percent of retirees would be hit by the claw-back. Fewer than 2 percent would be required to repay the whole amount.

No big deal, okay?

The media bought it. Headlines in the morning papers the next day generally ignored the claw-back. "Ottawa promises tough program to cut spending, bring down debt," said *The Globe and Mail*. Over at *The Financial Post*, changes in the Unemployment Insurance (now Employment Insurance) program were the top news.

The claw-back announcement was reported, but only as being of secondary interest. After all, only a few people were going to be affected.

That may have been true at the outset. But over the years, the virus in the system began to do its work, and today a large and growing number of retirees are being deprived of this benefit.

In the first edition of *Retiring Wealthy*, I made the following predictions. I stand by them today, almost a decade later.

- No one under age 30 today will ever collect Old Age Security unless he or she is absolutely destitute.
- Canadians who haven't yet reached 40—which includes a large number of late baby boomers—are going to be cut off from OAS if their current annual income is $30 000 or more.

- Anyone under 50 who earns more than $40 000 a year can forget about claiming OAS.

All this is happening, and will continue to happen, because of an insidious indexing mechanism that's been built into the claw-back formula.

Before I explain how it works, some background on OAS to put matters into perspective.

Old Age Security has been part of this country's social welfare fabric since 1952. It was originally intended to provide a basic retirement income for people over 65, and many older Canadians continue to rely heavily on payments from OAS and related programs, such as the Guaranteed Income Supplement (GIS) to survive. (The GIS is paid after a means test, and is available only to people at or below the poverty line.)

OAS payments are indexed to inflation and adjusted quarterly. As of the second quarter of 1999, monthly payments were $411.23, or just under $5000 a year. Not a lot, perhaps, but essential for many older people.

The rules governing OAS eligibility are somewhat complex. You must be a legal Canadian resident to apply, in most cases. However, if you lived in Canada for at least 20 years and now reside abroad, you can make an application from outside the country. You must have lived in Canada at least 40 years after the age of 18 to receive the full amount. Reduced benefits are payable if you were here at least 10 years.

There are special rules governing immigrants who came after 1977, Canadians who were under age 25 in 1977, and those who have resided abroad for extended periods after age 18. Check with the Income Securities Program Branch of Human Resources Development Canada for details if any of these situations apply to you.

So your payment will go with you if you'd prefer to live in the sunny south, as long as you meet the tests.

You don't have to retire, either. OAS payments are based on age, not working status. You can still be employed full time and collect.

You must make a formal application to receive OAS, however. Cheques won't automatically start arriving in your mailbox the month after your 65th birthday. You must furnish proof of age and meet the residence requirements.

Many people don't realize they have to apply until several months (or even years) after they become eligible. Not to worry; payments can be made retroactively for up to one year. But if you delay longer than that, you're out of luck.

However, all these rules may become somewhat academic in the years ahead, unless changes are made to the claw-back formula.

Let's go back to the 1989 budget speech in which the claw-back was introduced.

Mr. Wilson began by stressing the importance of our social safety net.

"It must be preserved," he told the Commons solemnly, "not only for those who require it now, but for the future as well."

Remember that reference to the future as I unravel this ball of wool for you.

The finance minister then continued, "The central purpose of the social safety net is to assist those most in need, not to subsidize those with high incomes."

Keep that statement in mind as well.

From there he went on to announce details of the claw-back (which also affects employment insurance, by the way). High-income Canadians (his term, not mine) who receive OAS would have their benefits taxed back at the rate of 15 percent of their net income above a certain threshold. This was set initially at $50 000.

"This measure maintains the universal character of these transfer programs," the minister concluded to warm applause from Conservative benches. "Everyone eligible for these programs will continue to receive their benefits, regardless of income. Those who need assistance most will continue to retain all their benefits. Recipients with high incomes will retain less. This preserves the social safety net and helps provide a sound financial basis for social programs into the future."

That was the rhetoric. Now let's look at the reality.

The income ceiling for avoiding the claw-back was set at $50 000 per person. It is now $53 215, a level it has been stuck at for several years. Above that threshold, the claw-back applies. The amount is based on net income, as reported on your tax return.

Net income covers income from all sources, including employment, all private and government pension payments, interest, rental

177

income, taxable capital gains, the taxable amount of dividend income, business and professional income, etc. From this amount, certain deductions are allowed. These include pension and RRSP contributions, child care expenses, support payments, moving expenses, carrying charges, and the like.

The decision to use net income as the threshold figure creates a serious inequity for OAS recipients who rely on investments for part of their income. Their investment income will include dividend payments. Because net income includes grossed-up dividends, some people are in the position of having their OAS benefits clawed back on the basis of income they never receive.

The gross-up provision provides that the actual amount of dividends received be increased by 25 percent for tax purposes. This is the figure used in the net income calculation. Later in the tax form you receive an offsetting benefit called the dividend tax credit. But it comes too late to affect the claw-back formula.

This situation penalizes OAS beneficiaries with high dividend income. For example, suppose Shirley Green has an income of $50 000, half of which comes from interest earned on GICs. She would not be subject to the claw-back.

Carolyn Jones also has an income of $50 000, half of which comes from investments. But in her case, the investment income is received in the form of dividends paid on preferred shares she owns. For tax purposes, this portion of her income is grossed up. This adds $6250 to her net income, pushing her over the claw-back threshold. As a result, she'll have to repay about $450 of her OAS benefit. Her income is exactly the same as that of Shirley Green, but she's worse off by hundreds of dollars because of the way in which the claw-back is applied.

But this unfair treatment is relatively minor when compared to what the government did with indexing. This is the hidden virus in the claw-back formula that will eventually achieve what Paul Martin tried to do and failed—cut off most Canadians from this benefit.

The claw-back threshold is indexed on the same basis as the tax brackets. This means the first 3 percent of inflation in any given year is not taken into account in the indexing. Only inflation over and above

3 percent is considered. Since Canada's inflation rate has been running well below 3 percent for several years, there has been no change in the threshold level.

The accompanying table shows what will eventually happen under this system, assuming an average annual inflation rate of 2 percent. Canadians with modest incomes by today's standards will find their OAS benefits eroded over time. Even if your income only keeps pace with inflation, a 30-year-old earning $30 000 a year today will have an income far in excess of the OAS threshold by the time he or she is eligible for benefits.

The Claw-Back Effect

Years From Now	Income			OAS Threshold
Today	$30 000	$40 000	$50 000	$53 215
5	33 122	44 163	55 204	53 215
10	36 570	48 760	60 950	53 215
15	40 376	53 835	67 293	53 215
20	44 578	59 438	74 297	53 215
25	49 218	65 624	82 030	53 215
30	54 341	72 454	90 568	53 215
35	59 997	79 996	99 994	53 215

Let's spend a moment with these numbers, because they illustrate dramatically the destructive seed inside the OAS system.

Start with the $30 000–a-year column. This is a relatively modest income by today's standards. Even though the income appears to grow as the years pass, it's an inflationary illusion. In fact, the purchasing power remains exactly the same. A 30-year-old whose income only keeps pace with inflation (the rate is 2 percent in this example) may have a salary of almost $60 000 a year when he retires at age 65, but it won't buy any more than $30 000 does today.

But if that person retires with income that is equivalent to his earnings during his final working year, he'll be subject to the OAS claw-back. The threshold at that point will be well below his income level because it doesn't move unless inflation exceeds 3 percent.

This sets up a situation in which even individuals of modest means by the standards of the day will be denied OAS benefits.

Now look at the $40 000 column. Few people earning this amount would classify themselves as rich. But look what happens to the OAS benefits of someone in this group. Using the same assumptions as before, she will cross the OAS threshold between year 10 and year 15. In other words, anyone now under age 40 who is earning about $40 000 a year and just keeps pace with inflation until retirement stands a good chance of having at least part of her OAS benefits clawed back.

If you're in the $50 000-a-year bracket, you'll cross the threshold within five years. So if you're under 50, forget about OAS.

Of course, if your income should rise at a faster rate than inflation, you'll cross the OAS threshold much sooner.

The bottom line, unless future governments change the policy, is that the proportion of Canadians over 65 able to benefit from OAS will steadily decline as the years pass.

However, there are a few strategies you can use to attempt to avoid the claw-back, or to at least minimize its effect. Unfortunately, the younger you are, the less likely it is that these will be of much help. All you can hope for is a change in the system.

Older people may be able to take advantage of these strategies to increase the amount of the OAS benefit they retain after tax.

These ideas are all based on an unusual quirk in the claw-back mechanism (which may itself be changed at some point, as Paul Martin tried to do with the Seniors' Benefit). The income threshold is an individual one. There is no provision for combined family income. So if one spouse is likely to have a relatively high income in retirement while the other income will be low, the objective should be to reduce the income of the higher-income spouse to below the threshold.

Here are some ways to do it.

- **Contribute to Spousal RRSPs.** Direct all RRSP contributions to the plan of the lower-income spouse (let's assume in this case it's the wife). This will build her retirement income, while reducing her husband's.

- **Split CPP benefits.** Have the majority of CPP benefits paid to the lower-income spouse if possible. See Chapter 15 for details.

- **Plan investments carefully.** Invest any income earned by the wife with a view to increasing her interest or dividend payments after retirement. Use the husband's income to live on.

Here's an example of how these strategies may help circumvent the claw-back. Suppose you were to turn 65 this year and your net income is $60 000. Your spouse is also turning 65 and has an income of $15 000 a year.

You would have some of your OAS benefits clawed back—about $1000, based on the current threshold. Your spouse would receive the full amount.

However, by using some of the strategies outlined above, you manage to switch $9000 in income to your spouse. You now have an income of $51 000, while your spouse receives $24 000. There is no difference in the total—in both cases, your household income is $75 000. But in this situation, no claw-back will apply. You've just put $1000, less regular taxes, in your collective pockets.

One word of caution. Before you embark on any of these strategies, do some careful post-retirement income projections. It may be that even by using these techniques, you won't be able to change the end result as far as the claw-back is concerned. Even worse, you could put more income into your spouse's hands while not reducing your own enough, with the result that both of you lose part or all of the OAS benefit.

Even if the entire OAS payment will be clawed back, you'd still be well-advised to apply for it. The monthly cheques can be invested and the interest earned can provide some small compensation for having to repay the benefits at tax-time.

In calculating your retirement income, I suggest you give careful consideration as to whether you'll include any provision for OAS.

The younger you are and/or the higher your income, the less likely it is you'll be able to retain any of the benefits under the claw-back system. If you build OAS into your retirement income projections and it ends up being taxed back, your lifestyle objectives could be compromised.

My recommendation is that you forget about OAS. Don't make any provision for it in your planning. If you do end up receiving an after-tax OAS benefit, treat it as a bonus. But don't count on it.

Now let's look at some of the basic rules governing OAS.

Eligibility. Anyone aged 65 or older who is a Canadian citizen or legal resident of Canada. If you're a resident, you must have lived here for at least 10 years after age 18. Non-residents are also eligible if they lived in Canada for at least 20 years after age 18.

When to Apply. At least six months before you're eligible to draw benefits. You can apply up to a year in advance.

How to Apply. You can get an application kit from any Human Resources Development Canada office—check the blue pages in your phone book for an address.

Required Documentation. Proof of age, in the form of a birth or baptismal certificate. If you were born outside of Canada, you'll also need to supply citizenship or immigration documents.

When You'll Collect. Payments start the month after your 65th birthday.

Payment Frequency. At the end of each month.

Indexing. OAS payments are fully indexed to inflation, with adjustments made every quarter.

Taxation. If you are not subject to the claw-back, your OAS payments will be taxed as regular income.

Guaranteed Income Supplement

The other major federal government income support program is known as the Guaranteed Income Supplement (GIS). The GIS is intended to help lower-income people, so hopefully you will never need to call upon it.

To be eligible for the GIS, you have be eligible for OAS and pass a means test. For a single person, the GIS is only available if income is less than $11 736, not including OAS. For a couple, the minimum is generally $15 312, although it can be higher in certain cases.

The maximum payment in the second quarter of 1999 was $488.72 a month for a single person or for someone married to a non-pensioner. For someone married to a pensioner, it was $318.33.

For more information about the GIS, contact a Human Resources Development Canada office.

Key Points in Review

1. Old Age Security is still around, as a result of the federal government's decision to abandon the proposed Seniors' Benefit. But the number of people who will be able to keep their payments in future will be diminished by the effect of the claw-back.

2. There are several ways to reduce the effect of the claw-back, or even eliminate it. These include the use of spousal RRSPs and splitting CPP benefits.

3. You can collect OAS even if you retire outside Canada, as long as you meet certain eligibility criteria.

4. The Guaranteed Income Supplement provides additional income support for OAS recipients of limited means.

17

Cashing In Your Chips

It is better to live rich than to die rich.
— Samuel Johnson

SAVING, PLANNING, CUTTING TAXES WHEN POSSIBLE, PREPARING FOR the future. It's all well and good—but only if you enjoy the benefits of all that labour and sacrifice.

Die rich and you'll have the fleeting satisfaction at the end of knowing your heirs will be well off. But you'll have missed out on a lot of fun. Being a miser should definitely not be one of your objectives.

Personally, I intend to enjoy my slowdown years to the fullest extent possible. (I don't plan to ever fully retire as long as I retain a keen mind, decent health, and a good word processor). I hope I have provided my children with the attributes they need to create a happy and prosperous life for themselves—a good upbringing, a close-knit family environment, as much education as they can handle, a sense of values, and whatever guidance and direction they needed. But leaving them a million dollars each when I go isn't on my list of priorities (sorry, kids). My wife and I have worked hard and been through a lot together. I think we're entitled to smell the flowers a bit when that time comes.

If your thinking runs along the same lines, the next few chapters will tell you how to do it. We're into the reward phase now. You've put together a solid retirement program over the years. Now you're about to start reaping your financial harvest in the most tax-effective way possible.

Government Programs

Let's start with the basics—the government programs. As I have already pointed out, you have to apply to Human Resources Development Canada to start obtaining benefits from these plans—it doesn't happen automatically. Canada Pension Plan payments can begin any time between ages 60 and 65 as long as you're "substantially retired" when you apply. This means that any employment or self-employment earnings must not exceed the maximum CPP pension payable for those aged 65 in the year you're making the claim. For example, in 1999 the maximum CPP pension for someone aged 65 was about $9000 a year. So your employment earnings could not have exceeded that amount if you were under 65 and wanted to apply early.

You have a 10-year window in which to apply for CPP benefits, from age 60 to age 70. You'll find information on the factors you need to consider in your decision in Chapter 15.

You become eligible for Old Age Security payments at age 65, and there's no advantage in waiting. You should arrange to apply during the year before you become eligible, even if all the benefit will be subject to the infamous claw-back rule.

Your next priority is to arrange for payment of your pension benefits, if you have a plan. For a defined benefits program, ask your human resources department to calculate what your entitlement will be, complete the appropriate paperwork, and arrange for a method of payment. A direct monthly deposit to your savings or chequing account is usually the most convenient.

For any other type of employer pension arrangement—money purchase plan, group RRSP, deferred profit sharing plan—some additional work is required. Your pension will have to be calculated based on the value of the assets that have accumulated to your credit by the date you retire. The longer your pension credits are left to compound in a tax-sheltered environment, the more money you will have to live on in retirement. So if you won't need income from an employer pension immediately, inquire whether arrangements can be made to defer the pension for a period of time, to allow the funds to continue to grow.

If you have an Individual Pension Plan (IPP), do a careful analysis of when you should start dipping into it. If you set up the plan fairly late in your working life, you're better off waiting as long as possible before initiating payments so as to allow the value of the portfolio to build to a respectable size.

While you're making pension arrangements with your employer, discuss other financial matters that may make life easier for you in retirement. Health insurance is an especially important consideration. Find out if your employer makes any provision to extend group health and dental benefits to retirees and, if so, make arrangements to advantage of it. Any group life coverage also needs a look. Many policies allow you to convert group life protection to a personal whole life policy when you retire, often without a medical. You may no longer feel you need this protection, but consider your position carefully before you pass up the option. If anything should happen to you after retirement, would your spouse have enough income to maintain his or her lifestyle? If not, you may want to continue some form of life insurance coverage (although it obviously gets pretty expensive at this stage). Although I don't feel that making a large provision for your heirs is of primary importance, life insurance, which is received tax free, is a good way to protect the value of your estate and to provide cash to cover the taxes that will come due when you die.

So don't be too quick to pass up a conversion option if it is offered. But don't automatically go for the employer program either; you might get a better deal on a new term policy, some of which have been especially designed for older people. Shop around before deciding.

RRSP Savings

Next on your agenda is your RRSP. You need to decide what to do with the money that's accumulated in your plan.

Essentially, you have five choices.

Leave the Money Where It Is. You're not required to collapse your RRSP until the end of the year in which you turn 69. So if you don't require income from this source right away and you haven't reached the age limit, there's no pressure to do anything at all, even though you're retiring.

Leaving the money in your RRSP for as long as possible is always a good financial strategy, because it maximizes the effect of tax-sheltered compounding.

For example, suppose when you retire at age 65, you've built assets of $200 000 in your RRSP. You don't need that money right away because you have a good pension plan and some additional income from part-time employment. By leaving it in the plan until the end of the year you turn 69, assuming a modest 6 percent annual return, you can add an additional $50 000 and change to your principal without making a single additional contribution.

If you were to retire at 60 and leave the money in your RRSP to the end of the year you turn 69, you would add more than $138 000 to the value of your plan. That's a great incentive for doing nothing until you have to.

Make Partial Withdrawals from the RRSP as Required. You may find yourself in a position where you don't want to close your RRSP, but you'd like to make use of some of the money that's accumulated—perhaps to take that round-the-world cruise you've always dreamed about. In this situation, a partial withdrawal of some funds may be in order. If this is the way you'd like to go, a little careful planning may save you some tax dollars.

For starters, decide whose RRSP the money should come from—your plan or your spouse's. Remember, RRSP withdrawals will be taxed at the marginal rate of whoever gets the money. So if you both have plans, the spouse with the lowest income should make the withdrawal.

The tax saving could be substantial. For example, suppose you're an Ontario resident and expect to have taxable income of $50 000 this year. Your spouse's taxable income will be $2000. You want to withdraw $8000 from an RRSP to purchase new furniture for your home. There's enough money in either plan to handle it.

If you make the withdrawal from your RRSP, it will cost you about $3100 in taxes, based on 1999 tax rates. But if the money comes from your spouse's RRSP, the tax will amount to about $1900—a difference of about $1200 in your favour.

Before you make the final decision, check the withdrawal rules for spousal RRSPs. If your spouse's plan was built with his or her contributions only, no problem. But if it's a spousal plan to which you contributed, any withdrawals made within three years of your last contribution will be attributed back to you for tax purposes. Be sure you don't run afoul of that technicality or all your careful planning will be for nothing.

Whenever you make lump-sum withdrawals from your RRSP, your financial institution is required to withhold some of the money for tax. The amount will vary depending on how much you take out at any one time. The federal rates are as follows (in Quebec they're slightly different):

Up to $5000	10%
$5001 to $15 000	20%
Over $15 000	30%

Keep this withholding in mind when you plan your RRSP withdrawals. Make sure the net amount you end up with after tax will be adequate for your needs. And, if possible, stagger your withdrawals to minimize the withholding tax. Two withdrawals of $5000 each will result in a total tax of $1000 being held back. One withdrawal of $10 000, on the other hand, will be subject to $2000 in withholding. I know that doesn't make a great deal of sense, but that's the way the system works.

This withholding formula is a headache for financial institutions because it encourages people who want to dip into their RRSPs to make several small withdrawals rather than one large one. That, in turn, leads to more time-consuming paperwork. To cut down on the practice, some companies place a limit on the number of withdrawals that can be made each year, or levy a charge on each withdrawal. Find out the practice of the trustee of your RRSP before proceeding.

Of course, any tax withheld on an RRSP withdrawal is credited to you when you file your annual return. At that time, your withdrawals will be treated as regular income and the tax you owe calculated accordingly. As a result, you will likely be required to pay additional tax on your RRSP withdrawals, so be sure you put some money aside to cover that.

Terminate the Plan and Take Out All the Money. Technically, you can wind up your RRSP any time you wish and withdraw all the cash. Unless you have a small RRSP and virtually no other income, however, this is not a wise way to proceed.

Collapsing your RRSP in this way guarantees you'll have to pay tax on your money at the highest possible rate.

To illustrate, let's say you're a British Columbia resident who has recently retired, and you decide you want to cash in all your RRSP savings. Your ordinary taxable income is a modest $30 000 a year, on which you pay relatively little to the government. So you figure, what the heck—why not get the money out of the old RRSP? After all, your tax rate isn't that high.

Have you got a shock coming! Let's say your RRSP is worth $50 000 when you collapse it. Based on 1999 tax rates, you'd be assessed taxes of almost $22 000 on your RRSP withdrawal. You'd be paying about 44 percent of your retirement money in taxes!

If your RRSP was worth $100 000, your situation would be even worse. You'd owe the government more than $48 000 in taxes, almost half the total value of the plan.

As you can see, closing your RRSP and taking the money out all at once is not exactly tax effective. In fact, it's one of the most financially destructive things you can do to yourself at this point in your life. Don't even consider it!

Use the Proceeds to Purchase an Annuity. If you want to (or must) close your RRSP, there are two choices that are much more tax effective than withdrawing the money. One is to buy an annuity.

An annuity is simply a contract between you and a life insurance company under which you pay them a certain amount of money in return for a guaranteed income. If the annuity is being purchased from RRSP funds, it's usually for life, although you can also buy a "term certain" annuity which will make payments to age 90.

Many people don't like the idea of annuities because they feel they're giving up control of their hard-earned money. Others prefer the thought of a steady, guaranteed income stream and not having to worry about managing the money and making reinvestment decisions.

You have to decide which category you fall into. Later in this book we'll look at annuities in detail and outline the many choices available to you.

Roll Over the RRSP into a RRIF. The other tax-effective choice is to convert your RRSP into a registered retirement income fund (RRIF). This is by far the most popular choice for retired Canadians because it allows continued control of capital while keeping open a range of other options, including annuities.

Think of a RRIF as simply the natural continuation of your RRSP. It can hold the same types of investments as your RRSP and is subject to many of the same rules. The main differences between the two are:

1. You cannot make contributions to a RRIF.
2. You must withdraw a minimum amount of money each year, based on a formula established by Revenue Canada.

You'll find a detailed explanation of RRIFs, and why I think they're the best choice for your RRSP money, later in this book.

Non-Registered Investments

Next, you need to give some thought to your non-registered investments and how they can best be used to generate retirement income for you.

This is a question that should be given top priority because, unlike your RRSPs, any income earned by your non-registered portfolio is being taxed annually. You should therefore review your non-registered holdings carefully to make sure they're producing the income you expect from them in the most tax-effective way possible.

Finally, you must put all the income pieces together to develop a total strategy that will generate income, keep taxes as low as possible, and provide inflation protection.

The ideal scenario would be as follows:

- **In the early years of retirement (age 60 to 65):** Try to live exclusively on income from your employer pension (if you have one), part-time earnings, and Canada Pension Plan. If necessary, supplement your income with cash from your non-registered portfolio as required.

- **In the middle years of retirement (age 65 to 69):** Use more of your income from non-registered investments to offset the effect of inflation. Add OAS payments to the income mix. Keep your RRSPs in reserve.

- **In the later years of retirement (age 70 on):** You now have no choice but to begin drawing against your RRSP savings. Use a RRIF for this purpose since it provides the most flexibility for adjusting income flow to meet your needs, while allowing the balance of your money to continue to grow tax sheltered. If your RRIF holdings are adequate, you can start dipping into your non-registered capital at this point for major expenses such as travel or a new car.

That's the ideal scenario. You may not be able to make it happen quite that way, but it's a good objective to aim for.

Cash Flow

The next area you need to consider is cash flow. Your income sources may be just fine, but are they going to provide the cash you need when you need it?

You see, it's one thing to retire wealthy. It's quite another to arrange your financial affairs in such a way that you'll always have enough cash to put food on the table.

There's an important distinction between wealth and cash flow. You'll become painfully aware of it the first time you find your bank account doesn't have enough money in it to cover your monthly expenses.

It's not that you don't have the wherewithal, of course. It's just that it's not immediately accessible. It's all tied up in your home, GICs, stocks, real estate, and a dozen other assets that aren't easily convertible to ready cash.

That's why it's important to make plans to ensure you'll have an adequate and regular cash flow after you retire. You want to be sure that all the wealth you're building can actually be put to use when it's required.

The time to begin the cash flow planning process is about five years before you intend to stop work. At that point you'll have a good idea of how much money your pension will generate (if you have one), the value of your registered and non-registered portfolios, your cash flow from CPP and OAS, and any other sources of income that may be available to you.

The first step is to determine how much income you can expect to receive from your pension and how often a cheque will arrive (usually it's monthly). Add to that the amount you'll receive from CPP and, if you'll be 65 at retirement, OAS. Any other government income, such as U.S. social security if you're eligible, should also be included. If you expect to have employment income from any source (for example, part-time work or consulting), add that figure as well. The total represents your basic monthly cash flow. Adjust the figure annually as you get closer to retirement to ensure it remains accurate.

Now refer to the expenditure projection you did at the start of this book. Break down the annual figure into a monthly cash requirement and compare the result with the cash projection you've just completed. Any shortfall (and there's likely to be one) will have to be made up by income from your registered and non-registered savings. This is where the real planning begins.

We'll start with your non-registered portfolio, because, as I've already stressed, it's a good idea to let your registered savings compound as long as possible in their tax-sheltered environment before you dip into them.

On the following worksheet, list all the assets in your non-registered portfolio and the amount of income each produces annually. Also note how frequently payments are made; that's an important factor in managing cash flow. Bonds, for example, usually pay interest every six months. Interest on Canada Savings Bonds is paid annually. Stock dividends are usually paid quarterly. Mutual fund distributions may be done monthly, quarterly, or annually; find out which policy applies for the funds you're holding. There are also several possible schedules for the payment of GIC interest.

In the "When Paid" column, write the month or months payment is expected if the income will be received on anything other than a monthly basis. For example, if you expect to receive a stock dividend at the end of every quarter, write *March, June, September, December* at the appropriate space.

Cash Flow Projection: Non-Registered Assets

Security	Anticipated Annual Income	Payment Frequency	When Paid
Cash and Equivalent			
_____	_____	_____	_____
_____	_____	_____	_____
_____	_____	_____	_____
_____	_____	_____	_____
_____	_____	_____	_____
Fixed Income			
_____	_____	_____	_____
_____	_____	_____	_____
_____	_____	_____	_____
_____	_____	_____	_____
_____	_____	_____	_____
Growth			
_____	_____	_____	_____
_____	_____	_____	_____
_____	_____	_____	_____
_____	_____	_____	_____
_____	_____	_____	_____
Totals	_____		

Now you have a picture of how much income you can expect to receive from your non-registered portfolio. Add this to the amount you projected from pension plan, government sources, and other income to obtain a revised total. Compare it again to your expenditure needs.

If it still falls short, see if there are ways to increase the amount. Review your non-registered portfolio to determine if it's set up in the most efficient way from an income-producing point of view. For example, a large portion of your portfolio may be in low-yielding common stocks that you purchased for their growth potential. As you get closer to retirement, you may want to (hopefully) take some profits and replace some of these shares with securities that generate more income. Here are some possibilities.

Preferred Shares. In many ways, preferred shares are closer to bonds than to common stock. They usually (but not always) pay a fixed rate of return in the form of a dividend, which is eligible for the dividend tax credit. Although they're traded on stock exchanges, they tend not to fluctuate dramatically in price the way common stocks do. Rather, the price of a preferred is usually affected most by changes in interest rates, the way bonds are.

Preferreds aren't as popular as they used to be, but there are still some good ones around. Since you're looking for income, you want to search out those that combine a good yield with a high degree of safety. Preferreds, like bonds, are rated for safety by the ratings services; P-1 is the best, P-5 the lowest. Pay attention to those ratings; some preferred shareholders have suffered heavy losses when the company that issued the paper went bankrupt. Since this is your retirement money, I suggest you not buy any preferreds with a rating of less than P-2. You'll find these tend to have a slightly lower yield than those farther up the risk scale, but you'll at least be able to sleep nights knowing the possibility of a default is remote.

You'll often find attractive preferreds issued by banks, trust companies, and utilities. Some of these are traditional preferreds, but the financial community also offers some variations. Here are a few examples:

- **Floating rate preferreds.** These are issues with variable dividends that fluctuate with movements in interest rates. Your return is usually calculated as a percentage of prime (70 to 75 percent is common). That means when interest rates decline, so will the return on these preferreds.

- **Fixed rate/floating rate preferreds.** A hybrid. They'll pay a fixed rate of return for a period of time, after which the return will float with interest rate movements.

- **Non-cumulative preferreds.** Issued by many banks and trust companies, these have become popular because of their relatively high yield. Non-cumulative means that if a payment is missed, it won't be made up later. That makes safety especially important. However, the senior issues carry little risk; the big Canadian banks have long histories of unbroken dividend payments, and all common share distributions would have to be eliminated before any preferred dividends could be skipped.

- **Convertible preferreds.** These carry a conversion provision that allows them to be exchanged for a specified number of shares of common stock. This may be at the owner's discretion or within a certain time frame. Usually they'll have a lower yield than other types of preferreds because of the conversion benefit.

Preferred shares may also be retractable, which means they can be sold back to the issuer at a specified price, usually on certain dates. Or they may be callable, which means the issuer can call them in for a specified price, again on certain dates.

When considering preferreds as an income option, remember to judge the yield on the basis of after-tax return. Use 1.3 as the factor to compare the return to an interest-bearing investment. For example, a preferred with a 6 percent yield will be about equivalent, after tax, to a GIC that pays 7.8 percent.

Dividends on preferred shares are usually paid quarterly.

High-Yielding Common Stocks. If you're in a position to sacrifice some immediate income for capital gains potential, high-yielding common stocks may be a better choice than preferreds. Many of the utility and bank stocks fall into this category, and sometimes their dividend yields can be very attractive. Just remember there's no guarantee on common share dividends. They will be the first thing cut if a company runs into financial problems.

Mortgage-Backed Securities. For a combination of steady monthly income and safety, you won't find many better investment choices than mortgage-backed securities (MBS). Many people aren't aware of them, but they're easily purchased and growing in popularity.

Mortgage-backed securities are shares in a pool of residential first mortgages that is assembled by a financial institution or mortgage lender and guaranteed by Canada Mortgage and Housing Corporation (CMHC). Each pool has its own term and coupon rate. Payments are normally made monthly, and are a blend of principal and interest.

The interest rate on MBS issues is usually very competitive. Most major newspapers carry MBS quotes in their business pages so you can see what they're paying; otherwise you can get the information from a stockbroker (brokerage houses are the main sellers of these securities).

For cash flow purposes, one of the biggest advantages of a mortgage-backed security is the regular monthly payment. You know how much you'll receive and you can plan accordingly. Occasionally, you may get a larger cheque than expected–this will happen when prepayments are made against some of the mortgages in your pool. If you don't like that idea, buy shares in a closed mortgage pool, which doesn't permit prepayments.

With an MBS, you have the peace of mind of knowing your investment is safe. CMHC is a crown corporation, so you have the federal government's guarantee of your principal and interest. And there's no limit on your protection, as there is with deposit insurance.

I think MBS certificates are a good choice for steady retirement cash flow; however, their yields have been quite low in recent years because of falling interest rates.

Monthly-Pay GICs. Most guaranteed investment certificates pay interest annually or semi-annually. However, most financial institutions also offer monthly-pay GICs, which are useful for managing cash flow.

You'll usually receive a slightly lower interest rate, however, and the minimum investment required may be higher than for an ordinary GIC.

Mutual Funds. An increasing number of mutual funds are being designed to produce steady cash flow and make distributions monthly. Your best bets here are dividend income funds and the more risky high-yield funds. There are also some bond funds available that offer monthly or quarterly distributions.

Systematic Withdrawal Plans. You don't have to be at the mercy of the distribution policy of your mutual funds. Many fund companies offer systematic withdrawal plans, which allow you to take out a prearranged amount every month. This is another good way to manage your cash flow. But find out if the company makes any charge for this service. And remember that if the amount you withdraw is in excess of the distributions, you'll gradually deplete your capital. Over the long term, that isn't likely to happen, however. In fact, your principal may actually grow if the fund does well, despite the steady income you're receiving.

REITs. Real estate investment trusts are an excellent way to increase the after-tax return from your non-registered investments, as I explained earlier in this book. Part of the distribution you receive will be sheltered by capital cost allowance, which means more money in your pocket.

Royalty Income Trusts. They're higher risk, but they can certainly improve your cash flow significantly. For purposes of retirement income, look for less volatile trusts. Those based on pipelines and electricity generation are good examples.

Bonds. Debt instruments of all types are favourite sources of retirement income. The main problem with bonds is the long time between payments—six months in most cases. You can get around that by building a portfolio that includes several bonds with different coupon dates. That will enable you to spread the payments more evenly.

Here's how doing some portfolio switching as retirement approaches can increase your income from non-registered investments considerably. Suppose you now have a portfolio that looks like this:

Security	Amount	Yield	Annual Return
Money market funds	$20 000	4%	$800
Fixed income funds	40 000	6%	2 400
Common stocks	25 000	2%	500
Equity funds	15 000	3%	450
Totals	*$100 000*	*4.15%*	*$4 150*

To improve your cash flow, you switch part of your savings into REITs and royalty trusts. Your sell all your low-yielding common stocks, replacing them with some higher-yielding commons, some preferreds, and some monthly-pay GICs. You leave your fixed income funds alone. The portfolio now looks like this:

Security	Amount	Yield	Annual Return
REITs	$10 000	8%	$800
Royalty trusts	10 000	10%	1 000
Fixed income funds	40 000	6%	2 400
Preferred shares	20 000	5.5%	1 100
Monthly-pay GICs	10 000	4.5%	450
High-yield common stock	10 000	4.5%	450
Totals	*$100 000*	*6.2%*	*$6 200*

These changes have increased the annual return on the portfolio by more than $2000–an improvement of about 50 percent over the original holdings!

If, after exhausting all other avenues, your projected cash flow is still less than your income needs, you'll have to consider drawing down your non-registered capital for the balance. If possible, hold on to your registered investments as a strategic reserve to be used later.

The time will come when you'll want to use your registered investments, of course (and after you turn 69 you'll have no choice). At that point, you'll want to work out an appropriate cash flow, based on your needs and the type of retirement income product you choose.

If you invest in an annuity, your monthly payment will be determined for you. With a RRIF you have more flexibility, as long as you meet the minimum withdrawal requirements of Revenue Canada.

That makes the management of a RRIF more tricky for cash flow purposes. You must ensure there is always enough money available in the plan to make the required payments. If you tie up all your assets in five-year GICs or stripped bonds that don't mature for several years, where is the money for the periodic withdrawals going to come from?

Cash flow management in a RRIF depends on the type of plan. If it's a GIC-based RRIF, you'll want to begin planning the maturity dates of your certificates well in advance of the time you start withdrawals to ensure funds will be available. Don't consider only the *year* of maturity. Think about what *months* GICs will be coming due. Make sure there will be a regular cash flow.

The same advice applies in the case of stripped bonds and coupons held in a self-directed RRIF. Pay close attention to the maturity dates, especially with strips purchased within 10 years of retirement.

Other good investments for generating regular cash flow inside a RRIF are mortgage-backed securities, monthly-pay GICs, some of the more conservative royalty income trusts, and fixed income mutual funds.

The final step in the cash management process is to combine your income from all sources into a cash flow calendar.

The next worksheet enables you to do that. Make some photocopies so you can revise your projections regularly.

Under each month, show the income you expect to receive, and the source. When you're finished, you'll have a clear picture of how much money you'll have to live on, and where it's coming from.

Retirement Cash Flow

Source	Amount											
	Jan	Feb	Mar	Apr	May	June	July	Aug	Sep	Oct	Nov	Dec
Pensions	___	___	___	___	___	___	___	___	___	___	___	___
CPP	___	___	___	___	___	___	___	___	___	___	___	___

Source	**Amount**											
	Jan	**Feb**	**Mar**	**Apr**	**May**	**June**	**July**	**Aug**	**Sep**	**Oct**	**Nov**	**Dec**
OAS	___	___	___	___	___	___	___	___	___	___	___	___
Other Govt. Payments	___	___	___	___	___	___	___	___	___	___	___	___
Earnings	___	___	___	___	___	___	___	___	___	___	___	___
Investments (Non-registered	___	___	___	___	___	___	___	___	___	___	___	___
Annuities	___	___	___	___	___	___	___	___	___	___	___	___
RRIFs	___	___	___	___	___	___	___	___	___	___	___	___
Other	___	___	___	___	___	___	___	___	___	___	___	___
Totals	___	___	___	___	___	___	___	___	___	___	___	___

Key Points in Review

1. As you approach retirement, carefully assess what your primary sources of income will be after you stop work and compare them to projected expenses.

2. There are five possible ways to draw income from your RRSP savings. Converting to a RRIF offers the most control and flexibility.

3. Try to hold some income sources in reserve so they will be there if inflation starts eroding your buying power.
4. Do some careful cash flow planning. You want to be sure your monthly income will be adequate to cover all basic expenses.

18

RRIFing It

Men at some time are masters of their fates.

— William Shakespeare

LET ME DECLARE MY BIAS AT THE OUTSET. I FIRMLY BELIEVE THERE IS no better choice for retirement income than a RRIF.

I've heard all the arguments in favour of annuities—how they provide steady cash flow for life, how they are worry-free, how they can be purchased with guarantees that protect your heirs in case of an early demise.

All those points are valid. But a RRIF is still the better way to go.

The annuity is for the person who wants the security of a fixed income for life. The RRIF is for the person who wants to remain in full control of his or her money, even if that involves a degree of risk.

Not that registered retirement income funds are inherently risky—no more so than RRSPs. The degree of risk is what you make it. You can have a RRIF that invests exclusively in ultra-safe Treasury bills, one that holds most of its assets in stocks or equity funds, and everything in between.

In short, you determine the measure of risk you're prepared to accept.

The main advantage of a RRIF is control. You keep possession of your capital, rather than turning it over to a life insurance company in exchange for an annuity. You retain the ability to make the investment decisions relating to your retirement funds. You decide how much money to withdraw each year, subject to certain government-mandated minimums. And, if there is any money left when you die, you can decide to whom it should pass.

Those are the main reasons that RRIFs have become the preferred option of most people when the time comes to cash in their RRSPs. But there's still a lot of confusion about these plans and how they work. Hopefully, this chapter will clarify all.

RRIF Guidelines

Here are some of the key points to be aware of when considering your RRIF options.

Timing

You must wind up your RRSP no later than the last day of December in the year in which you turn 69. But you can set up a RRIF any time before then that you wish–there's no minimum age limit. And there's no rule that says you cannot have both an RRSP and a RRIF at the same time, as long as you're under age 70.

This creates a tax planning opportunity in certain circumstances. If you are 65 or older but haven't yet retired, you may want to consider using part of your RRSP money to set up a RRIF that pays out just enough to allow you to make use of the pension income tax credit. Depending on your tax bracket, you can receive up to $1000 a year tax free.

Number of Plans

You can open as many RRIFs as you like–as with RRSPs, there's no legal limit on the number of plans. However, I don't advise having multiple plans for several reasons:

1. The difficulty in monitoring several plans.
2. The nuisance of having to deal with several cheques each month, rather than just one.
3. The problems you may encounter in trying to ensure each plan will generate enough cash flow to avoid dipping into principal.
4. Potentially higher administration costs.
5. Difficulty in maximizing your foreign content, which is calculated on the basis of each separate plan.

If you have more than one RRSP spread among a number of companies, each will be after you to consolidate your RRIF with them. Arrange for interviews with each and find out exactly what they will do for you. Choose the company that offers the best combination of low fees, regular reporting, plan flexibility, and service.

Investments

You can invest your RRIF money in anything you like, as long as it's a qualified security by Revenue Canada standards and your financial institution will accept it. Your priorities should be safety and cash flow, with some growth potential. More on this in the next chapter.

Maturity Date

In the past, a RRIF had to be collapsed by the time you turned 90, and all the assets paid out. That is no longer the case. You can keep your RRIF for the rest of your life, as long as enough capital remains to sustain it.

Beneficiary

As with an RRSP, you can make your spouse the beneficiary of your plan. This will allow the invested funds to pass to him or her tax free if you should die. However, you should also look at the option of making your spouse the "successor annuitant" to your plan. In this case, if you die the assets in the RRIF's portfolio remain intact. All that changes is the name on the cheque. But a word of caution: a successor annuitant cannot change the age that was used to calculate the minimum withdrawal amount from the original RRIF. So if your spouse is younger, you may not wish to take this approach.

Types of RRIFs

There are almost as many different types of RRIFs as there are types of RRSPs. You have to decide which you prefer; most people tend to continue with the same type of plan they used with their RRSP. Your options include:

- **A savings plan.** Operates like a savings account, except that it's tax sheltered. Generally not recommended because of the low return.

- **A self-directed plan.** You make all the investment decisions yourself. Self-directed RRIFs usually cost about the same as a self-administered RRSP.

- **A mutual fund plan.** Your money is invested in a selection of mutual funds of your choice. These plans work best when set up with a company offering a variety of well-managed mutual funds with free switching privileges and a systematic withdrawal plan.

- **GIC plans.** Your funds are invested in guaranteed investment certificates of varying maturities. As certificates come due, the money is automatically reinvested for the same term, unless you specify otherwise.

- **Guaranteed income plans.** These guarantee a regular monthly income over the life of the RRIF. In practice, they operate in much the same way as an annuity.

- **A managed plan.** The investment decisions are turned over to a portfolio manager who handles everything for you. A special fee will be charged for this service.

Costs

RRIFs cost no more than RRSPs in most cases. Pay any administration fees outside the plan (rather than having them deducted from the RRIF's assets) to avoid having them as a drain, however small, on your assets.

Deposit Insurance

RRIF assets invested in cash, a savings plan, or GICs with maturities of not more than five years will be covered by deposit insurance up to $60 000 if the company holding the plan is a CDIC member. If it's a credit union, provincial insurance plans will protect your assets; the limits will vary depending on where you live. No other type of RRIF asset is protected by deposit insurance, although other types of coverage may apply depending on who your money is invested with. Insurance companies and stockbrokers have their own forms of protection; ask for details. Also, some assets carry their own protection. Canada Savings Bonds, for example, aren't insured but they're fully guaranteed by the federal government.

Minimum Withdrawal

Once a RRIF is set up, the government requires you to start making annual withdrawals from it after the first year. These withdrawals will be taxed at your normal rate. They may be for any amount you want, provided they aren't less than the minimum set by a Revenue Canada formula.

This formula is based on your age or, if you make such an election at the time the RRIF is set up, on the age of your younger spouse. For all RRIFs that were set up prior to December 31, 1992, the minimum withdrawal until age 78 is calculated as follows:

$$\text{Minimum Payment} = \frac{\text{Value of RRIF at start of the year}}{90 - \text{Your age at start of the year}}$$

The calculation is easy. Just subtract your age on January 1 from 90, and divide the value of the RRIF on that day by the result. For example, suppose you were 70 at the start of the year, and had \$100 000 in your RRIF. Your minimum payout for the year would be calculated as follows:

$$\text{Minimum Payment} = \frac{\$100\ 000}{90 - 70} = \$5000$$

Your minimum withdrawal this year will be one-twentieth of the plan's value or \$5000. Next year it will be one-nineteenth of the value, and so on until age 78. At that point, this formula is no longer used. Instead, your minimum withdrawal is calculated using a special table.

For any RRIF set up after December 31, 1992, the above formula may be used until you, or your younger spouse if that's the option you've chosen, turn 71. At that point, the minimum withdrawal is based on government tables that are reproduced here.

Minimum RRIF Withdrawals

Age	Percentage of RRIF to Withdraw
71	7.38%
72	7.48%
73	7.59%
74	7.71%
75	7.85%
76	7.99%
77	8.15%
78	8.33%
79	8.53%
80	8.75%
81	8.99%
82	9.27%
83	9.58%
84	9.93%
85	10.33%
86	10.79%
87	11.33%
88	11.96%
89	12.71%
90	13.62%
91	14.73%
92	16.12%
93	17.92%
94 on	20.00%

Let's look at what your annual income would be under these rules. The following table applies to all RRIFs created after the end of 1992. All other assumptions are the same as in the previous table, and assume an average annual compound rate of return of 8 percent.

RRIF Withdrawals

Age on Jan.1	Plan Value on Jan.1	Income Earned	Annual Payment
71	$100 000	$8 000	$7 380
72	100 620	8 050	7 526
73	101 144	8 092	7 677
74	101 559	8 125	7 830
75	101 854	8 148	7 996
76	102 006	8 160	8 150
77	102 016	8 161	8 314
78	101 863	8 149	8 485
79	101 527	8 122	8 660
80	100 989	8 079	8 837
81	100 231	8 018	9 011
82	99 238	7 939	9 199
83	97 978	7 838	9 386
84	96 430	7 714	9 575
85	94 569	7 566	9 769
86	92 366	7 389	9 966
87	89 789	7 183	10 173
88	86 799	6 944	10 381

Age on Jan.1	Plan Value on Jan.1	Income Earned	Annual Payment
89	83 362	6 669	10 595
90	79 436	6 355	10 819
91	74 972	5 998	11 048
92	69 927	5 594	11 272
93	64 249	5 140	11 513
94	57 876	4 630	11 575
95	50 931	4 074	10 186
96	44 819	3 586	8 964
97	39 441	3 155	7 888
98	34 708	2 777	6 942
99	30 543	2 443	6 109
100	26 877	2 150	5 375

Note that, using these assumptions, your RRIF reaches its maximum value at age 77. After that, the capital starts to diminish.

Of course, you're free to choose another type of withdrawal plan, as long as you take out at least the required minimum each year. You can also change your withdrawal program at any time.

One option is to withdraw the same amount of money each year—in other words, you decide to use your RRIF as a level-payment annuity. By doing this, you'll receive more money in the early years than you will by using the minimum formula. But as you grow older and the payments stay the same, you'll fall behind the amount you would have received under the minimum plan. As well, the purchasing power of your RRIF payments will steadily decline because of inflation.

Another negative feature of this formula is that the value of the invested capital in your RRIF begins declining immediately because of the large amounts you're withdrawing. This will be financially damaging if you want to switch to another income option as you grow older.

Therefore, I don't recommend a formula like this unless you have some other sources of income that will help offset the impact of inflation in your later years.

There are many other possible combinations. Ask the organization handling your RRIF to give you a computer printout of the options that interest you before making a decision.

One of the beauties of a RRIF is that, once you select a payout formula, you're not locked in. You can change it if you find it's not working out as you expected. And you may make withdrawals of capital from your plan at any time if you require extra funds. Just remember, you'll pay tax on any such withdrawals at your marginal rate. As well, inquire whether the company holding your RRIF charges any withdrawal fees.

When choosing a payment schedule, do so with the Old Age Security claw-back in mind. Take a look at how the formula you choose will affect the chance you'll have to repay part or all of your OAS cheques. If it's feasible, try for a formula that will keep your total income under the claw-back threshold for as long as possible.

Don't forget you can use your spouse's age, if he or she is younger, as the basis for the withdrawal formula you select. The impact of this will be to reduce the amount of your payments, and to spread them over a longer period of time.

Maximizing Your Returns

Now that you understand the basics, let's look at some of the strategies you can use to maximize the returns on your RRIF.

The first is timing—when should you set up a RRIF? If you open a plan too soon, you may find you're receiving income you don't really need and paying more tax than necessary. On the other hand, if you wait too long you may find yourself having to make investment commitments at inopportune times. The timing decision will, in the end, be a personal choice but generally I suggest waiting as long as possible in order to maximize the tax-sheltered growth in your RRSP.

The more money that's allowed to build in your RRSP, the greater the RRIF income it will generate for you. That's why it's a good idea not to start tapping into it any sooner than you need to, unless it's to set up a small plan to allow you to claim the pension income credit. You have to collapse your RRSP by the end of the year you turn 69, but you're not required to make withdrawals from a RRIF during the year you set up the plan. So hold off as long as you can.

If you need money, it's a good idea to draw first on your non-registered portfolio, even if it means selling some of your securities. This will keep your taxes lower and allow continued tax-sheltered growth of the assets in the RRSP.

Next, give careful thought to the type of RRIF plan you select. The greater your return on your RRIF assets, the larger the payout you can expect from the plan. Unlike an annuity, therefore, you actually have the opportunity to increase your retirement income through good money management.

You should therefore choose a plan that offers a chance for above-average returns. Self-directed plans, mutual fund plans, and managed plans are the best bets.

Next, you must decide how much of your RRIF is to be in growth assets. If you have adequate growth securities in your non-registered portfolio, your RRIF can be placed entirely in fixed-income investments. However, if you don't have much in the way of stocks, equity funds, or other growth assets, you should consider including some in your RRIF. You may be depending on it for income for many years, so you should include some growth potential in the plan, at least at the outset.

Don't go overboard, though. I recommend your total growth assets not exceed 25 percent of your registered and non-registered portfolios up to age 70; 20 percent between 70 and 75; 15 percent to age 85; and 10 percent after that.

If you're like many Canadians, at least part of your RRIF will be invested in GICs. There are two things you can do to maximize your return from these investments.

The first is to buy some index-linked GICs for your plan during periods when interest rates are low. These GICs have the potential to produce higher returns because your payments will be based on the performance of a specific stock index. Don't overdo it, though—if markets dive, you could end up with a zero return on this type of security, although your capital will be protected. I suggest not having more than 25 percent of your GIC assets in index-linked securities.

Also, stagger the maturity dates of your certificates. No one, not even the most astute economic forecaster, can accurately predict where interest rates will be at any given time. If interest rates are low when all your GICs mature, the return on your RRIF investments will drop sharply. Having about 20 percent of your GICs maturing every year will enable you to smooth out the interest rate cycles and ensure a relatively steady income flow for your plan.

You can use staggered GIC maturities to provide a steady cash flow for your RRIF. Another way to do this in a self-directed RRIF is with stripped bonds. You can start this process in a self-administered RRSP. Simply purchase a number of strips at discount prices, some of which will mature every year after you retire. When the time comes to collapse your RRSP, simply shift them into your RRIF. This will ensure cash is always becoming available in your RRIF to meet your payout requirements.

Finally, here's a strategy to use when your RRIF capital peaks. If you are still going strong, and are starting to worry a bit about what happens when your RRIF income starts to decline, you should seriously consider cashing in part or all of your RRIF and using the proceeds to purchase a life annuity. Because of your advanced age, a life annuity purchased at this time will pay you a respectable amount. The income will, of course, be guaranteed for as long as you live.

This is a good way to use the strong points of both RRIFs and annuities to ensure a comfortable income flow throughout your retirement years, while holding the tax people at bay for as long as possible.

Key Points in Review

1. A RRIF is the best way to convert your RRSP capital to an income stream because of the flexibility and control it offers.

2. Although you can have as many RRIFs as you want, it's a good idea to consolidate all your RRSP assets into a single plan.

3. Consider naming your spouse the successor annuitant to your plan, rather than the beneficiary.

4. The federal government requires that you make a minimum annual withdrawal from a RRIF, starting in the year after the plan is created.

5. You may withdraw as much money as you like from a RRIF each year, provided the minimum legal requirement is met.

6. Income from a RRIF is taxed in the same way as employment income. You don't get any tax breaks when the money is withdrawn.

7. Keep a percentage of your RRIF in growth assets as an inflation hedge.

8. If you reach the point where the assets in your RRIF are starting to diminish, consider converting part or all of it to a life annuity.

19

RRIF
Investment Strategies

*Dollars do better if they are
accompanied by sense.*

— Earl Riney

RRIFS ARE DIFFERENT FROM RRSPS. AFTER MANY YEARS OF RRSP
conditioning, that's often difficult for a new RRIF investor to grasp. But
it's essential that you do so, otherwise you and your RRIF could end up
pulling in opposite directions.

While you were contributing to your RRSP, your primary goal was
to build as large a capital base as possible, consistent with the amount
of risk you were prepared to take. So growth is the main objective of an
RRSP portfolio.

In the case of a RRIF, however, growth is no longer the number one
goal. Now you need to focus on income, with an increased emphasis on
safety. Growth drops to third on the priority list.

This means you'll probably need to reconfigure much or all of your
RRSP portfolio when the time comes to convert to a RRIF. You should-
n't eliminate all growth potential from your plan, but you may want to
structure the plan differently so your growth assets (stocks and equity
funds, primarily) can contribute to the cash flow you'll need.

Planning a RRIF portfolio has been made more difficult by the low-
interest-rate world in which we have been living. In the past, people
could rely on safe fixed-income securities to generate the cash flow they

required from their plan. That is no longer the case. You need to look for alternatives, and the older you are the more difficult finding them becomes.

Here's an example. Let's suppose you retire this year at age 65 and plan to start withdrawing money from a RRIF next year. You are still 65 next January 1 (your birthday is in July), and your RRIF is worth the tidy sum of $300 000. Using the formula I explained in the last chapter, the minimum annual withdrawal from your RRIF in your first full year of retirement will be $12 000. That represents 4 percent of the total value of the plan.

Now 4 percent isn't difficult to make up. Depending on where interest rates are at the time, a Government of Canada bond or a GIC will likely generate enough interest income to cover the payment with some left over.

Let's assume your RRIF earns an internal return of 5 percent that first year. So $15 000 comes into the plan, while $12 000 is paid out. At the start of the next year, when you are aged 66, the RRIF has increased in value to $303 000. Again applying the formula, your minimum withdrawal that year will be $12 625, or about 4.2 percent of the asset value. Your 5 percent fixed-income security will still cover that, but the margin is thinner.

Let's leap ahead to the year in which you are 71 years of age on January 1. Let's say that at this stage the RRIF value is back to $300 000. According to the government's minimum withdrawal tables, you must take out at least 7.38 percent of the plan's value this year—a total of just over $22 000. Now you're in some trouble if you want to stick with fixed-income securities. You can't find any GICs or quality bonds that pay anything like that high a return. So what to do?

Higher-Yield Securities

You have a choice. One option is to start drawing down capital to make up the difference. But that sets you on a slippery slope, because every year more of your capital will need to come out of the plan to meet the minimum payment requirement. Alternatively, you can look for other types of securities to help to increase the cash flow from your plan.

They do exist. It's a matter of deciding whether you can accept the increased risk that accompanies them. Here are some of the options.

High-Yield Bond Funds

These funds invest in a portfolio of lower-rated corporate bonds, to generate better yields. Sometimes known as "junk bonds," these securities are issued by companies or governments that could potentially face financial difficulties in the future—which is why they are forced to pay a higher interest rate to borrow money. There are two main risks in purchasing this type of security: default risk, which means the issuer doesn't have enough money to pay interest when due or to redeem the notes; and market risk, which could result in the value of your bonds being driven down by a so-called "flight to quality." That's exactly what happened to junk bonds in the late summer of 1998, and these funds were hit hard as a result.

REITs

As we saw in an earlier chapter, real estate investment trusts offer the potential for above-average cash flow. Many people don't like to hold them in a RRIF because the tax benefits are lost. But you should consider them if you want to increase the income stream.

Royalty Income Trusts

When the market for royalty trusts caved in during 1998, many investors sold their units at a loss and muttered "never again." Unfortunately, in doing so they have ruled out one of the best weapons available for combating low interest rates. Royalty income trusts offer a return well in excess of anything you can expect from even the most generous GIC. The trick is to choose those with the least downside risk for your plan.

The cash flow from any royalty trust will depend on the success of the underlying business. If profits decline, so will the payments. The trusts most vulnerable to boom-and-bust cycles are those based on the resource sector—oil and gas trusts and coal trusts in particular. We saw just how sensitive they are in 1998, when oil prices dropped dramatically. In response, the distributions from oil and gas trusts fell, as did the market value of the shares. When oil prices rebounded in early 1999, shares in these trusts followed suit.

For RRIF investing, I recommend you build a small portfolio of royalty trusts that covers several industries. You might include a retail trust (e.g., North West Company), a pipeline trust (e.g., Koch or Pembina), an electrical-generating trust (e.g., Trans-Canada Power), a staple food supplier (e.g., Rogers Sugar Income Fund), and an energy distribution trust (e.g., OPTUS Natural Gas Distribution Trust). These are not risk-free, of course, but the portfolio approach will greatly reduce the downside potential and the yields will be much higher than you can expect to receive from bonds or GICs.

High Income Funds

A few mutual fund companies have developed funds that invest in a portfolio of REITs and royalty trusts. The most prominent are the Guardian Monthly High Income Fund and the BPI High Income Fund. The portfolios are designed to minimize risk, although that didn't prevent them from taking a big hit when the royalty trust market hit the skids in 1998. As a result, many investors were scared off and missed a good opportunity to acquire high yields at low prices.

Systematic Withdrawal Plans

It's a good idea to continue to maintain some growth potential in your RRIF as protection against inflation, even at modest rates. But those growth assets can't just sit in your plan untouched, or you'll never be able to produce enough cash flow to meet the ever-increasing minimum withdrawal requirements as you get older.

The solution is to set up a systematic withdrawal plan (SWP) for your growth securities. The easiest way to do this is to use conservatively managed equity mutual funds as your core holding.

Systematic withdrawal plans are, at the core, very simple but some people have difficulty understanding them. Let's say you want to hold 20 percent of your RRIF in growth securities, and that works out to about $50 000 in assets. You have no other foreign content in your plan, so you decide to use the entire allocation here. After checking the options carefully, you decide to invest it all in the Fidelity International Portfolio Fund.

You tell your financial adviser you want to establish an SWP for the fund that will produce $400 a month in cash flow for the RRIF. The necessary paperwork is done and the plan is set into place. Each month, that $400 will be there for you. It can be generated from several sources: realized capital gains within the fund, interest earned by cash holdings, and dividends. If your fund holdings do not generate enough cash to meet the monthly requirement, some of your units will be redeemed to make up the difference. That may appear to be a draw-down of capital, but it will likely be only temporary. Over time, a well-managed equity fund should generate a return that will more than cover the value of your withdrawals. Consider the Trimark Fund, for example. If you'd invested $100 000 in this fund when it was set up in 1981 and requested payments of $833 a month (10 percent of your original investment per year), you would have received total income of over $172 000 to the end of 1998. But far from being exhausted, your capital would actually have grown to more than $700 000 over that time because of the fund's performance. In other words, over about 17 years, you took out more in income than the amount you initially invested—but your capital grew more than seven times in value.

You don't have to worry about the tax consequences of a systematic withdrawal plan inside a RRIF because all the money, whatever the source, is taxed at your standard marginal rate when it is withdrawn.

So the key to RRIF investing is to ensure that you have enough high-income securities in the plan to meet your cash flow needs without exposing yourself to too much risk. On the facing page is an example of a RRIF portfolio that you can use in setting up your plan.

You may have to vary the percentages at times, depending on interest rate levels, to produce the cash flow you need to cover your minimum withdrawal requirements. However, I suggest you use this as a base model and fine tune from there. If interest rates rise, the percentage of higher risk securities can be decreased and the percentage of GICs and bonds increased.

Sample RRIF Portfolio

Type of Security	Percentage of Portfolio
Money market funds	10%
GICs	20%
High-grade bonds or bond funds	20%
High-yield bonds	10%
REITs and royalty trusts or high income funds	20%
Equity funds (systematic withdrawal plans)	20%

Key Points in Review

1. A RRIF investment portfolio should be structured quite differently from that of an RRSP. With a RRIF, growth is no longer a main priority. Cash flow and safety take precedence.

2. In times of low interest rates, it is difficult to generate enough income within a RRIF to cover the minimum withdrawal requirement. The older you are, the harder it becomes to avoid dipping into capital.

3. To produce better cash returns, it may be necessary to include some securities that carry a higher risk level than would normally be recommended for a RRIF. These may include high-yield bonds, real estate investment trusts, and royalty income trusts.

4. You should retain a small growth component in your RRIF. However, it must be set up in such a way that it contributes to the total RRIF income. A systematic withdrawal plan is the best way to achieve this.

5. Use a portfolio model for structuring your RRIF, but modify it as necessary to meet changing conditions.

20

LIRAs and LIFs

*It is plain poverty, no doubt, to need a thing
and not to have the use of it.*

— Xenophon

"I HAVE A LOCKED-IN RRSP. I'M OUT OF WORK AND NEED THE MONEY. What can I do?"

This is one of the most frequent questions I receive about retirement planning and RRSPs–people who have locked-in plans and are frustrated because they cannot get at the money.

It's a situation that arises when people leave their employment and opt to have pension credits transferred into an RRSP. The government in its wisdom has decided that in this situation Canadians must be protected from themselves. So money transferred in this way is "locked in"–the funds can only be used for retirement income and nothing else. These plans are called locked-in retirement accounts (LIRAs) in some provinces, or simply locked-in RRSPs.

Owning a LIRA is rather like having a trust fund you cannot touch until you reach a certain age. The money is yours, but it isn't. You cannot access the assets of a locked-in plan under any circumstances unless you take steps to convert them to a retirement income stream.

Those strict rules have caused a lot of grief. Over the years, I have received some heart-wrenching letters from people who have a tidy sum tied up in a LIRA but cannot make use of the money to get them through a financial emergency. In many cases, early conversion to retirement income is not a satisfactory answer. The people are relatively young and the crunch they are in is short term—unemployment is the usual problem. What they really need is a lump sum to tide them over, which they could get by making a withdrawal from an ordinary RRSP. But in this case the money is out of reach.

I have a great deal of trouble with this situation. The money rightfully belongs to the individual, and to my mind governments have no right to dictate how and when it can be used. If people choose to make a withdrawal and pay the appropriate taxes, they should be allowed to do so. No one should presume to know better than us what our financial priorities are.

The bureaucratic argument would be that the money in a LIRA was accumulated specifically for purposes of retirement, and Canadians should not be allowed to squander it. But that logic was defeated the moment Ottawa introduced the Home Buyers' Plan, which allows people to direct money away from retirement and into housing. More recently, the federal government has decided that retirement savings may also be diverted to pay for continuing education. So the precedent for encroaching on money put aside for retirement is now well-established. It's true that locked-in accounts cannot be used for either of these programs—at least not yet. But the rationale for this rule is foggy. Retirement savings are retirement savings, whatever the mechanism used. If one group of savers is allowed to use the money for other purposes, why not everyone? It's a question the government should ponder.

As things now stand, however, you have only two ways to access money in a locked-in RRSP. One is to use the funds to buy an annuity. The other is to convert the plan to a life income fund (LIF).

LIFs are relatively new on the scene—just a few years ago, the annuity was the only permitted route. LIFs are similar to RRIFs in some ways, but very different in others. And, unlike RRSPs and RRIFs, they are administered by the provinces, which means the regulations governing them will vary somewhat across the country. Most provinces now have LIF legislation in place, so they are available almost everywhere (Prince Edward Island and the Northwest Territories are the exceptions).

In some jurisdictions, there is a minimum age for setting up a LIF, usually 55. In other provinces, no such limitation exists.

As with a RRIF, you are required to make a minimum annual withdrawal from a LIF. The formula for calculating this amount is usually the same as for a RRIF. However, unlike a RRIF, there is a ceiling on how much you can withdraw from a LIF in any given year. The purpose of this restriction is to prevent you from draining all the funds from the plan—another manifestation of big brotherism at work. This maximum withdrawal figure can also vary from one province to another. The accompanying table shows the Ontario scale as it applied for 1999.

Maximum Annual Withdrawal for an Ontario Life Income Fund (1999)

Age on Jan. 1	Maximum Withdrawal (Percentage of LIF Balance on Jan. 1)
48	6.19655%
49	6.23197%
50	6.26996%
51	6.31073%
52	6.35454%
53	6.40164%
54	6.45234%
55	6.50697%
56	6.56589%
57	6.62952%
58	6.69833%
59	6.77285%
60	6.85367%

Age on Jan. 1	Maximum Withdrawal (Percentage of LIF Balance on Jan. 1)
61	6.94147%
62	7.03703%
63	7.14124%
64	7.25513%
65	7.37988%
66	7.51689%
67	7.66778%
68	7.83449%
69	8.01930%
70	8.22496%
71	8.45480%
72	8.71288%
73	9.00423%
74	9.33511%
75	9.71347%
76	10.14952%
77	10.65661%
78	11.25255%
79	11.96160%

As you can see from the table, the restrictions are pretty tight. You can never withdraw more than about 12 percent of the value of your plan in any given year. And the margin between the minimum and maximum withdrawal rates is very small. For example, at age 71, the minimum withdrawal from a LIF is 7.38 percent while the maximum is set at 8.45 percent. That's a range of only slightly more than one percentage point. On a $100 000 LIF, that's a margin of just slightly more than $1000.

The table ends at age 79 because in Ontario and most other provinces, you are required to convert the capital remaining in your LIF to a life annuity when you turn 80. That's the other major difference between RRIFs and LIFs. A RRIF can be held for as long as you live, allowing you to maintain control and to use the balance remaining for estate planning purposes.

Two provinces have recognized the inherent unfairness of this setup: Alberta and Saskatchewan. In both you can invest your money in a locked-in retirement income fund (LRIF). These are identical to LIFs in that there are both minimum and maximum annual withdrawal limits. However, there is no requirement to convert a LRIF to a life annuity at age 80, thus leaving the choice to each individual–where it should be. Other provinces would do well to take a close look at the LRIF concept.

Until that happens, I suggest you wait until the last minute to convert a LIF to a life annuity. This will allow more capital to build tax sheltered in the plan, thus enabling you to purchase more annuity income. The only exception would be a case in which interest rates rise sharply and you want to take advantage of the higher payments that annuities offer at that time. However, even in that situation I suggest you don't convert until you are at least age 75.

The investment strategy for a LIF will be similar to that used in a RRIF. In both cases, cash flow and capital preservation are the main priorities. See Chapter 19 for details.

Key Points in Review

1. Money in a LIRA (also known as a locked-in RRSP) cannot be withdrawn, even in a financial emergency.

2. There are only two options for converting locked-in plans: buy a life annuity or, in most parts of the country, move to a life income fund (LIF).

3. LIFs are administered by the provinces, so regulations vary across Canada.

4. As with a RRIF, you must withdraw a minimum amount from a LIF each year. However, there is cap on maximum annual withdrawals to prevent people from depleting their plans.
5. In most provinces, the assets remaining in a LIF must be used to purchase a life annuity at age 80. Alberta and Saskatchewan are the two exceptions.
6. Investment strategies for a LIF should be similar to those used in a RRIF.

21

Annuities–
Security for Life

*There is nothing more demoralizing than
a small but adequate income.*

— Edmund Wilson

IF PEACE OF MIND MEANS KNOWING THERE WILL BE A CHEQUE IN THE
mail every month after retirement, no matter what storms are brewed by
the economic gods, then you may want to consider buying a life annuity with your RRSP money.

It's not a course I generally recommend, especially during periods of
low interest rates. But there is no doubt that a life annuity represents a
high degree of security. You can be reasonably (but not completely) con-
fident there will always be money available on a regular basis, no matter how long you live, no matter what investment decisions you make.

But, as with everything else in this world, you must give up something to get something. With an annuity, it may be control over your
capital and a lack of inflation protection. It doesn't necessarily have to
be that way–there are annuities that deal with these concerns. But you
pay a price for them too.

You also should be aware that your annuity contract is only as good
as the financial strength of the insurance company that is behind it. In
the past, insurance company failures were virtually non-existent. But
that changed in the nineties, with the collapse of Confederation Life
being the most spectacular, but not the only, failure. The insurance

industry provides a measure of protection for annuity clients in this situation through its agency, CompCorp. But the limit on annuity coverage is only $2000 a month. Beyond that, you're at risk if the company you deal with goes down in flames. The best way to protect yourself if your annuity payments will be larger is to deal with more than one company, so all your payments are protected.

There was a time when annuities were the number one choice (indeed, the *only* practical choice) of retirees when the time came to draw on their RRSP capital.

But when the federal government made RRIFs a viable option, the life annuity business declined. The life insurance companies–the only people who are allowed to provide life annuities–have responded by overhauling their product and improving its image. Life annuities, which had been fairly straightforward, became more complex as insurance firms dressed them up in new clothes and gave them some eye-catching accessories in a bid to restore their appeal.

That's not to say that some of the bells and whistles aren't of value to the potential buyer–they are. But they make the choice of a retirement income option that much more difficult.

The bottom line is that you should not dismiss the idea of using some of your RRSP funds to buy an annuity without looking closely at the alternatives. There are situations in which an annuity should be seriously considered–and the older you get, the truer this becomes.

The purpose of this chapter is to provide an overview of the annuity options available and to offer some suggestions for making the right decision.

Let's start with the basics. An annuity, in its simplest terms, is an exchange of capital for income. You pay a company a certain amount of money for which it undertakes to provide you with a steady income, either for a fixed term or for life.

This income is actually a mix of interest and repayment of principal, which is why annuity payments are usually higher than the amount you'd receive if you simply invested the capital yourself in a guaranteed investment certificate.

There are several types of annuities available, but only two can be purchased with RRSP money. One is a *life annuity* which, as the name suggests, will provide payments for as long as you or your spouse survives. These are offered only by life insurance companies, although they can be sold by other firms acting as brokers. The other is a *term certain annuity*, which makes payments to age 90 (or until your spouse turns 90 if he or she is younger), then cuts out. These can be obtained through insurance firms or financial institutions such as banks and trust companies.

Non-registered assets may be used to buy a *prescribed annuity*, which will provide regular income for the period you select. These are available from a variety of financial institutions.

The advantage of a life annuity over a term certain annuity is that you can't outlive it. An increasing number of people today are living past age 90. The last thing you need if you are among the long-lived is to have your income suddenly cut off. The Canadian life insurance industry uses this as a major selling point for life annuities, and it's certainly worth thinking about.

A word of warning before you venture into the world of annuities. Like most other life insurance company products, they have been made far more complicated than they need to be. Be prepared for all kinds of variations and combinations, each carrying a different price tag, each guaranteed to make your head spin. That seems to be the way the insurance industry likes to operate: dazzle the client with numbers and get them to sign while they're still reeling. Don't be bulldozed; find out exactly what is being offered and at what price. Then take your time assessing the relative merits of the income products available to you.

The income you'll receive from an annuity will be determined mainly by five factors: the amount of money you have to invest, your sex (men get higher payments than women because they tend to die sooner), your age when payments begin (the older you are, the more money you'll get), the number of bells and whistles you select, and the level of interest rates at the time you make your purchase (the higher, the better). By using these variables properly, you can develop an annuity strategy that will give you the maximum possible payback.

Before you start, here are some terms you need to understand when shopping for a life annuity.

Single Annuity. Issued to you personally. Payments will be calculated on the basis of your life expectancy.

Joint Life Annuity. Also called *last survivor annuity.* A guaranteed payment for both you and your spouse, which will continue for as long as one of you remains alive.

Guarantee. A promise from the issuing company that you or your estate will receive a specified amount of money, no matter what happens. Think of it as a form of insurance. If you die without a guarantee the month after you purchase an annuity, your heirs will receive nothing. With a guarantee, they'll at least get a return equal to the amount you would have been paid over the guarantee period. This may be paid either in instalments or as a lump sum, depending on the terms you choose.

A typical guarantee will run for five, ten, or fifteen years, although some companies offer them for longer periods. However, the longer the guarantee you choose, the less your income payments will be. Using the insurance analogy again—and why not, since these are insurance company products—you'll pay a higher premium for a longer guarantee.

Many financial advisers recommend you take a guarantee, especially if you're buying a single annuity. But it's very costly, and the amount of protection you receive declines every year. It's also one of the few forms of insurance I'm aware of where the premiums continue long after the coverage runs out (you'll continue to receive the lower annuity payment even after the guarantee expires).

Only you can decide if it's worth it; certainly the younger you are and the better your health, the less chance your heirs will ever benefit from the guarantee. If you're buying a joint annuity and you're both in good health, I suggest you seriously consider bypassing the guarantee; the odds are at least one of you will outlive it.

Impaired Annuity. If you're in poor health when you apply for a life insurance policy, the odds are you won't get coverage. If you do, you're likely to be charged a premium rate.

With an annuity, however, poor health can translate into a financial advantage. If your medical report indicates that your life expectancy is below normal, some companies will issue what's known as an *impaired annuity.* You'll receive higher monthly payments (perhaps by as much as 15 percent) for your money. The trick is to then turn around and surprise them by living far longer than anyone expected!

Increasing Income and Indexed Annuities. In the old days, annuity payments were fixed for life. But high inflation in the seventies and early eighties, plus competition from RRIFs, forced the insurance industry to come up with alternatives that protect annuity buyers from cost-of-living increases—for a price, of course.

There are two basic types of income-protection annuities available. One is known as an *increasing life annuity.* This type of plan simply increases your payment by a set percentage each year, usually between 1 and 4 percent, regardless of movements in the consumer price index. Alternatively, you can choose an *indexed annuity.* This plan will increase your payments each year in line with the inflation rate, although some companies put a cap on the amount of annual increase that's allowed.

With both these annuities, your initial income will be much lower than you'd receive with an ordinary, level-payment plan. However, you'll make up for that initial shortfall over time, as your payments increase—assuming, of course, that you live long enough.

If you don't have any other inflation protection in your retirement income program, you should look carefully at these annuity options. No one should begin retirement with an income that will remain relatively constant, unless it's much more than you initially need and you can afford to keep adding to your savings.

Income-Reducing Annuity. The other side of the coin. Payments from these joint annuities decline when the first spouse dies, on the somewhat dubious theory that one can live more cheaply than two. The income for the surviving spouse may drop by anywhere from one-third to three-quarters of the original payment.

There's potential for genuine financial hardship for your loved one in arrangements like this. Suppose, for example, he or she needs increased medical care in old age. Cutting the annuity payment substantially may make that difficult or impossible. These plans aren't particularly popular, with good reason.

Integrated Annuities. These plans are structured in such a way that the payments are reduced on a dollar-for-dollar basis as Canada Pension Plan and Old Age Security benefits kick in. The result is a level income for life. Integrated annuities are most useful to people who retire early and need higher monthly payments to tide them over until they are eligible to begin drawing government benefits (age 60 for CPP, 65 for OAS).

Variable Annuities. These plans invest your money in a fund, with your payments based on the fund's performance. Because of this unpredictability factor, they shouldn't be considered if you're relying on this money as the prime source of your income.

Cashable Annuities. In the old days, an annuity, like a diamond, was forever. Once you were in, there was no going back. The decision was made and you had to live with it.

Now, however, you can keep your financial options open with a cashable annuity. If you decide you want to get out, you can arrange to have your annuity cashed in (the technical term is "commuted") at its current value. At that point, you can use the money to buy another annuity or to invest in a RRIF, in which case no tax will be payable. Or you can have the cash paid directly to you, as long as you don't mind paying tax on it at your top rate.

As with everything else in the annuity world, you have to pay for this flexibility in the form of lower monthly payments.

Renewable Annuities. Normally, the interest rate on which your annuity payments are based is locked in for the duration of the plan. However, it is now possible to buy an annuity for which the period of the rate guarantee is shorter than the term of the plan. At the end of each interest rate period, you can use your remaining cash value to buy another renewable annuity, a life or fixed-term annuity, or a RRIF.

This type of annuity is worth considering if interest rates are low at the time of your purchase, as they were throughout most of the nineties. Rather than lock in a low rate for the rest of your life, a renewable annuity enables you to choose a shorter term in the hope rates will be higher when the time comes to renew.

Usually, however, the shorter the term you select, the lower the interest rate paid and, therefore, the less income you'll receive. Again, you pay for flexibility.

Deferred Annuity. One way to avoid the problems created by annuity shopping when interest rates are down is to buy a deferred annuity when rates are high (as they will almost certainly be again at some point). This is simply the life insurance industry's equivalent of a guaranteed investment certificate. The primary difference from an ordinary GIC that you'd buy from a bank or trust company is that with a deferred annuity, the proceeds from the plan must be used to be purchase an annuity (or be redeemed) by a certain date. This may be a specific number of years, or may relate to the investor's age.

There are also some other differences from an ordinary GIC of which you should be aware.

- **Beneficiary.** You can designate a beneficiary for a deferred annuity, who will continue to receive payments if you die. This is not possible with regular GICs.

- **Pension tax credit.** Income from a deferred annuity is eligible for the pension tax credit. Ordinary GIC interest is not.

- **Creditor protection.** If the beneficiary of the deferred annuity is your spouse, a child, or a parent, creditors cannot make a claim against the invested principal. They can, however, go after payments made to you.

- **Liquidity.** Most deferred annuities can be redeemed prior to maturity, with an interest rate adjustment. Ask the company with which you're dealing about its policy in this regard. In most, but not all, cases, bank and trust company GICs cannot be cashed before maturity.

- **Security.** GICs from banks and trust companies are protected by deposit insurance up to $60 000, as long as the term does not exceed five years. Life insurance companies are not members of the Canada Deposit Insurance Corporation. However, CompCorp protects deferred annuities to the same dollar limit as deposit insurance. There is no maximum term.

A deferred annuity enables you to lock in your interest rate when rates are high, but to delay receiving payments until you need them. So you can go shopping for an annuity several years before you actually expect to draw the money. This is an important advantage that allows you to set up the maximum possible income flow from your annuity.

The level of interest rates is an extremely important factor in buying an annuity. If you lock in for a long term at a time when rates are low, you'll end up sacrificing thousands of dollars in retirement income.

So time your annuity purchases for maximum return. If interest rates are low when you're shopping, postpone the decision or buy a renewable annuity, which will allow you to get back into the market under more propitious circumstances.

Here are some other strategies to use if you decide an annuity is the route you want to go.

1. Do some comparison shopping. The rates paid on the same annuity will vary from one company to another at any given time, sometimes substantially. The problem is that, despite some diligent searching, I have not been able to find any independent source for comparative rates. *The Toronto Star* used to publish annuity rates regularly, but has now discontinued doing so. I could not find any site on the Internet that offered this information, and my contacts at the Canadian Life and Health Insurance Association could not come up with any suggestions. So you may have no choice but to ask for quotes from several different companies. Alternatively, you can call an annuity broker. He or she will do a computerized search to obtain the best rate for you, usually at no charge (they're paid a commission by the insurance company that gets the business). You'll find them listed in the Yellow Pages under Annuities.
2. Wait as long as you can. The older you are when you buy an annuity, the greater the return. The reason, of course, is that the actuaries calculate you won't be around as long to collect. Nothing personal. Just statistical probability.
3. Understand the tax consequences. Although annuity payments are a blend of principal and interest, the full amount will be taxed at

your regular rate if the plan has been purchased with registered funds. You are, however, allowed to claim the pension tax credit for the first $1000 you receive each year.

Annuities purchased with non-registered funds are treated differently. In this case, only the interest portion of the payment is taxed. This interest is deemed to be averaged over the full term of the annuity for tax purposes, resulting in a tax deferral that can be significant on a long-term contract. Payments from these annuities are also eligible for the pension tax credit.

4. Be clear about the variations. As I pointed out at the start of this chapter, there are many variations of annuity products in the marketplace. Often, these are offered in combination with RRIFs, with the goal of achieving a more attractive combination of steady returns, flexibility, and inflation protection.

   Some of these plans can be extremely complicated. If you're not clear on exactly what you're getting for your money, I suggest you pass.

5. Consider converting RRIF assets. You should consider converting part or all of your RRIF to a life annuity when you reach a point when the capital in your plan starts to decline. The reason is that as the assets in the RRIF decline, so will the payments you receive. (You could always increase them, of course, but that would only speed up the capital erosion process). By moving to an annuity at this point, you'll ensure a steady income stream for the rest of your life. And because you'll likely be quite old when this happens, your annuity payment will be higher.

As you can see, annuities can be complicated but they also can be of great use in the right circumstances. Don't write them off because they seem like an old-fashioned concept. Just be sure that you use them efficiently, and that you get the best possible return for your money.

Key Points in Review

1. Life annuities guarantee a steady, predictable income stream for as long as you live. That peace of mind is very important to some retirees.

2. The nineties saw three insurance companies go under, including high-profile Confederation Life. To protect yourself against future failures, limit the amount of annuity business you give to any one company.

3. Entering into a life annuity contract when interest rates are low is generally not a good idea.

4. The amount of an annuity payment is governed by five factors: sex, age, the options you select, prevailing interest rates, and the capital you have to invest.

5. A guarantee will ensure that your heirs receive a specific amount from the insurance company if you should die early.

6. You can buy annuities that will increase payments annually by a set rate or in line with the cost of living.

7. Deferred annuities offer a way of locking in when interest rates are high.

8. Comparison shopping is highly recommended when buying an annuity. Rates will vary among companies. An annuity broker may be helpful in this regard.

22

Your Home as a Source of Income

Maybe they call it take-home pay because there is no other place you can afford to go with it.

— Franklin P. Jones

IN YEARS PAST, YOUR HOME WAS JUST YOUR HOME. A PLACE TO HANG your hat and put your feet up.

Today, however, your home can become a source of retirement income for you—perhaps a significant source, depending on your situation. You can even continue to live in the house while at the same time drawing income from it.

One of your primary financial goals before you retire should be to ensure your mortgage is entirely paid off. A debt-free home will open up several financial options for you that would not otherwise be available.

Being mortgage-free at retirement shouldn't be difficult. Most Canadian mortgages are amortized over 25 years, so anyone who bought a house before age 40 should have it paid off by age 65. The exceptions will be those who trade up to a more expensive home in later life, and those who have tapped into their equity through a secured personal line of credit for which the house was put up as collateral. If you're in either situation, you won't have the same kind of financial freedom as someone who owns an unencumbered property at retirement.

But let's assume that you are, or will be, in a mortgage-free position. What are your options?

The first is to use your home equity to take advantage of one of the few tax breaks Canadians have left—the principal residence exemption. Any profit you make on the sale of the family home is free and clear—it is not considered a taxable capital gain. This can result in a significant pool of retirement capital to draw on, but only if you are prepared to sell your home and move into downsized accommodation. The difference between the selling price of your old home and the cost of the new place can be invested to generate additional retirement income.

This is common retirement planning strategy, and it is certainly worth considering if your home is a typical suburban four-bedroom, big backyard type of place. Most people when they retire don't need, or even want, so much space. They prefer something that is more suited to a child-free couple. And they are often very happy to let someone else look after the maintenance, the gardening, and all the myriad other chores that come with a large home. If that sounds like it could be you, then you are definitely a candidate for downsizing.

How much capital can you free up in this way? As an example, suppose you bought a house in a major city like Vancouver, Calgary, or Toronto 30 years ago, for which you paid $100 000. Assuming it has been well looked after and the neighbourhood is still desirable, that same house today will probably fetch at least $300 000 and perhaps more. The mortgage has long since been paid off, so all the cash after a sale, less commissions and other expenses, is yours.

You then have two choices. You can take part of the money and use it to buy a small residence, perhaps a two-bedroom condo. Or you can rent. You should look carefully at the financial implications of each before you decide.

Let's consider the rental option. If you insist on having a luxury suite in the heart of downtown, it probably won't make any financial sense. But if your tastes are more modest and you live in a major metropolitan area, you can probably find very nice rental accommodations in one of the nearby satellite communities (e.g., Abbotsford near Vancouver or Newmarket near Toronto) at a reasonable price. In smaller cities, finding reasonable rental space should not be difficult unless there is a housing shortage for whatever reason.

Work through the math carefully, making sure to take taxes into account. Let's assume you sold a house and realized $300 000, net after all expenses. You invest the money in a balanced portfolio of mutual funds and it returns 8 percent a year on average, or $24 000 in annual income. About one-third of that goes in taxes (a blend of interest, dividends, and capital gains will be taxed at a lower rate than pure interest income). So you are left with $16 000 a year net after taxes. In order to come out with some extra money in your pocket, your monthly rent cannot exceed $1300. Here's how it works out:

Gross income	$24 000
Taxes	8 000
After-tax income	16 000
Annual rent at $1300 a month	15 600
Additional annual income	400

Of course, you can always dip into capital to supplement your income, but that will gradually erode your nest egg.

Now let's assume that instead of renting, you buy a place for $200 000. In all cases, additional expenses such as utilities and maintenance are constant.

You now own your home and have $100 000 to invest in your mutual funds portfolio. This generates gross revenue of $8000 a year. You have a cost that you didn't incur by renting–property tax, which we'll put at $3000 a year. Let's see how it all works out.

Gross income	$8 000
Taxes	2 664
After-tax income	5 336
Property tax	3 000
Additional annual income	2 336

Don't assume from these examples that buying is automatically better than renting. It depends on what prices and costs you are working with. But these illustrations give you an idea of how to calculate the relative benefits of buying or renting in your personal situation. Just fill in your own numbers.

Of course, if you decide you'd rather stay in the family home, you won't be able to generate any additional investment income by using the trading down approach. What then?

There are three other ways to tap into the capital in your home after retirement. All involve borrowing against the equity in your house in one way or another.

One option is to put a new mortgage on the property. If you use the proceeds to build an investment portfolio, the interest on the loan will be tax deductible. If your mortgage rate is 7 percent and you're in a 40 percent tax bracket, the after-tax interest rate on your loan will therefore be 4.2 percent.

For this strategy to make sense, your investments must yield more after tax than the interest you're paying on the loan. This means you should concentrate on generating capital gains, dividends, or rental income from your portfolio, all of which have built-in tax advantages. The difficulty is that investments that produce these types of income tend to be somewhat higher risk than interest-bearing securities like GICs, term deposits, money market funds, and the like. So to achieve the results required to make this strategy work, you'll have to accept an increased possibility of losses.

However, as long as interest rates remain low, this strategy can certainly work. If you invest in a mutual fund portfolio that yields 8 percent annually on average, you'll come out ahead. Here's an illustration. We'll assume you pay tax at only 30 percent on your mutual fund income because of the advantage given to dividends, etc.

New mortgage on home	$150 000
Mortgage rate	7%
After-tax annual interest cost	6 300
Gross revenue from portfolio @ 8%	12 000
Taxes	3 600
After-tax revenue	8 400
Net profit	2 100

The second option is a variation on the first. In this case, you obtain a home equity personal line of credit. You'll still have to put a mortgage on the property, but a PLC gives you greater flexibility in drawing on the funds and allows you to repay the loan according to your own schedule, rather than the fixed schedule of a regular mortgage.

A home equity PLC is simply a preauthorized credit line based on the value of your equity in your home. You don't even need to have fully paid off the original mortgage to use it. You aren't charged interest until you actually start drawing against the credit line, and then only on the amount you actually use. The interest rate will be close to the financial institution's prime rate, and will be adjusted up or down monthly in accordance with movements in the prime. Repayment formulas vary. Some financial institutions require only that you pay the interest owing each month. Others want up to 3 percent of the month-end total, principal plus interest. In all cases, however, you may make repayments above the minimum amount at any time, without penalty.

Interest on PLC loans is also tax deductible if the money is invested. (There are a few exceptions here, including investments in commodities and raw land, but presumably you aren't going to consider speculations like that for your retirement money.) Again, this lowers the after-tax cost of the loan. But, as with an ordinary mortgage, you'll probably have to assume additional risk if you're going to generate enough after-tax income to make the whole process worthwhile.

Also, don't lose sight of the fact that both these strategies cost money up front. In either case, you'll have to put a new mortgage on your home, with the associated legal and other expenses that process involves.

Your third choice—and one that is intriguing more retired people—is to use a reverse mortgage. The name derives from the fact that, whereas you make monthly payments against an ordinary mortgage, a reverse mortgage makes payments to you! And in tax-free dollars, to boot!

How can this be? Here's the story.

In the mid-eighties, a Vancouver accountant named William Turner decided there had to be a way out of the financial squeeze that was forcing many retired people to make an agonizing choice—to sell their home to raise cash or see their standard of living deteriorate. After two years of research, he adapted a concept that was already being used in Britain and the United States to Canadian needs and introduced the first reverse annuity mortgage to this country, calling it the Canadian Home Income Plan (CHIP). This was in 1986 and to this day CHIP remains the only lifetime reverse mortgage program available.

A reverse mortgage allows older people to use the equity in their home to generate income in the form of a monthly annuity payment. As icing on the cake, Turner obtained a ruling from Revenue Canada that annuities purchased under his plan would not be considered taxable income—in other words, the payments would be received tax free. He also persuaded Ottawa to agree that any money received through the plan would not affect eligibility for government means-tested income support programs, such as the Guaranteed Income Supplement.

Not surprisingly, the CHIP plan has attracted a lot of interest among retired people. The program, which is now backed by the Royal Bank of Canada, Toronto-Dominion Bank, and Hongkong Bank of Canada, has underwritten more than $150 million in reverse mortgage loans since its creation.

The concept is relatively simple. A mortgage is taken out against the property. The homeowner may draw the money in a lump-sum cash payment, as a combination of cash and income, or as tax-sheltered guaranteed income. If an annuity is chosen, it will continue to pay regular income for life or, if it's a joint and last survivor annuity, for as long as one spouse remains alive.

No payments are ever made against the mortgage loan, nor is title to the house affected in any way—it always remains with the owner. If you wish, you can sell the house later, rent it, or move—the plan offers a great deal of flexibility.

When the owner dies (or the last surviving spouse in the case of a joint plan), the house is sold. The principal and accrued interest on the loan are repaid at that time. Anything remaining from the proceeds of the sale becomes part of the estate. CHIP reports that the vast majority of their clients discharge their mortgage with at least 50 percent equity remaining in the home.

The loan proceeds don't have to be used for annuity income. There are many clever financial planning strategies that can be implemented. For example, one man received a $300 000 loan under the plan.

He already had the same amount in taxable GICs. These were redeemed and the money given to his daughter—an early inheritance, if you like. He then invested the proceeds from the loan in new GICs for himself, the interest from which was tax sheltered (this is possible because the interest on the loan exceeds the return from the investment). The net result was more after-tax cash for him and a large sum of tax-free money for his daughter (we have no gift tax in Canada, remember).

Other CHIP clients have used the money to buy a sun-belt residence, to pay for renovations on their home, or simply to live a more comfortable lifestyle.

On the surface, it looks foolproof. You keep living in your home for as long as you like, all the while enjoying the benefits of the extra money. And it costs you nothing. Basically, your heirs foot the bill, because a large part of the money that would normally come to them from the sale of the house will go instead to the mortgage company.

But there are some potential drawbacks to consider before signing up.

For one, this plan doesn't work very well for young retirees. You're eligible once you turn 62, but the older you are, the better. That's because the younger you are when you start, the less money you can draw. Also, the younger you are, the longer you can be expected to live, which means more unpaid interest will accumulate on your mortgage loan over the years.

Also, you can only tap into a relatively small percentage of your equity using a reverse mortgage, because of the nature of the plan. Forty-five percent of the appraised value is the maximum allowed, and it could be substantially less depending on the circumstances.

The accompanying table shows how much a couple can expect to receive from a reverse mortgage at various ages. It assumes they take 25 percent of the money as a lump-sum payment up front and the balance as a lifetime, tax-free annuity. The numbers are based on conditions as they prevailed in spring 1999.

Until recently, the CHIP program was only available in urban areas of British Columbia, Ontario, Manitoba, Alberta and Quebec. However, the company is extending it across the rest of the country, including some rural areas, so inquire about availability where you live.

Reverse Mortgage Payouts

Home Value	Allowable Mortgage	Initial Payment (25%)	Monthly Benefit
Age 65			
$125 000	$20 189	$5 047	$89.03
$250 000	41 554	10 386	183.26
$500 000	84 282	21 070	371.69
Age 75			
$125 000	$39 527	$9 861	$219.08
$250 000	80 228	20 057	444.67
$500 000	161 632	40 408	895.85
Age 80			
$125 000	$49 026	$12 256	$309.97
$250 000	99 226	24 806	627.36
$500 000	199 628	49 907	1 262.15

Source: Canadian Home Income Plan (CHIP)

If you want more information, you can contact the Canadian Home Income Plan by calling 1-800-563-2447, toll-free.

Before I leave this chapter, there's one other point I'd like to make. So far, I've focused entirely on financial considerations in discussing your housing needs after retirement. But there's a lot more involved.

Where you live will be a major component of your lifestyle decision. If staying in your present home is extremely important to you, one of your priorities should be to make sure things work out that way. On the other hand, if you feel the place is too big and represents too much work, you may be looking forward to moving.

Give your decision some careful thought before acting. I have some friends who decided to sell their four-bedroom house in the Toronto suburb of Don Mills after the husband retired because they didn't feel they needed as much space. Instead, they bought a new townhouse in an area north of the city. It didn't take them long to discover they'd made the wrong choice. Their new place turned out to be too small for a lifetime of accumulated furniture and memorabilia. And they found they didn't like being so far away from their friends and social activities. Within two years they had sold the townhouse (fortunately at a substantial profit) and purchased a new home not far away from their old one.

So don't let financial matters be the only consideration in deciding whether you'll stay or sell after you retire. Consider the neighbourhood, proximity to your friends and children, easy access to your golf course or bridge club, the strain (and the cost) of moving, and other important lifestyle factors.

If moving does turn out to be your choice, try to talk to residents of the area you're considering and hear what they have to say about it. Better still, rent in the area for a while, if that's feasible. Nothing will help your decision more than the actual experience of being there.

Key Points in Review

1. Pay off your mortgage before you retire. A debt-free home will open up several financial options you may never have thought about.

2. Any profit made on the sale of a principal residence in Canada is tax exempt.

3. If you decide to sell your house and move to a smaller place, give careful consideration to whether buying or renting new accommodation makes the most sense. You'll have to do some comparison shopping and crunch some numbers first.

4. You can free up investment capital by taking a new mortgage on the home or applying for a homeowner's line of credit. Interest on the loan will be tax deductible if the money is used for investment purposes.

5. A reverse mortgage allows you to receive tax-free income while never having to make a repayment during your lifetime. However, this type of mortgage is only available in certain parts of the country.

6. Don't let financial considerations be the only factor in deciding whether to stay in your home or to sell. Consider your lifestyle and your proximity to family and friends. It's no good having more money if you're unhappy as a result.

23

Taxing Times

The avoidance of taxes is the only intellectual
pursuit that still carries any reward.

— John Maynard Keynes

IT WASN'T TOO LONG AGO THAT THE NUMBER ONE COMPLAINT OF retired people was the difficulty they were having in making ends meet. Television programs during the seventies and eighties frequently ran items about the poor senior citizen who was living on cat food, or the couple who could only afford meat once a week, or the retired mechanic whose pension had been eaten away by inflation, forcing him to move in with his daughter and son-in-law.

Perhaps it's a measure of how far we've come that we don't hear or read many stories like that any more. That isn't to say there still aren't seniors who must desperately struggle to stretch their limited budget from month to month. There most certainly are such people, a lot of them. But they aren't as much in evidence today. Instead, the complaint I now hear most often from seniors is about the high taxes they have to pay!

My standard response is that they should be thankful they are in the position of having to pay taxes at all. It's a sure sign that they are relatively well off, which is exactly where we all want to be when the time comes to stop work. Not surprisingly, that does not mollify them, and I understand why. The plain fact is that in recent years there have been a number of changes in the tax system that have been clearly aimed at Canada's seniors, to the point where they felt they were being targeted by Ottawa. They have a case.

In the first edition of *Retiring Wealthy*, I wrote about a woman who had called into a radio phone-in show on which I was appearing. She was in her seventies, and extremely bitter. She and her husband had worked hard all their lives and had put money aside in pension plans and RRSPs for their retirement, she said. Now they had settled back to live on the fruits of their labour—and the government was taxing it all away!

Nothing I could say would placate her. I pointed out that she and her husband had enjoyed the benefit of years of tax-free compounding and that they were getting special tax concessions because of their ages. She remained furious. She was absolutely convinced the whole retirement planning system in this country is a massive fraud, which people didn't learn about until it was too late in their lives to do anything about it.

"I am frustrated, disillusioned, and angry," she concluded. "And I don't know what to do about it."

If she is still living, she must be even more angry and frustrated today. She and her husband actually had a pretty easy time of it back then, compared to their tax situation today.

Let's quickly review the key changes that have been introduced in recent years, and how they affect older people.

1989: The Old Age Security claw-back is introduced by the Progressive Conservative government of Brian Mulroney. Phased in over three years, it becomes fully operational in 1991. The finance minister of the day, Michael Wilson, insists only very wealthy seniors will be affected. But the legislation allows for only partial indexing of the income threshold at which the claw-back cuts in, ensuring that, over time, an increasing number of seniors will have to repay part or all of their OAS benefits.

1994: In his first budget, Liberal Finance Minister Paul Martin announces plans to subject the age tax credit, which everyone receives at age 65, to an income test. As a result, anyone with net income over about $26 000 saw their age credit eroded. People with net income over $49 100 lost it entirely. The change costs anyone who loses the total credit about $900 a year in additional tax.

1995: Mr. Martin extends the reach of the OAS claw-back to hit certain categories of people that had previously escaped.

1996: Continuing his methodical tax assault on older people, Paul Martin reduces the maximum age for owning an RRSP to 69 from 71. This one move had a triple impact. First, it forced people to move to a RRIF sooner than they might otherwise have done, thus allowing the government to begin collecting taxes on their retirement income two years earlier. Second, it took away two years of RRSP contributions from people who work into their seventies. Finally, it cost the RRSP holder who didn't need cash immediately two additional years of tax-sheltered compounding.

Also in 1996, Mr. Martin removed the tax deductibility for RRSP and RRIF administration fees. Not a big deal, perhaps, but it costs top bracket taxpayers with a self-directed plan about $70 a year in additional tax.

But those two measures in the 1996 budget were nothing compared to Mr. Martin's last bombshell. He proposed a new Seniors' Benefit, which would take effect in 2001. The idea was to cut government support for older Canadians by several billion dollars, and there is little doubt that would have been the ultimate result. The plan would have deprived retired people of the benefits of OAS payments, the age tax credit, and the pension tax credit, and replaced all these with a new tax-free payment system. The announced purpose of the measure was to target benefits more effectively toward poor seniors. But it quickly became obvious that many middle-income people would be hard-hit, losing thousands of dollars in OAS payments while having to pay more tax each year because of the disappearance of the credits. The net result would be a plan that would penalize those Canadians who successfully planned for their retirement, and could actually have the effect of reducing the incentive to contribute to an RRSP.

The Seniors' Benefit brought out the heavy artillery. Seniors' groups across the country mobilized their forces in opposition to it, led by representatives of the Canadian Association of Retired Persons (CARP). Many financial professionals weighed in with criticisms of the program's impact on retirement planning. In the end, the opponents scored a rare success. In the summer of 1998, Mr. Martin ran up the white flag and announced the Seniors' Benefit was being abandoned in its entirety. No fixes—it was dead.

Seniors' organizations rejoiced—apparently forgetting that all the other tax changes that negatively affected them remained firmly in place.

So this is the situation in which we find ourselves as we enter the twenty-first century. Governments, both federal and provincial, continue to seek out ways to wring more tax dollars from a segment of the population that continues to grow larger and is perceived as being increasingly well-off. Retirees, for their part, are fighting hard to keep more of what they see as a lifetime of hard-earned savings and to fend off what they regard as a series of blatant tax grabs.

Tax Reduction Strategies

What can you do? How can you structure your affairs so as to legally reduce the amount of money that Revenue Canada will take each year? Here are some ideas that may help.

Review Your Non-Registered Investment Portfolio

Completely review all the securities that you hold outside your RRSP, RRIF, LIF, or whatever. Make sure that they are as tax effective as possible.

Take a look at the accompanying table. It shows the tax structure for the province of Ontario as of 1999. The numbers will vary in other provinces and the territories, but the pattern will be exactly the same.

Ontario Tax Rates—1999

Taxable Income	Interest	Dividends	Capital Gains
$7 045 to $7 294	17.00%	4.58%	12.75%
7 295 to 9 328	17.34%	5.01%	13.01%
9 329 to 11 735	30.67%	8.96%	23.01%
11 736 to 19 794	24.19%	6.99%	18.14%
19 795 to 29 590	23.72%	6.39%	17.79%
29 591 to 46 735	36.27%	22.33%	27.20%
46 736 to 51 199	37.44%	23.04%	28.08%
51 200 to 59 180	39.49%	24.29%	29.62%
59 181 to 60 155	44.05%	30.04%	33.04%
60 156 to 62 391	48.17%	32.53%	36.13%
62 392 and up	48.75%	32.92%	36.57%

Source: Ernst & Young LLP

Note the different tax rates that apply to investment income. Interest is taxed at the top rate—the same rate you pay on employment income. But both dividends and capital gains get a tax break.

In the case of dividends, it is the dividend tax credit. The principle behind this credit is that dividends are paid out of after-tax corporate earnings. So, in theory, since tax has already been paid on them, they shouldn't be taxed again in the hands of investors. Of course, they are taxed—just not as heavily. As you can see, dividends are the most tax-efficient way to receive investment income out of the three possibilities shown here.

Now take a look at how attractive the dividend tax rate is for people with relatively low incomes. You can have total taxable income of up to $29 590 and still have a single-digit tax rate applied to your dividends.

Capital gains don't fare as well, which is ironic since capital gains usually involve more risk than dividend income. For capital gains, the first 25 percent of the profit is tax free. You pay at your marginal rate on the other 75 percent. This strange situation grew out of the now-dead $100 000 lifetime capital gains exemption. Before that exemption was introduced, only half of your gains were taxed. But since the government—this was the Mulroney regime—was giving you the first hundred thousand tax-free, they decided to increase the rate on gains after that amount. Naturally, when Liberal Finance Minister Paul Martin abolished the exemption, he didn't cut the inclusion rate back to 50 percent. So now we have the weird situation in which you're better off earning dividends than capital gains—at least as far as Revenue Canada is concerned. That's bad tax policy, but no one seems ready to do anything about it. The best thing for you to do is to position your non-registered investment portfolio to take advantage of it. You'll find a number of tips on how to do this in Chapter 14.

Make Use of Unused RRSP Contribution Room

Just because you have retired, it doesn't necessarily mean that you can no longer contribute to an RRSP—yours or your spouse's. You may still have unused RRSP contribution room accumulated from years past. Check your most recent notice of assessment from Revenue Canada. If so, you can use up those credits by continuing to make RRSP contributions, even though you no longer have any earned income. I strongly recommend you use them all up before your RRSP (or your spouse's) has to be wound up, which is by the end of the year in which you turn 69.

Hide Retiring Allowances from the Tax People

If you retire early, or lose your job, you're likely to receive a severance benefit from your employer. A portion of that money can be rolled directly into your RRSP, over and above your normal contribution limit, thus allowing you to escape immediate taxes on it. However, this tax advantage is gradually disappearing, another casualty of Mr. Martin's tax grab campaign.

These rollovers are calculated on the basis of $2000 for every year or part-year of service up to and including 1995, plus an additional $1500 for each year before 1989 that you weren't a member of a company pension plan or deferred profit sharing plan (DPSP).

There's an important technical point here. A year, for purposes of this calculation, means any calendar year in which you worked for the company. Suppose you started on December 15, 1990 and left in 1995. You would receive credit for six years of employment, up to and including 1995, even though in the first of those years you only spent two weeks in the organization.

The amount you can shelter from tax can be substantial, depending on your length of service. For example, if you qualified for 30 years of credits, you'd be entitled to the following RRSP retiring allowance contribution, depending on your pension plan status:

Pension plan member for the full eligible period: $60 000
No pension plan: $95 000

If you'll be receiving a retiring allowance you want to tax shelter, be sure to make the appropriate arrangements with your employer in advance. Ideally, any eligible amount should go directly from your employer to your RRSP. If it is paid to you and you then make the RRSP deposit, you can still claim a deduction. However, tax will be withheld on the payment and you'll only get that money back when you file your return.

Apply for Old Age Security, Even if It Will All Be Taxed Back

If you're in a high income bracket, you may wonder why you should even bother applying for OAS, if it's all going to be taxed away by the clawback. The reason is that you won't have to repay the money until the tax deadline, April 30 of the year following. In the meantime, it could be earning interest for you. If OAS payments average $412 a month and you invest your cheque in a money market fund paying 4 percent, you can earn about $100 in interest over a 12-month period. It may not be a lot, but when the government is taxing away your benefits right, left, and centre, every little bit helps.

Claim the Pension Income Credit

The first $1000 of pension income qualifies for a special tax credit, called the pension income credit. It's worth $170 off your federal tax. When the provincial tax saving is added, the total reduction is around $250, depending on your province of residence.

Only specific forms of pension income qualify, however—in fact, the list of exclusions in the tax guide is actually longer than the list of eligible pension income sources. You can claim periodic payments from an employer pension or deferred profit sharing plan, payments from an annuity purchased with RRSP money, and the taxable portion of payments from an income-averaging annuity contract. You can also claim income from a RRIF if you are 65 or older during the tax year, or you received the RRIF money because a spouse died.

You may not claim CPP or QPP payments, Old Age Security, lump-sum withdrawals from an RRSP, lump-sum payments from a pension plan, retiring allowances, a retirement compensation arrangement, or income from a variety of other sources (consult the tax guide if you're unsure).

Contrary to widespread belief, there is no age limit for claiming the pension credit, except in the case of a RRIF. If you have income from a qualifying source, this credit is available to you. Complete the appropriate chart at line 314 in the tax guide and claim your prize.

Claim the Age Credit—If You Can

To be eligible for this tax credit, you must meet both an age test and an income test. If you were 65 or older before the end of the tax year, you've passed part one. If your net income was less than $25 921, you qualify on that count as well and can claim the full age amount of $3 482. That will reduce your total tax bill by about $900, with the exact amount depending on where you live.

If your net income is more than $25 921 but less than $49 134, you'll be able to claim part of the credit. (Obviously, the higher your income, the less you'll get.) You'll find a form at line 301 of the tax guide that will lead you through the calculation.

Transfer Unused Credits

You're allowed to claim certain tax credits for yourself if your spouse is unable to use them, including the pension credit and the age credit, as well as credits for disability, tuition, and education. Any amounts not needed to reduce your spouse's taxable income to zero are eligible. You'll have to complete schedule 2, which comes with the tax return, to do this.

Transferring credits can be especially valuable in cases where one spouse has a very low income. Take, for example, a couple in which the 66-year-old wife receives only Old Age Security plus a small private pension of $2000 a year. She's not liable for any taxes. But she has pension and age credits that she can't use.

Her husband can transfer these credits to himself, and reduce his tax bill by over $1000 in the process. If the wife were eligible for the disability credit (perhaps because of a severe hearing impairment), he could transfer that amount as well, adding another $1000 and change to his savings.

Deduct Carrying Charges and Interest Expenses

If you have a non-registered investment portfolio, there are several types of expenses that you may be able to deduct. These include interest paid on an investment loan, safety-deposit box fees, professional money management fees (RRIFs and RRSPs excepted), and accounting fees related to your investment income.

Claim All Medical Expenses

Your tax-deductible medical and dental costs may increase after you retire. This can be as a natural consequence of the aging process or because you no longer have a group health and dental plan, or for both these reasons.

The medical credit will provide some relief. But, unfortunately, you'll only be able to recover a portion of your total costs. You'll receive no credit for expenses up to 3 percent of your net income, to a maximum of $1614 (1998 tax year). For anything above that, you get a 17 percent federal tax credit. With provincial taxes taken into account, you'll end up recovering about a quarter of your costs above the threshold.

That's small compensation for a large medical bill. So you should make sure you know the rules in order to take maximum advantage of it. Many people aren't aware of the wide range of expenses that can be claimed for the medical tax credit. They include everything from premiums paid for private health insurance plans (including travel insurance while outside Canada) to full-time attendant care. All the things you'd expect are on the list: doctors' fees, hospital bills, dental charges, prescriptions, glasses, and the like. But you can also claim a variety of costs you might not regard as truly medical. For example, if you begin to lose your hearing–not uncommon as you get older– the cost of hearing aids is deductible, as is the cost of any repairs to them. If you're physically disabled, the costs of modifying your home to make it more convenient for you to function may be claimed. A blind person may include the cost of a seeing-eye dog. You can even claim medical expenses incurred abroad. The rule of thumb is: if it's a genuine medically-related cost, claim it. All Revenue Canada can do is say no.

You may claim expenses that occurred in any 12-month period ending in the tax year for which you're filing a return, as long as they weren't deducted in the previous year.

Since the tax credit is the same no matter who claims it, have the lower-income spouse do so. The 3 percent net income threshold will be less, and you'll end up with a larger tax refund. For example, if a wife has a net income of $50 000 annually, she'll have a medical expense threshold of $1500 (3% x $50 000 = $1500). If her husband has net income of $30 000, his threshold is only $900 (3% x $30 000 = $900). They'll be able to claim an extra $600 in expenses if he includes the bills on his return.

See if You're Eligible for the GST/HST Credit

You may not be claiming the GST/HST credit now because your income is too high. But if you expect it to drop in retirement, you may be entitled to receive a regular cheque from the government. The maximum net family income you can receive and still be eligible for a credit is $33 880. Remember, if you are eligible for the credit you have to make a new claim every year.

Check Out Provincial Tax Credits

Most provinces offer their own tax credits to seniors. Although in virtually all cases only lower income people can make use of them, it doesn't hurt to check them out when you're completing your tax return. You might get a pleasant surprise.

Make Sure Your Assets Pass to Your Spouse

In most circumstances, you can keep your retirement savings out of Revenue Canada's hands when you die by willing them to your spouse. The tax people will only come calling when your assets pass to the next generation.

This requires a little planning, however. It's important, for example, that your spouse be designated as the beneficiary for your RRSP. For a RRIF or LIF, your spouse should be named as beneficiary or successor annuitant, depending on which way you decide to go. If your retirement plans are left to your estate, they may be taxed. At the very least, they'll wind up in probate and it may be some time before your spouse can get access to the funds.

You have an opportunity to designate a beneficiary at the time you open an RRSP or RRIF, or join a pension plan. Some people fail to specify anyone, however, in which case your estate will get the proceeds of your plan.

If you don't know who your beneficiary is, ask. If it's your estate, arrange to have the beneficiary switched to your spouse, unless you have some strong reason for not doing so. It could save your loved one a lot of financial headaches if anything should happen to you.

Plan for the Next Generation

Sooner or later, both you and your spouse will be gone and another generation will inherit your assets including, perhaps, some of your retirement savings or benefits. The whole subject of estate planning is for another book, but there is one important point about which you should be aware when preparing for that day.

You can, in special circumstances, pass some of your retirement savings on to a child or grandchild who is financially dependent upon you, even if your spouse is still living. This can be done with the proceeds of both an RRSP and a RRIF.

The definition of a financially dependent person for these purposes is very tight, however. The income of the child or grandchild has to be less than the basic personal tax amount in the year before your death. If the dependent child or grandchild is physically or mentally disabled, the proceeds from your RRSP or RRIF can be transferred directly into an RRSP in the youngster's name. The money can also be used to buy an annuity.

In the case of children who are not disabled, the only way to avoid tax is to purchase an annuity that provides payments for a term not longer than 18 years minus the age of the child at the time of purchase. Thus, if a child were thirteen years old when the annuity was bought, the term could not exceed five years. The annuity payments will be taxed as ordinary income in the child's hands.

The inherited money could also be included in a child's income, in which case it would be taxable–but perhaps at a lower rate than the estate would pay.

Take Out More Insurance

When you die, the assets in any registered plan you own (RRSP, RRIF, etc.) are considered to have been taken into income in the year of your death. The result in most cases is that half the money goes in taxes. One way to protect your heirs from the effect of this is to take out a life insurance policy that will cover the expected tax bill. It won't be cheap, but it may end up costing less than the taxes would.

Don't Run Afoul of Tax Technicalities

There are all sorts of nitty-gritty rules governing the management of RRSPs, RRIFs, LIFs, and pension plans. Make a mistake, and Revenue Canada could sock it to you, hard.

I'm not going to give the full list here. It makes for incredibly boring reading; if you want all the details, pick up a copy of Revenue Canada's guide titled *RRSPs and Other Registered Plans for Retirement*. But here are two important points to be aware of.

1. Don't exceed the foreign property limit in your RRSP or RRIF. That is more easily said than done in the case of a RRIF/LIF. That's because the book value of your plan—on which your foreign content allowance is based—will change every time you buy or sell a security (any security, not just foreign ones) or make a withdrawal from the plan. This can create so many headaches that some financial institutions arbitrarily impose a lower foreign content limit on RRIFs (15 percent is typical) to ensure the plan isn't constantly getting into penalty territory.

2. Don't miss your instalment payments. Once you stop receiving a regular salary, you may have to begin remitting tax to Revenue Canada on an instalment basis if a significant portion of your income comes from sources that do not withhold tax at source (e.g., investments). Payments are due quarterly, on the fifteenth of March, June, September, and December. The tax department usually won't hit you with interest and penalty charges in the first year, but once you've received official notice of your obligation to pay quarterly, you'll have to send in a regular cheque or face the expensive consequences. Ask your district taxation office to send you the booklet *Paying Your Income Tax by Instalments*, which contains all the details.

You may also wish to ask the federal government to withhold tax from your CPP and OAS payments. This is not something I normally recommend—it's always best to defer paying taxes for as long as possible. But having tax withheld at source will reduce the amount you will have to pay by instalment, and will also help to ensure that you don't find yourself cash-short when tax-filing time comes around.

To have tax withheld, complete form TD3, *Request for Income Tax Deduction on Non-Employment Income*, and send it to the nearest Income Security Programs office of Human Resources Development Canada.

Key Points in Review

1. Policy changes by the federal government in recent years have imposed an increasingly heavy tax burden on seniors.
2. Every effort should be made to maximize tax-advantaged income from a non-registered investment portfolio.
3. You can still make RRSP contributions after you retire if you have unused carry-forward credits.
4. The retiring allowances rule can be used to tax-shelter certain lump-sum payments from your employer.
5. Be sure to transfer any unused tax credits from your spouse.
6. If you have a lot of money in registered plans, do some estate planning to ensure as much as possible goes to your heirs.

24

Sun-Belt Retirement

*Winter is not natural. There's a perfectly good
reason it is silent out there. Anything with legs or
wings and two brain cells to rub together has left.*

— Arthur Black

AFTER A LIFETIME SPENT IN WHAT IS, TO PUT IT KINDLY, NOT THE MOST
salubrious of climates, you can hardly blame Canadians who decide to
live out their retirement years in places where the sun shines all year
round.

Florida, Arizona, California, and Hawaii have all become retirement
meccas in recent years. More adventurous snowbirds have flown to
places as far afield as the Caribbean, the Bahamas, Costa Rica, Mexico,
and southern Europe.

If you're inclined to join the exodus to the sun after you retire, you'll
need to do some careful advance planning. Financial considerations are
important, of course. But there are other matters to take into account-
housing, family, medical facilities, and social ties among them.

The first, and most important, decision is whether you plan to cut
your ties with Canada partially or totally. You can spend your winters in
the warmth and still remain a Canadian resident, with all the pluses and
minuses that involves. Or you can sever your connection with Canada
entirely and take up full-time residency in another country.

You retain your Canadian resident status for tax purposes if you
maintain a home in this country and live here over half the year. Even

if you are abroad for more than six months each year, Revenue Canada may take the view you're still a Canadian resident for tax purposes if you retain ties to Canada, such as real estate, bank accounts, investments, club memberships, a Canadian driver's licence, etc.

Being a Canadian resident makes you eligible for continued coverage under your provincial health care program, a benefit that many older people are reluctant to surrender. However, "residency" for purposes of health insurance varies from one province to another, so make inquiries first.

Continuing as a Canadian resident also ensures you will receive any social benefits to which you are entitled. Some of these may be lost under certain conditions if you leave the country–Old Age Security benefits, for example, may be discontinued after six months if you take up residency abroad and did not live in Canada for at least 20 years after the age of 18. But if you meet the qualifications for continued payment, you'll be able to draw OAS while sunning on the beach, and you can even arrange to have your money directly deposited to a U.S. bank if you take up residence in that country.

Any benefits earned under the Canada Pension Plan are payable no matter where you live. Direct deposit to a U.S. account can also be arranged for these payments.

Of course, retaining Canadian residency also makes you liable to pay Canadian taxes, which are much higher than those in the most popular snowbird destinations, including the United States. You'll have to weigh the economic pros and cons.

Your country of residence is more than just a matter of money. You may wish to continue to keep a home in Canada because you don't want to spend muggy summers in Florida or the hurricane season in the Caribbean, or because you want to be closer to your family and friends for part of the year–or perhaps simply because you love what is, after all, a very beautiful, if normally cold, country.

If you decide to move abroad, make inquiries about residency requirements at the embassy or consulate of the country you're considering. Moving to the U.S. has become easier in certain situations as a result of the Free Trade Agreement, but you'll still need to meet their qualifications. You'll have to obtain a green card–which could take some time—or meet what they call a "substantial presence" test, which is based on a period of residency in that country. Check with a U.S. immigration representative for full details.

Whether or not you choose to remain a Canadian resident, you may decide to purchase a sun-belt home for the winter months. After all, there's nothing wrong with spending November to April in Florida or Hawaii and arriving back just in time for the spectacular blossomings of May.

So let's spend some time looking at sun-belt real estate—and some of the problems that can develop if you're going shopping for a winter residence for the first time. I'll use Florida for the examples that follow, because it's the most popular choice for Canadians and the area with which I have the greatest familiarity since we own a winter home in Fort Myers Beach. But most of the points that follow will be applicable to any other warm climate as well.

Things to Consider

The first thing to understand is that buying a place in a hot climate is not like buying a home in Canada. Many considerations come into play that you've probably never dreamed of. Here are a few examples.

Climate Zones. All of Florida is warm in the winter compared to Canada, but some areas are much warmer than others. Your comfort level will be influenced by which one you choose. The state has three main climate zones:

- **The North.** This is a belt across the top of the state that includes the Panhandle, Jacksonville, and the capital, Tallahassee. It can be quite cool in winter, with even the occasional snowflake. The average daily temperature in January in Tallahasee is only 53 degrees Fahrenheit (12 degrees Celsius). Also, this zone is much more susceptible to the winter and spring storms that track from south-west to north-east across the U.S. You are much more likely to find yourself under a thunderstorm or tornado watch here during the winter and early spring than you are in any other part of the state.

- **The Middle.** The central part of the state encompasses such popular vacation destinations as Tampa/St. Petersburg, Sarasota, and Orlando. Winter temperatures are much milder; the average daily temperature in Orlando in January is 60 degrees Farenheit (15 degrees Celsius).
- **The South.** The extreme tip of the state is warmest of all in the winter. It includes Miami, Fort Lauderdale, Key West, Fort Myers, and the lovely community of Naples. Average January temperature in Miami Beach is 69 degrees Fahrenheit (19 degrees Celsius), the same as in Key West.

Insects. They thrive in the heat. Termites, roaches, fire ants, no-see-ums (my wife's pet peeve)—you name it, it's around. In Canada, many buyers insist on having a house checked by a home inspector before closing a deal. In Florida, a check by a pest control expert is equally important. As well, you will need to pay for year-round pest control maintenance, unless it is covered by condo fees.

Storage Areas. Warm-weather homes usually don't have basements (although those built on stilts may have usable space underneath). This makes storage a chronic problem; be sure there's adequate room for all your possessions. Garages, which serve as junk-collectors in Canada, are also rarer in the South; carports tend to be more popular.

Flooding. Florida is nothing more than a big sandbar. If you want to live near the sea, high water should be a concern if you are on ground level. Some coastal communities now require that land be artificially elevated before new homes are constructed, to reduce the flood risk. But older buildings have not been subject to these requirements in most cases. Check out the flood risk and the elevation above the high water mark on any property you're considering before going ahead.

Hurricane Shutters. All areas around the Gulf of Mexico and the Caribbean Sea are potential hurricane targets. If the property you're considering does not have hurricane shutters you may have to install them, and they aren't cheap. For our three-bedroom home, the price tag was about $12 000 U.S.

Landscaping. If you're buying a condo, you don't have to worry about it. Otherwise, keeping a property neat and tidy in a subtropical climate can be even more difficult than it is in Canada in June. That beautiful palm tree on the front lawn will have to be sprayed regularly to keep it healthy. An orange tree may seem wonderful—until the fruit falls to the ground and starts rotting, attracting all kinds of unwelcome insects. If you're not planning to take up permanent residence, you'll need to hire someone to come in regularly to do the yard work for you. Expect to pay upwards of $100 a month for the service. Alternatively, you can look at places with "maintenance-free landscaping," which basically means your yard will be pebbles instead of grass. That eliminates the need for mowing, but you may still have the falling oranges to contend with.

Sprinkler Systems. Underground sprinklers are much more common in the South than in Canada. They're especially useful if the house is going to be vacant for long periods and you want to keep the vegetation green during the winter dry months.

Pools and Heaters. Pools are a common accessory in more expensive Southern homes. It may not surprise you that many of them are not heated—after all, this is the sun belt, right? Unfortunately, even the mildest parts of the sun belt can get rather cool at times. If the pool isn't heated, you may find the water too chilly for your liking, especially in January and February. In my experience, a system of solar panels is the least expensive to operate (the sun does all the work). However, even they might not be adequate to keep your pool at a toasty eighty degrees during the depth of winter, when even south Florida temperatures can fall into the low forties at night. In such cases, a supplementary propane gas heater may be needed, at a cost of about $1200. So if you're looking for a place with a pool and you find one that's already heated, consider it a plus.

Of course, you will have to have your pool maintained regularly. If you don't, you'll be greeted by a foul-smelling algae pit when you arrive for the winter. You should arrange for weekly visits by a qualified person. Cost will be $50 to $100 a month.

Screening. Many Florida residences have a screened balcony, porch, or lanai. If you look at one that doesn't and the real estate agent insists it's not really needed, don't believe a word of it. Unless you want to retreat inside at sunset when the mosquitoes and no-see-ums emerge in their zillions, you need screening—and even that is not 100 percent effective. If you like the idea of enjoying a barbecue dinner outside on a soft Florida night, a screened lanai is an absolute essential.

Sea/Canal Frontage. If the place is on tidal water and you've never had experience with the sea before, there are a host of things to watch out for. One is the condition of the seawall, if there is one. If it needs repairs, they can be costly, and you can't get insurance to cover such expenses. If the house has a dock, check the pilings. They must be replaced periodically, which is also expensive. Many Florida canal homes have davits or lifts for raising boats out of the water. See if they're working properly. I once encountered a davit that wasps had virtually destroyed by packing it with mud as they built a nest.

Condo Rules. If the property you're considering is a condominium, get a copy of the rules and study them thoroughly before you buy. Some of the regulations can be strange. For example, some friends purchased a condo home in Boca Raton. After investing a lot of money in hurricane shutters, they discovered that the rules did not permit homes to be shuttered unless there was an actual hurricane warning. Since hurricanes occur in the summer months, when they were back in Canada, that created a big problem for them.

Financial Issues

The financial considerations involved in buying a sun-belt property can also differ from your Canadian real estate experience. Here are some of the money problems to be aware of:

Prices. They'll vary depending on where you buy, but if you're used to the prices in expensive cities like Toronto and Vancouver or popular vacation areas such as Whistler and Muskoka, you'll find costs in the more popular parts of Florida are comparable once the exchange rate is taken into account. Of course, much depends on the area you choose. You can find some wonderful Florida properties for a fraction of what you'd pay in Canada if you go hunting in the Panhandle or some of the less fashionable inland areas. On the other hand, some areas are outrageously expensive. You'll pay a big premium for addresses like Palm Beach, Boca Raton, Fort Lauderdale, Sanibel, Naples, and some parts of Sarasota.

Don't expect to make a killing on your investment. Generally, Florida resale prices tend to be soft, especially for condos. That's because the market is usually saturated with such properties, due to the older age of the population in the most popular resort areas (people become ill or die and the house goes up for sale). A few areas of the state have experienced significant price gains in recent years, however, most notably the south-western area around Naples.

This chronic oversupply makes most of Florida a buyer's market. You can afford to be choosy and to drive a hard bargain. It's not unusual for properties to stay on the market for a year or more; I've seen some that have gone for two or three years without moving. The longer the "For Sale" sign has been on the front lawn, the better your chances of getting a good buy.

The other side of this coin is that it may take a long time to sell the property when the time comes for you to do so, and you may take a loss in the process. I have several Canadian friends who have owned Florida property at some time in their lives. Most enjoyed the place while they had it, but few ended up making any money when they sold.

However, you can add to your retirement income by buying and selling Florida properties if you're the handy type. The trick is to buy a run-down property in an area where values are on the rise, fix it up, add some attractive extras (e.g., pool, dock) and then resell. Some friends of ours in Fort Myers Beach did this three times, pocketing a profit of around $100 000 each time. The downside, of course, is that you're always living in a construction zone.

Mortgages. Mortgage interest rates used to be lower in the U.S. than in Canada, but that has not been the case in recent years. But you can lock them in for a long period if you wish—5- and 30-year mortgages are common.

You may have to pay more up front when you take out a mortgage in the States. Many lenders charge "points" for initiating a mortgage; these are a percentage (1 or 2 percent is common) of the total value of the loan. The charge is supposed to cover a variety of costs, but it's mainly an interest rate buy-down. Usually (but not always), you'll find that the more points you're charged, the lower the interest rate will be.

Since there are many more mortgage lenders in the States than in Canada, you'll have to shop around for the best deal. And you'll need to do a lot of calculations to figure out whether you're better off paying points and taking a lower rate, or putting out nothing up front but carrying a higher interest charge. A mortgage broker can be very helpful in cutting through the maze of numbers on your behalf. Your real estate agent will undoubtedly be able to recommend one.

Another problem you may encounter is the reluctance of many U.S. financial institutions to lend money to aliens (that's us, folks, not some weird creatures from space). The reason is that many companies sell their mortgage contracts to third parties, and they are reluctant to accept Canadian or other foreign owners because of the potential problems of collection in the event of default. Maybe they think we're bad risks.

Property Taxes. Of course, you'll have to pay property taxes on your sun-belt residence. But the rate of tax may depend on whether or not you're moving there permanently. Some communities offer a substantial discount to permanent residents that is not available to snowbirds who reside in Canada and only come down for the winter. This seems to defy logic, since seasonal residents put less strain on community services, but that's the way it works. Ask about the policy in the area you're considering.

Insurance. You'll need to carry flood and hurricane protection, which you may not have on your Canadian home policy. These riders can be very expensive. It costs about three times more to insure our Florida home than it does our residence in Toronto, even though the values are roughly comparable.

Estate Taxes. This has been a major area of concern to anyone buying property in the United States. Canadians used to face death duties on U.S. property that could only be described as confiscatory. However, a new Canada-U.S. tax protocol that came into effect at the end of 1995 eased the situation considerably by increasing the amount that is exempt from U.S. estate taxes to $600 000.

Foreign Property Declaration. Effective with the 1998 tax year, Revenue Canada requires you to report any foreign property you own if the total cost is more than $100 000. Purchasing a sun-belt property may put you into that category. If so, be sure to make an annual declaration to that effect. You won't pay any extra tax; the measure is mainly intended to prevent Canadians from earning undeclared income from offshore investment accounts.

Renting Your House. If you rent out your sun-belt home for part of the year when you're not there, the tax people are going to come sniffing around. If the property is in the U.S., both Revenue Canada and the Internal Revenue Service (IRS) are going to want their share. As far as Canadian taxes are concerned, income from your U.S. property will be treated in the same way as any other rental income. You'll be allowed to deduct appropriate expenses to arrive at your net rental income, so be sure to keep all your receipts.

If you are a "non-resident alien" (which I'll explain in more detail shortly), any rental income from a U.S. property is subject to a 30 percent withholding tax in that country, with no deductions allowed. However, there is an exception if you want to treat your property as a business. To do this, you have to complete IRS form 1040NR, "U.S. Nonresident Alien Income Tax Return," and attach a letter providing full details about the property.

Selling Your House. If the time comes to sell your U.S. house, the buyers, or their agent, are required to withhold 10 percent of the gross price and remit it to the IRS. You then have to file form 1040NR to report a gain or loss. If you and your spouse owned the property jointly, you must each file a return. If you want more information about how all this works, get a copy of IRS publication number 519, titled *U.S. Tax Guide for Aliens.*

Other Considerations

So much for housing. There are a number of other matters you also have to deal with if you decide to take up residency abroad.

Income taxes are clearly a major consideration. The big issue that will have to be resolved is who you have to pay them to. The rules will vary depending on which country you go to, but we'll focus on the U.S. because it is the most common destination of Canadians.

If you spend a significant amount of time in the States, you may be classified as a "resident alien." To determine if this is your situation, take their "substantial presence test." It works like this:

> For the current year, count every day spent in the U.S. as one day. For last year, count every day as one-third of a day. For the year before that, count every day as one-sixth of a day. If the total exceeds 182 days, you meet the substantial presence test. If so, you have to file a U.S. tax return and report your worldwide income.

So, for example, suppose you spent 125 days in the U.S. in each of the past 3 years. That's about 4 months a year. Here's the calculation.

$$\text{This year} = 125 \times 1 = 125 \text{ days}$$
$$\text{Last year} = 125 \times 1/3 = 42 \text{ days}$$
$$\text{Prior year} = 125 \times 1/6 = 21 \text{ days}$$
$$\text{Total} = 188 \text{ days}$$

Even though in this case you never spent more than about four months in the U.S. in any one year, you qualify as a resident alien of that country.

You can get around this if you meet three conditions:

1. You were in the U.S. less than 183 days in the current year.
2. Your tax home is in Canada, meaning you are employed in this country or live here regularly.
3. You have a "closer connection" to Canada than to the U.S. This can be determined by a variety of things, from where you vote to the church to which you belong.

In this case, you have to advise the IRS by filing form 8840, "Closer Connection Exception Statement." You'll find a copy in a useful pamphlet published by Revenue Canada, titled *Canadian Residents Going Down South*. The pamphlet also outlines your obligations either as a resident alien or non-resident alien in the U.S. If you plan to spend any significant amount of time in that country after you retire, I strongly recommend that you get a copy of it.

If you do end up paying any U.S. income tax as a result of all this, you may be able to claim a foreign tax credit when you file your Canadian return.

RRSPs and RRIFs are another issue that will inevitably come up if you take flight from Canada. Of course, if you remain a Canadian for tax purposes, nothing happens. Your retirement plans are subject to the same rules as before.

But if you should become a resident of another country, that all changes. Again, everything will depend on which country you choose and the tax treaty that prevails between that nation and Canada.

In the case of the U.S., the value of an RRSP when you become a U.S. resident is considered capital, and is therefore not taxable. Any income earned within the plan after you become a U.S. resident may continue to compound tax-free. You only become liable for U.S. taxes once you start making withdrawals from the plan, and then only on those amounts that relate to income earned in your RRSP *after* you became a U.S. resident, plus any unrealized capital gains. This makes it a sound strategy to take any capital gains in your RRSP before you leave Canada, thereby reducing the U.S. tax for which you'll eventually be liable.

If you've lost money in your RRSP to the extent that the plan's value is less than it was at the time you became a U.S. resident, you'll face no U.S. tax at all.

You will have to pay a withholding tax of 25 percent in Canada when you make withdrawals from your RRSP after you become a non-resident by moving to the U.S. Periodic payments from a RRIF or annuity are subject to a 15 percent withholding tax. (Withholding rates may differ if you move to another country; the standard rate on pensions, RRIFs, and annuities is 25 percent, but any tax treaty provisions take precedence.)

If you become a non-resident, Revenue Canada will regard the with-holdings as your full payment. This means you'll pay tax at a much lower rate than would have been the case had you stayed home. Of course, some tax may be assessed in the U.S. (or wherever else you're living). But if you're in the States, such tax will only be payable on a portion of your withdrawals, as we've seen. Plus, you should be able to claim a credit for your Canadian withholdings against your U.S. taxes payable.

These changes in the rules make it advantageous to keep your RRSP if you decide to move to the States. Your investments will continue to grow, tax sheltered, just as if you'd stayed in Canada.

To get this tax break, you have to make a declaration to the IRS that you intend to make use of this provision of the tax treaty. This requires a special election, which is made with the first U.S. return you file. You'll be required to supply detailed financial information about your RRSP at that time.

The same rules apply to registered retirement income funds (RRIFs) as well. They're simply regarded as a substitute for an RRSP.

Pension income may also receive a tax break if you move to the U.S. Employee and employer contributions made to the plan on your behalf prior to taking up U.S. residency are considered capital, in the same way as your RRSP, and therefore won't be taxed.

Pension payments originating in Canada are also subject to with-holding tax if you become a non-resident. The standard rate is 25 per-cent, but what you pay will be determined in the provisions of the tax treaty between Canada and the country you're moving to.

Several other types of Canadian income may also have tax withheld at source if you leave. These include most interest payments, dividends, rents, CPP, and OAS.

For a period in the late nineties, RRSP and RRIF investors faced a real problem when they moved to the States. Because of a sudden enforcement of an old rule by the U.S. Securities and Exchange Commission (SEC), they found they could no longer manage their plans. Canadian brokers and planners were prohibited from taking orders from U.S. residents, even though the registered plans remained here, which effectively froze most of the assets. Fortunately, saner heads prevailed and the issue was resolved in mid-1999.

There is another side of RRSP/RRIF investing that needs careful consideration if you decide to leave Canada for good. Should you run the risk of leaving your registered assets in Canadian dollars and perhaps seeing the loonie fall in relation to the currency of your new country of residence?

The best way to avoid this danger is to switch a large proportion of your investments into securities denominated in the currency of the country in which you'll be living. I'll continue to use the United States as an example, since most Canadians who retire abroad go there.

You can convert Canadian dollar securities into U.S.-denominated assets quite easily, even in registered plans such as RRSPs and RRIFs. The foreign content limitations and the rule that says you cannot hold foreign currency in a registered plan are not the impediments they may seem at first glance.

U.S. dollar–denominated bonds from Canadian issuers such as the federal and provincial governments are considered to be 100 percent Canadian content for RRSP/RRIF purposes. So are mutual funds that invest in these securities.

Some financial institutions issue U.S. dollar term deposits and GICs, which are considered Canadian content for RRSPs. As well, some Canadian stocks are denominated in U.S. dollars and pay dividends in that currency. Ask your broker for a list.

In the case of non-registered investments, there are no barriers of any kind in switching to a U.S. dollar–based portfolio. It's simply a matter of selecting which securities you want to move. U.S. equities, as a group, tend to outperform Canadian stocks, so that could be a plus if you want to maintain a growth component in your portfolio.

You won't be able to protect yourself in currency terms in cases where your income originates in Canadian dollars–OAS, CPP, an employer pension plan, and the like. You'll have to accept a degree of currency risk, although you may wish to convert your funds to U.S. dollars as soon as they're received to minimize this risk.

Yet another financial consideration is the cost of living. Canada is a very expensive country, for a variety of reasons. Sun-belt living may be cheaper, even given the weakness of the Canadian dollar in recent years. Living costs in Florida, for example, are generally less expensive for such important budget components as food, clothing, and gasoline.

Finally, you need to consider the new Canadian departure tax. The government doesn't call it that, of course, but a departure tax is really what it comes down to—and it may make it financially difficult for you to take up residence in another country, depending on your situation.

It works like this. On the day you leave the country, Revenue Canada takes the position that you sold all your stocks, bonds, mutual funds, and other securities. This is called a *deemed disposition.* You must declare any capital gains (or losses) that result from this fictitious sale on your final Canadian tax return. If you have a lot of invested money, the tax liability could be huge.

There are a few exceptions to the deemed disposition rule. You don't have to declare any Canadian real estate that you own, any Canadian business property (if the operation is run from a permanent Canadian address), pensions and other rights, stock options, or certain property of short-term residents.

You can, if you so choose, defer paying the tax on property subject to this rule until it is actually sold. The catch is that you have to provide Revenue Canada with "acceptable security" to ensure they will eventually get paid.

You must also provide RevCan with a list of all your worldwide assets if their fair market value totals more than $25 000.

As you can see, leaving Canada can be expensive, and it will certainly entail a lot of paperwork.

If, after all this, you're still thinking about retiring elsewhere, spend considerable time in that country before making up your mind. A few weeks won't do. You may love Florida in dry March but hate it in mid-July when the humidity builds, the insects swarm, and thunderstorms boil up from the Gulf of Mexico almost every afternoon. Southern France may be a delight in summer. But when the cold mistral howls in winter, you may be reminded of Saskatchewan.

Choosing your country of residence is one of the biggest decisions you'll face in your retirement years. Do the research and take the time to get it right.

Key Points in Review

1. Many Canadians decide to spend some part of their retirement years in a warmer climate. The key decision is whether or not you want to remain a resident of Canada for tax purposes.

2. Buying foreign real estate can be something of an adventure. Make sure you know the potential problems before you plunge in.

3. Finding a U.S. company that will give a mortgage to a non-resident can be a challenge. A mortgage broker can help out here.

4. If you rent out your property in the United States, both Revenue Canada and the Internal Revenue Service will want their share. By the time the tax people have been satisfied, you may be just as well off leaving the house empty.

5. As a Canadian, when you sell a U.S. property, the buyer must withhold 10 percent of the gross price. You'll then have to file a U.S. return.

6. You could be subject to U.S. income tax even if you only spend four months a year in that country. But there are ways to get around the problem.

7. Special rules govern RRSPs and RRIFs if you move to the States, and they work in your favour. So keep your registered plans intact. However, it's best to realize any capital gains before you leave.

8. To protect your buying power and reduce currency risk, convert at least some of your assets to the currency of the country in which you will be living.

9. Canada's new departure tax will make it expensive for you to become a non-resident if you have a large investment portfolio.

25
Putting It All Together

Action may not always bring happiness but
there is no happiness without action.

— Benjamin Disraeli

KNOWLEDGE IS A VALUABLE ASSET, BUT IT IS NO SUBSTITUTE FOR action. All the information in this book will not help you achieve a wealthy retirement if you don't translate it into meaningful planning and commitment.

Wishing and dreaming won't make it happen. Only you can.

I once read an anecdote in a book called *The Light Touch*, by Malcolm Kushner, which illustrates the point. I've embellished it somewhat for my purposes.

It's the story of a religious old man who wanted a sign from God that He truly existed.

Not a little sign, either. A BIG sign.

One summer evening he went outside, looked up at the sky, and said, "God, if you really listen to your flock here on Earth, then please, please—let me win the Lotto 649 before I die."

With that, he went inside and began to pray. Every day he prayed ceaselessly, stopping only to perform the necessities of life and for sleep.

A year went by in this way. He did not win the Lotto 649.

Disillusioned and despondent, the old man went outside and again addressed the sky.

"Lord," he said, "you have failed me. I have prayed, but you have not heeded me. Oh Lord, you have deserted me."

With that, the skies darkened, lightning flashed, and there was a great peal of thunder. Then came the voice of the Almighty, deep, stern, yet compassionate.

"Give me a break, old man," He said. "At least buy a ticket!"

The Lord helps those who help themselves. It's true when it comes to money, too.

So how do you go about it?

Well, you've made a start by reading this book. But you may have come this far without completing the various worksheets I've provided to help you get a handle on your current financial position and to do some projections for the future.

If that's the case, I suggest you make that your next step. You can't begin putting together a meaningful retirement plan unless you have a clear picture of where you are now and where you want to go.

Yes, it may be somewhat time-consuming at the outset. But we're talking about perhaps a quarter to a third of your lifetime here. Isn't it worth a few hours?

Resources

Once you know where you stand, decide whether you need some professional assistance in formulating your plan and achieving your objectives. There are several types of experts you can turn to for help, depending on your requirements. They include the following.

Human Resource People. If you're an employee, the people who administer your pension plan and benefits should be able to provide assistance in projecting your retirement income, based on your service and income records to date. They should also be able to advise you about the continuation of benefits once you retire. If you're a trade union member, you may also be able to get help from that source. Remember, though, that pension benefits may be upgraded and insurance policies may change, so review your position every year or two.

Financial Planners. These are financial professionals who can advise you on a range of issues, from taxes to investing. They can also set up a retirement savings program for you, based on your goals and your means.

You should exercise care in selecting a planner, however. This is by and large an unregulated profession; in most provinces anyone can call themselves a financial planner even if they have no professional qualifications. One good test of a person's credentials is to ask if he or she is a member of the Canadian Association of Financial Planners (CAFP), a professional organization that is working hard to raise the standards of the industry. The Association publishes a list of its members in each province; you can write to their national office at Suite 1710, 439 University Avenue, Toronto, Ontario M5G 1Y8 for information. You can also call them toll-free at 1-800-346-2237 (in Toronto call 416-593-6592). They also have a useful Web site where you can find a qualified financial planner with any particular specialties that you require, from estate planning to cross-border taxation. The address is **www.cafp.org**.

Financial planners are compensated in several ways. A fee-for-service planner charges on an hourly basis and should, as a result, offer completely unbiased advice. You will also encounter financial planners who are compensated by commission, based on investments you make with them. In this case, you should ask up front about any potential conflicts of interest in the advice you receive. This doesn't mean such planners will necessarily steer you wrong. But if you know where they're coming from, you'll be in a better position to assess the value of their recommendations.

Some planners earn their income by a combination of these methods. Some are employed by large organizations and are paid a straight salary.

The members' registers published by CAFP indicate how a particular planner is compensated and what rates you can expect to pay on a fee-for-service basis. They also indicate what products each planner is licensed to sell, so you have a good idea at the outset of what to expect. If you prefer a particular payment method, you can locate appropriate planners through the Web site.

Retirement Counsellors. These are a specialized type of financial planner who concentrate on retirement planning. They frequently also act as brokers for various types of retirement plans, including RRSPs, RRIFs, and annuities, as well as for a variety of investments like GICs and mutual funds. Often, there is no charge for their counselling services, but they collect a commission on any products you buy from them.

Investment Counsellors. Despite the similarity in the name, these are a very different breed. Investment counsellors are professional money managers who, for a fee, will assume responsibility for managing your portfolio. They usually charge a percentage of the portfolio's asset value and aren't normally interested in accounts of less than $100 000. Brokerage firms and many trust companies offer this service.

Stockbrokers. The term has become a misnomer. These days, brokers handle a lot more than stock. They'll happily sell you mutual funds, bonds, strips, mortgage-backed securities, tax shelters, second-hand GICs, and just about any other financial product you can think of. Most of the brokers I've encountered are solid, knowledgeable people—although they are, bottom line, in the selling business, a point you should never forget. As in any profession, there are a few rotten apples in the barrel, however. If you have any concerns about the way in which your account is handled, talk to a senior person in the firm right away. Don't let the situation drag on.

Mutual Fund Sales People. Many people sell mutual funds as one of many investment products—brokers and financial planners, for example. Then there are those who specialize in this area. Some are employed by a specific company; the giant Winnipeg-based Investors Group is an example. Others handle a variety of funds from several managers. You will not normally be able to buy no-load mutual funds through these representatives, however, since they receive no commission for them.

Banks. They're now firmly in the business of providing retirement planning counselling, and most branches have access to a least one person who has been specially trained for that role. The banks are anxious to get your RRSP and RRIF business, and will go out of their way to be helpful. But don't lose sight of the fact that they have a vested interest in promoting their own products and services, from discount brokerage to wealth management.

Trust Companies. Most now offer some type of retirement counselling as an extension of their financial planning services. Trust companies have special expertise in estate planning, which may be an important consideration to you. Like banks, they also provide a range of retirement products.

Insurance Companies. They hold the exclusive franchise on life annuities, although brokers and planners may sell them on their behalf. The insurance industry also has a range of other retirement products. The problem is that they often tend to be unduly complicated. Be sure you understand exactly what you're buying before signing up.

Accountants. They're a good source of assistance if tax planning is an important part of your retirement program or if you're considering retiring abroad. Be sure, however, that your accountant is up to date on all the latest rules. The big, well-known firms are expensive, but are generally very knowledgeable. CA firms are also the place to go for setting up an Individual Pension Plan.

Lawyers. Normally they are not a good source for financial help, unless they specialize in tax law. You may need their services if you wish to emigrate, however.

An important rule relating to professional advice is not to obtain more than you require. None of it comes free; if you don't pay for it directly, you'll pay indirectly through commissions.

The financial industry does offer some free services as you approach retirement age, however, and you should take advantage of them.

Most banks, trust companies, and credit unions have special discounts and privileges for "seniors"—which in some cases means anyone over 50. These typically include free chequing privileges, bonus interest on GICs, a reduction on safety deposit box charges, free travellers' cheques, and the like.

You'll also be able to take advantage of special seniors' discounts offered by transportation companies, cinemas, and merchants—if you have the courage to claim them. Some people don't because they say it makes them feel old.

I can sympathize with that. A couple of weeks after my 55th birthday, we were driving north from Florida and stopped at a Shoney's restaurant for their fabulous buffet breakfast (if you've never tried it, you've missed one of the great eating experiences of life). I noticed on the menu that seniors, which in this case meant anyone 55 or more, received a 10 percent discount. I told the waitress I qualified, fully expecting she would take one look at my youthful countenance and demand to see some ID. She didn't. I got the discount, but felt depressed the rest of the day.

Still, you can save a lot of money by taking advantage of the many discounts offered to older people. So swallow your pride and ask when the time comes. After all, you're only as old as you feel.

That's about all I can tell you. Now it's up to you. If you make a commitment and put together a carefully structured plan, you can indeed be among the growing number of Canadians who will retire genuinely wealthy.

Make no mistake. It will require time, effort, and maybe some sacrifice. But then, what in life that's worthwhile does not?

Any time you feel your resolve weakening, think about the ultimate reward. Twenty, thirty, maybe even more years of living the way you want, free and independent. A home by the sea, a trip around the world, time with your family, a second career—all are possible and achievable. It's in your hands now!

Appendix: Sources
of Information

If you'd like more information about retirement planning in general or greater detail about a specific issue raised in this book, here are some sources that may be helpful. This is not an exhaustive list by any means, but it will at least get you started.

Books

The Canadian Snowbird Guide, by Douglas Gray (McGraw-Hill Ryerson). This is the most comprehensive book available for those who want to spend part or all of their retirement years in sunnier climes. It offers all sorts of useful tips on snowbirding in the U.S., Mexico, Costa Rica, and elsewhere. There's a very good section on the tax implications of U.S. living.

David Tafler's Guide to RRIFs, by David Tafler (ITP Nelson). Veteran financial writer Tafler, who is editor and publisher of *CARP News*, provides a detailed, step-by-step approach to setting up and managing a RRIF. The book also includes information on annuities, LIFs, and estate planning.

David Tafler's 50+ Survival Guide, by David Tafler (ITP Nelson). A pot-pourri of useful knowledge for older people, covering a wide range of topics including health, travel, and money.

Gordon Pape's Buyer's Guide to RRSPs, by Gordon Pape and David Tafler (Prentice Hall Canada). A comprehensive guide to RRSPs, published annually. Includes specific investment recommendations for RRSPs and RRIFs.

Revenue Canada Publications

Canadian Residents Going Down South
Emigrants and Income Tax
Pension Adjustment Reversal Guide
RRSPs and Other Registered Plans for Retirement
When You Retire

Web Sites

Canadian Association of Financial Planners
www.cafp.org

Locate a local planner with the specialties you're seeking and the payment method you prefer.

Canadian Association of Retired Persons (CARP)
www.fifty-plus.net

You'll find lots of interesting information here on everything from travel to health. There are also discussion groups, contests, a "Fifty-Plus Store", jokes and more. You can even buy a car on-line at five percent over dealer cost. What you won't find, surprisingly, is much in the way of financial information.

Human Resources Development Canada—Income Security Programs
www.hrdc-drhc.gc.ca/isp

You'll find just about everything you need to know about the Canada Pension Plan, Old Age Security, Guaranteed Income Supplement, and other federal programs for older people at this site, including the answers to the most commonly asked questions.

Miningco
www.miningco.com

Don't be put off by the strange name. This is an omni-link site where you can find cross-references to all kinds of information. Click on the "Finance and Investing" button on the main menu and then on the "Investing Canada" subdirectory (for some reason I could not establish a direct link so had to go by this route). Once you get there, you'll find a dazzling array of links to just about every financial and retirement topic you can imagine. Some of them are valuable, some are useless, so plan to spend some time sorting through them all.

Quicken
www.quicken.ca

There are a lot of useful calculators here that will help you with your retirement plan. Try the life expectancy test; you may be surprised to discover how long you are likely to live. Plan accordingly. Other features allow you to look at the effects of inflation, calculate the tax savings produced by an RRSP contribution, find out what type of investor you are, and more. A very useful Internet stop.

Revenue Canada
www.rc.gc.ca

To its credit, RevCan has created the most comprehensive source for Canadian tax information on the Internet. You can download virtually all of their publications, including the ones mentioned here. All their forms are also available for download.

RetireWeb
www.retireweb.com

Scott Parkinson of the Hutchison Avenue Software Corporation in Montreal has set himself the challenging goal of becoming "the most comprehensive and understandable source of a on-line retirement information in Canada." Ambitious, certainly, and some of the aspects of the site, such as the section dealing with the psychological aspects of retirement, have yet to be developed. But you will find a lot of valuable financial information, some good calculators, and a lot of useful links here.

Gordon Pape
www.gordonpape.com

I would be remiss not to mention my own Web site here. Although there isn't a lot of information that relates specifically to retirement planning, you can access and download my CBC radio transcripts, which often deal with related topics. There is also some free investing advice, including my weekly Mutual Fund Minute audio feature and a Question and Answer forum, plus links to all the mutual fund companies. The site also offers two newsletter subscription services and my On-Line Mutual Funds Database.

Index